I0754809

THE LIFE

OF OUR

BLESSED LORD AND SAVIOUR

JESUS CHRIST:

AND

THE LIVES AND SUFFERINGS

OF HIS

HOLY EVANGELISTS AND APOSTLES.

BY

REV. JOHN FLEETWOOD, D. D.

WITH AN INTRODUCTION TO THE AMERICAN EDITION,

BY PROF. S. SEAGER.

NEW YORK:
MILLER, ORTON & CO., 25 PARK ROW.
1857.

CONTENTS

LIVES OF THE APOSTLES.

INTRODUCTION TO THE AMERICAN EDITION.

EVERY new contribution to the stock of Christian knowledge must be regarded as a substantial benefit to the cause of truth in any age; but at a time unprecedented for the multiplication of books, whose chief aim is to furnish light reading, giving the mind occupation without the trouble of thinking, a work which tends directly both to develop the intellect, and sanctify the heart, can not fail to commend itself to the public. Such a work is "Fleetwood's Life of Christ." The wide-spread fame it has acquired, both in Europe and in this country, among evangelical Christians generally, furnishes conclusive evidence of its intrinsic merit. The various editions heretofore published were too voluminous, and consequently too expensive to be accessible to the great mass of readers. A good book should be made, as far as practicable, like the sunlight and the rain, the common property of all. To bring this invaluable volume within the reach of every class, and give it the extensive circulation it so justly deserves, Geo. H. Derby & Co. issue the present edition, in a cheap form, retaining, however, every thing of importance in the elegantly illuminated Glasgow edition.

Biography, truthfully written, possesses an interest scarcely equaled by any other species of composition. But when remarkable incidents are recorded, which claim to have occurred during the lifetime of one long since departed, we must be satisfactorily assured of the authenticity of the original record, and of the faithfulness of the successive transcribers. The more extraordinary those events are, the more positive and definite must be the evidence in support of them. Fortunately, in the present instance, the facts themselves, and the men who record them, rest for their credibility and faithfulness on the inspiration of the Holy Spirit.

The author of this volume has collected, with great discrimination, into a beautifully-connected narrative, and arranged, as far as practicable, in chronological order, all the most striking events in the life of the Saviour, from his glorious advent to his more glorious return to heaven, interspersing the whole with such reflections as seemed necessary, both to give unity to the plan of the work, and to illustrate, in the most impressive manner, the grand design of his mission. The ornamental in style is purposely avoided, while a simplicity and clearness of diction, admirably corresponding to that of the New Testament, is carefully studied. Those soul-inspiring truths which, for ages, were the burden of prophecy, and into which "the angels desired to look," are too sublime to admit the artificial adorning so profusely lavished upon works of mere taste.

> "They need not the aid of foreign ornament,
> But are, when unadorned, adorned the most."

How puerile appears the rhetorician's art, in attempting to improve the inimitable narration of the evangelists, when recording those stupendous miracles of Jesus, which form so large a part of his public life! Who would allow the marshaling of words, and the rounding of periods, however skillfully performed, to take the place of the simple "Lazarus, come forth," "Peace, be still," "Take up thy bed and walk?" Well was it said, "never man spake like this man." Even the enemies of revelation have been forced to award to the precepts of Christ, a beauty of style and a loftiness of sentiment, which commanded their admiration. All lovers of the genuine sublime in writing, will ever delight in reading the Holy Scriptures, and more especially those portions which record the life, death, and resurrection of the Lord Jesus. The prophecies of the Old Testament which specified so minutely the coming of the Just One, couched in the simplest language, truths so vast in their range, so lofty in their conception, that the prophets themselves, unable to comprehend them, "searched what, or what manner of time the Spirit of Christ which was in them did signify, when it testified beforehand the sufferings of Christ, and the glory that should follow;" and even the angels, in rapt astonishment, desired to look into the "mystery of godliness, God manifest in the flesh." In Jesus, the divine Messiah, the types and symbols of the first covenant receive so lucid an interpretation, as fully to justify the apostle in calling them "the shadow of good things to come."

Does the sincere inquirer after truth hesitate to repose perfect confidence in Christ, as the long-promised Saviour? Let him stand at the bier of the widow's son, and hear that creative word, "Arise;" or look upon that motly throng of traffickers, impiously desecrating the temple of the living God, while Jesus enters and drives them, awe-struck and silent, before him, none attempting to resist his authority, but submitting to a power they did not comprehend; and he will be led to upbraid himself for his incredibility, while he joyfully acknowledges, "truly this is the Son of God." Faith gathers new vigor by the contemplation of those wonderful miracles, which attest so fully, that in Jesus dwelt "all the fullness of the Godhead bodily." How vastly superior is the evidence upon which the disciple of Christ rests his confidence, to that afforded to the most heaven-favored of former times! Every thing under the old dispensation was of necessity prospective, every thing promised the ushering in of a more glorious period; insomuch that the eye of Christian faith watched the signs of the times, and caught with rapturous delight, the star in the east, which was to guide the wise men of Bethlehem. But "God, who at sundry times and in divers manners, spake in times past to the fathers by the prophets, hath in these last days spoken unto us by his Son." Thus we are furnished with a key, to unlock the treasures of wisdom which were so long inaccessible to prophets and kings. The life of Christ serves the double purpose of illustrating God's administration, during four thousand years, while the world was in process of preparation for his advent; and also, of demonstrating practically the infinitude of His love who "spared not his own Son, but delivered him up for us all." We are enabled to form some idea of the magnitude of sin, by the nature and extent of the satisfaction which Infinite Justice required, and in view of which, God could "be just and the justifier of him that believeth in Jesus." Behold our atoning Saviour! He who wept at the grave of Lazarus as a sympathizing man, raised him from that grave like "the Mighty God." He who, as a "man of sorrows and acquainted with grief," "had not where to lay his head," possessed "all power in heaven and in earth." In accommodation to our weakness, God has condescended to approach us in the person of his Son, constituting his humanity, a temple in which his divinity might dwell. How glorious, how sublime is such a dispensation! No longer do we grope in a land of shadows. The former things have indeed passed away. "The law and the prophets were until John; since that time the kingdom of God is preached and every man presseth into it." While John the Baptist, than whom a greater had not appeared before him; standing on the transition point between the old dispensation and the new, inquires, "Watchman what of the night?" the least in the kingdom of Christ, answers, "The morning cometh." Taking his stand point on the threshold of the Christian temple, whose glory was so far to exceed that of the former, the disciple of Jesus occupies the very focus of all the light which had dimly gleamed on the vision of patriarchs and prophets, from the morning of creation, and, gazing backward over the long series of preparatory events, rejoices to find himself emerging into the broad sunlight of a day, which shall shine more and more, till the consummation of all God's purposes in relation to our race.

Long had the human mind plied its utmost energies to grasp the idea of the infinite. To aid its conception, every imaginable form of matter, animate and inanimate, was sought, but still there was an impassable gulf between the creature and the Creator. But in Christ, the attributes of a perfect man, and also those of the invisible God, were mysteriously blended exhibiting the divine character in a palpable form.

> "'T was this Almighty Word that all things made;
> He grasps whole nature in his single hand:
> All the eternal truths in him are laid,
> The Ground of all things, and their Head,
> The circle where they move, and center where they stand."

Thus, "God, who commanded the light to shine out of darkness, hath shined in our hearts, to give the light of the knowledge of the glory of God in the face of Jesus Christ." From the hour when, on the mount of transfiguration, a voice from "the most excellent glory," fell upon the ears of Peter, James and John, designating Christ as the beloved of the Father, and the sole object of hope and of trust to the world; he had been recognized as "the brightness of the Father's glory, and the express image of his person." Every act of his was a solemn protest against all doubt and unbelief, and an intelligible response to the painful query, ever and anon agitating the minds of even his own disciples, "art thou he that should come, or do we look for another?" The apostles, though slow to apprehend the ineffable grandeur of the Saviour's character and mission, came at length to the full conviction, that he was the veritable impersonation of the eternal Jehovah. They saw in him a circumstantial fulfillment of the ancient prophecies; they beheld his miracles; they marked his guileless life; and with a faith which appropriated his infinite sacrifice to themselves, they claimed him as their God. From that moment he was to them the "chief corner stone laid in Zion, elect, precious."

Another important view, in which the evangelists everywhere represent Christ, is his absolute sinlessness. This view derives its value from its connection with the atonement, and from the necessity, that he who was to be a model for a sinning race should himself be sinless. The most searching scrutiny of those who were interested to convict him, resulted in the verdict "I find no fault in him." Behold the evidence of moral perfection in the tempers which were the unvarying habit of his life. Standing on the hill which overlooked Jerusalem, he gazed upon its grandeur, and, with tears, bewailed the ruin which brooded over the people who were even then plotting his destruction. From the cross, where he was expiring in agony, he prays, "Father, forgive them, they know not what they do." Follow him through the awful eclipse of the grave, and his first acts, after his resurrection, were an exhibition of moral sublimity, infinitely surpassing the proudest deeds of heroes and conquerors. The simple declaration, "Peace be on you," and the accompanying gift of the Holy Ghost, were but the earnest of that love with which he loved his own to the end.

During the succeeding forty days, he was mainly occupied in establishing the faith of those upon whom would soon devolve the mighty work of "going into all the world to preach the gospel to every creature." He appeared to them on various occasions, to prepare them for his departure, and to "leave them an example that they should follow his steps." When the time had fully come, that he should be received up into glory, having performed his last visit to the family of Lazarus and his sisters, he returned as far as Bethany, and there, in presence of a select company of his friends, while in the very act of blessing them, "he was taken up, and a cloud received him out of their sight." Here closes the great mission of Christ as a Redeemer, and his Mediatorship in Heaven begins.

Let us now contemplate him, not only as possessing, in a pre-eminent degree, the elements of a stainless, holy character, but harmoniously uniting in himself every divine attribute in infinite perfection — exhibiting that absolute completeness of every conceivable excellence, which renders him the fit object of supreme, unceasing adoration and praise, to every order of intelligences, forever and ever. His life, like his character, was a perfect unit. He was never diverted for a moment from the glorious work which brought him to earth. The salvation of a revolted empire was the single, all-absorbing object, to the accomplishment of which every thing was made subservient. This having been attained, he resumed his place at the right hand of the Father, where he "ever liveth to make intercession for us."

"Thence shall he come,
When this world's dissolution shall be ripe,
With glory and power to judge both quick and dead;
To judge the unfaithful dead, but to reward
His faithful, and receive them into bliss."

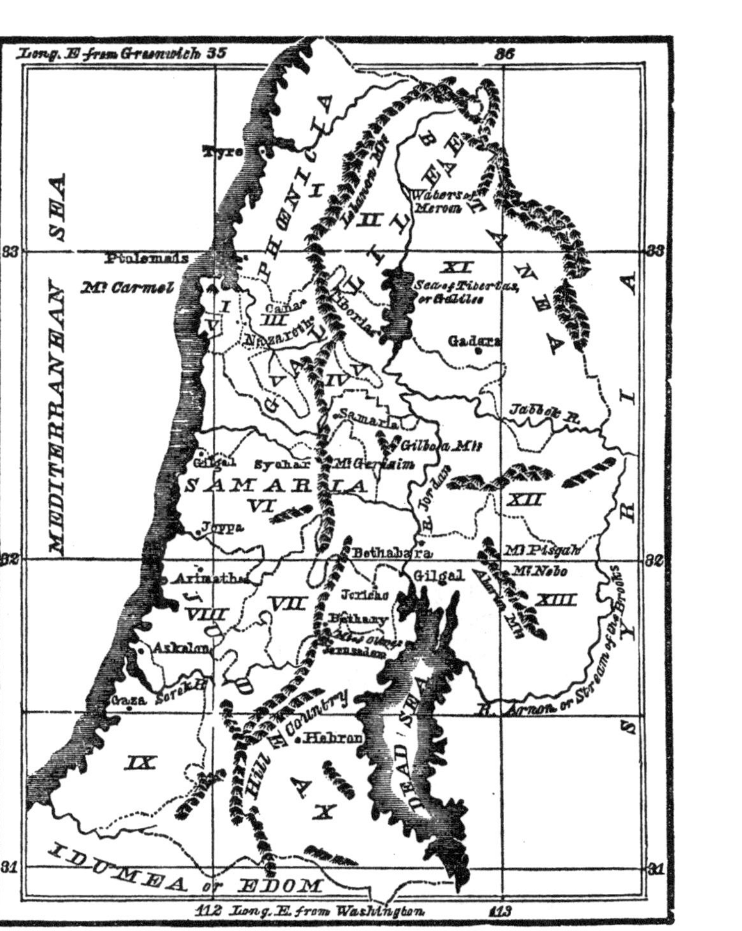

THE HISTORY

OF THE

LIFE OF JESUS CHRIST.

CHAPTER I.

PRESAGE OF THE BIRTH OF CHRIST — PREDICTION OF THE BIRTH OF JOHN THE BAPTIST— SALUTATION OF THE BLESSED VIRGIN BY THE ANGEL— VISITATION OF THE VIRGIN MARY TO ELIZABETH — BIRTH OF THE BAPTIST.

NO event that ever did, or perhaps will happen, can more remarkably display the wisdom and power of the great Jehovah, than the glorious manner in which he brought life and immortality to light, by the gospel of his only Son, manifested in the flesh.

History, as it refers merely to human events, is a pleasing and instructing subject; but that which relates to our immortal interests, certainly claims our most serious regard.

If we survey the stupendous works of the creation, we shall find that few arrived at perfection at once. This observation is amply confirmed by the various productions in the natural, and changes in the moral world. The Supreme Being, who conducts all his operations according to infinite wisdom, appears to have retained the same maxim in regulating his kindest dispensations to the sons of men. The divine will was not revealed, at first, in its clearest evidence, and fullest splendor. The dawn, in a spiritual as well as in a natural sense, preceded the meridian glory; the former revelation was but a type, or earnest of the latter, and, in comparison with it, intricate and mysterious.

The all-gracious God, as it seemed best to his unerring wisdom, was pleased, by degrees, to open and unfold his glorious councils; and man, by degrees attained to the knowledge of the great plan of salvation, and the means used by its great Author to promote and establish it.

Some time before the incarnation of the blessed Jesus, an opinion prevailed among the pious part of the Jews, that the great Jehovah would condescend to favor them with a clear revelation of his divine will, by the mission of some eminent person, qualified from above to instruct them in the same. This opinion was founded on the predictions of the ancient prophets, who had described, with the utmost beauty and clearness, the person, character, and glory of the Messiah, appointed, by God, in his own time, to declare his eternal counsels to mankind.

Relying on the fulfillment of these prophecies, the devout persons among the Jews imagined the time appointed by God was near at hand, and that the appointed Messiah would shortly make his appearance, and therefore are said to "have awaited night and day for the consolation of Israel." The people, at that time grievously oppressed by the Roman power, and consequently anxious of regaining their liberty, as well as revenging themselves on their tyrannical oppressors, wanted the accomplishment of the prophecies with the most solicitous desire. But this opinion of the approach of a general deliverer extended much farther than the country of the Jews; for, through their connection with so many countries, their disputes with the learned men among the heathen, and the translation of the Old Testament into a language now almost general, their religion greatly prevailed in the east, and consequently their opinion, that a prince would appear in the kingdom of Judea, who would dispel the mists of ignorance, deliver the Jews from the Roman yoke, and spread his dominion from one end of the world to the other.

While the eastern world was fraught with these sanguine hopes, the angel Gabriel, who had appeared to Daniel the prophet, with a certain information as to the period of the Messiah's coming, as well as his transactions in this lower world, was sent to Zacharias, a pious priest, while he was executing his office before God, in the order of his course, (which was to burn incense when he went into the temple of the Lord,) to foretell that a child would spring from him and his wife Elizabeth, though they were stricken in years, who should be endowed with extraordinary gifts from heaven, and honored with being the forerunner of the Saviour of the world.

Zacharias, when he saw the angel, though he probably knew him to be of heavenly extraction, could not judge the subject of his mission, and therefore discovered a mixture of fear and surprise, but the heavenly ambassador cheered his desponding soul with this kind address: "Fear not, Zacharias, for thy prayer is heard, and thy wife Elizabeth shall bear thee a son, and thou shalt call his name John." That he waited, day and night, for the consolation of Israel, he well knew; which is all we can understand by his prayer being heard; for it was unnatural in him to think, that he and his wife Elizabeth, who were advanced in years, should have a son; nay, he intimates his doubts concerning it in these words: "Whereby shall I know this? for I am an old man, and my wife well stricken in years." Besides, he was a priest of the course of Abia, whose particular office was to pray on behalf of the people, for public and national blessings; so that it is very reasonable to think that on all occasions of public worship he prayed most earnestly for the accomplishment of the prophecies relative to the appearance of the long-expected Messiah, who was promised as a general blessing to all the nations of the earth.

That this was the great subject of his prayer, appears from the declaration of Gabriel: The prayer thou hast directed with sincerity to an Almighty ear, concerning the coming of the Messiah, "is heard; and, behold, thy wife Elizabeth shall bear thee a son," who shall prepare the way for the mighty Redeemer of Israel. The good old priest was as much astonished at the subject of his mission as he was at the appearance of the messenger; and esteeming it impossible that his wife, thus advanced in years, should conceive a son, weakly demanded a sign, to confirm his belief in the fulfillment of the promise, though he knew the authority of the angel was derived from the God of truth. But as it is the lot of humanity to err, Zacharias had, for that time, forgot that nothing was impossible to Omnipotence, as well as that it were not the first time the aged were caused to conceive, and bear children.

The least reflection would have reminded him, that Sarah had conceived and borne Isaac, when she was far advanced in years; and that Samuel was born of a woman, who was reputed, and even called, barren.

His curiosity was, indeed, gratified, but in a manner that carried with it at once a confirmation of the promise, and a punishment of his unbelief. As he had verbally testified his doubt of the fulfillment of the prediction of the angel, he was punished with the loss of his speech, which was to continue to the very day in which the prediction should be accomplished: "Behold, thou shalt be dumb, and not able to speak, until the day that these things shall be performed, because thou believest not my words, which shall be fulfilled in their season."

Zacharias soon received an awful testimony of the divinity of the mission of Gabriel, who was no sooner departed than he was struck dumb; for when he came to pray in the course of his office during the oblation of his incense, he could not utter a word; and was under a necessity of making signs to the people that an angel had appeared to him in the temple, and that he was deprived of the faculty of speech, as a punishment for his doubting the fulfillment of an event which he had been foretold concerning him.

Soon after Zacharias departed to his own house, (the day of his ministration being accomplished,) his wife Elizabeth, according to the prediction of the angel, conceived, and retired into a private place, where she lived five months in the uninterrupted exercise of piety, devotion, and contemplation on the mysterious providence of the Almighty, and his amazing goodness to the sinful children of men.

When Elizabeth was advanced six months in her pregnancy, the same heavenly ambassador was sent to a poor virgin, called Mary, who lived in obscurity in Nazareth, under the care of Joseph, to whom she was espoused. This man and woman were both lineally descended from the house of David, from whose loins it was foretold the great Messiah should spring.

This virgin being ordained by the Most High to be the mother of the great Saviour of the world, was saluted by the angel in the most respectful terms: " Hail, thou that are highly favored; the Lord is with thee: blessed art thou among women!" Such an address, from so exalted a being, greatly alarmed the meek and humble virgin; to allay whose fear, and encourage whose heart, the angel related, in the most sublime terms, the subject of his embassy, which was to assure her that she was the chosen of God to the greatest honor which could be conferred on a mortal, and which would perpetuate her memory; an honor no less than that of being mother of the promised and long-expected Messiah, who upon earth shall be called Jesus, because he should save his people from their sins, be the restorer of human nature, and the procuring cause of eternal bliss to sinners, who had forfeited the favor, and incurred the resentment of an offended God: that this divine person was the son of the Most High God: to whom should be given, by his Almighty Father, a throne in the heavenly kingdom, and on which he should preside, and which, being the whole church of Christ, the house of Jacob, the spiritual Israel, or the kingdom of the Messiah, should continue forever and ever.

The astonished virgin, unmindful that Isaiah had long since prophesied, " that a virgin should conceive and bear a son," thought her virginity an insurmountable barrier to the fulfillment of the prophecy, especially as such an event had never occurred since the creation of the world, and therefore required of the angel an explanation of the manner in which such a circumstance could be effected.

This desire by no means implies her not remembering, that with God all things were possible, but only serves to prove the weakness of her apprehensions on the one hand, or her diffidence and sense of her unworthiness on the other.

The angel, therefore, perceiving the uprightness of her disposition, notwithstanding some little proof of human weakness, and shortness of sight, vouchsafed an immediate answer to her inquiry: "The Holy Ghost shall come upon you, and the power of the Highest shall overshadow thee;" or, in other words, This miraculous event shall be brought about by the aid of the Holy Spirit, and wonderful exertion of the power of the Most High. As thy conception shall be effected by the immediate influence of the Holy Ghost, "therefore also that holy thing which shall be born of thee shall be called the Son of God." To confirm her faith in the glorious message, the heavenly messenger observed to her, that her cousin Elizabeth, notwithstanding her advanced years, and reputed barrenness, was about six months pregnant, assigning this incontestible argument for the miraculous incident: "For with God nothing shall be impossible."

This reply not only removed all her doubts and fears, but filled her with inexpressible joy, so that she even anticipated the promised felicity; for she, with the rest of the daughters of Jacob, had long indulged a hope of being selected by God to be the honored mother of the Saviour of Israel; and therefore, on her being assured that such happiness was destined her by the great Disposer of all events, she thus expressed her reliance on the fulfillment of the Divine promise, and perfect acquiescence in the will of the Almighty "Behold the handmaid of the Lord! be it unto me according to thy word."

The angel had no sooner departed, than Mary set out for the mountainous country of Judea, though at a very remote distance from Nazareth, in order to rejoice with her cousin Elizabeth, in the joyful news that she had received from the angel concerning her. The rapture and delight which filled the minds of Mary and Elizabeth, on the occasion of this salutation, can alone be conceived from the affecting description recorded by the evangelist Luke, who is peculiar for the beauty of his style, and elegance of his expressions.

That evangelist writes, that the salutation of Mary had such an effect upon Elizabeth, that on hearing of the miraculous event that had befallen the virgin, the babe leaped within her, and that she, being inspired with a holy delight on the approaching prospect of the nativity of her Saviour, exclaimed with rapture, "And whence is this to me, that the mother of my Lord should come to me."—Luke i: 43. Nor did her ecstasy ceas with this token of humility and joy on the importan event, in the ardor of which she evinced that propheti influence, which, while it amazed the blessed virgin, could not fail of establishing her belief in what the angel had foretold; for she repeated the very words expressed by the angel, in his salutation of the holy virgin, "Blessed art thou among women;" together with a quotation from the Psalms, "and blessed is the fruit of thy womb."

Mary conceived the Seed long promised, and earnestly desired: the Seed in whom all the nations of the earth were to be blessed, according to the words of the Psalmist: "His name shall continue as long as the sun; and men shall be blessed in him: all nations shall call him blessed." The happy virgin, catching the holy flame from the aged Elizabeth, broke out into an humble acknowledgment of her unworthiness, and the wonderful grace of the Almighty, in appointing her to the exalted honor of bearing the Redeemer of Israel, as expressed in these known words, "My soul doth magnify the Lord," &c.

Thus having, by this visit, confirmed herself in the belief of the prediction of the angel Gabriel, when the period of Elizabeth's pregnancy approached, she returned to Nazareth, having resided in Judea about three months.

Soon after the departure of Mary, Elizabeth brought forth a son, the appointed harbinger of the King of Glory; and on the eighth day after his birth, according to the Judaical custom, he was circumcised, and called, agreeably to the appointment of the angel, John, alluding, in the Hebrew tongue, to the gracious display of the wisdom and goodness of God, who was about to manifest himself to the world by the spreading of the gospel of his Son, of whom this John was the appointed forerunner.

The promise being thus fulfilled, the aged priest was restored to his speech, and immediately broke out into praise and rapture at the marvellous works of God, in strains which astonished all around him.

This surprising event greatly alarmed the people of the adjacent country, who were divided in their opinions concerning a child, whose birth was attended with so many extraordinary circumstances. Indeed, these incidents were worthy of general admiration; that he who was to be the forerunner of the mighty Saviour of Israel should not make his entrance on life in an obscure and uncommon manner, but with particular tokens of the favor of heaven, in order to attract the observation of his countrymen, and excite their attention to that ministry which he is called to by the blessed God, even the preparation of the people for the reception of the Messiah, who was shortly to appear in the flesh.

It is observable, that the Baptist from his infancy, displayed great qualities, both of mind and body; for such was his strength of constitution, through the blessing of the God of nature, that he lived till near the thirtieth year of his age, when his public ministry began, in the mountainous and desert country of Judea, bereft of almost all the comforts of life. But at length the prophecy of the good old Zacharias, relating to his future elevation, was literally fulfilled: "Thou, O child, shalt be called the Prophet of the Highest; for thou shalt go before the face of the Lord to prepare his ways; to give knowledge of salvation to his people, by the remission of their sins, through the tender mercies of our God, whereby the dayspring from on high hath visited us, to give light to them that sit in darkness and in the shadow of death, to guide our feet in the way of peace."

As Joseph had betrothed Mary, according to the method of the Jewish espousals, before they came to cohabit together as man and wife, she was found to be with child; at which he was so much confounded that he resolved to put her away. Yet he purposed doing it privately, probably to prevent that exemplary punishment which the law inflicted on those who had violated the faith of their espousals before the marriage was completed, (Deut. xii: 23, 24,) or endure the infamy of a public divorce.

While he was ruminating on this interesting event, he was overtaken with a pleasing slumber, and received a communication from above, which fully revealed the cause and manner of Mary's pregnancy, dispelled his doubts, and encouraged him to take home his falsely-suspected spouse: "Joseph, thou son of David, fear not to take unto thee Mary thy wife; for that which is conceived in her is of the Holy Ghost."

The pious Joseph complied with the voice of Heaven most cheerfully; for no sooner did the morning dawn appear, than he rose from his couch, and obeyed the commands of the Most High, by relating to his espoused wife his being assured of her innocence, and immediately restored her to her former favor.

While he related to her the manner of this extraordinary revelation by a messenger from heaven, he discovered in her a remarkable chastity of heart, entirely conformable to so mysterious an operation, and knew her not, till she had brought forth the great Redeemer of Israel.

Thus was fulfilled that which was foretold by the prophets, and particularly the prediction of Isaiah, which imported that a virgin should bring forth a son: "Behold, a virgin shall conceive, and bear a son, and shall call his name Immanuel, which being interpreted, is God with us."—Isa. vii: 14. Matt. i: 23.

CHAPTER II.

General Decree for Taxation Published — Birth of Christ — Declaration of the same to Shepherds — Circumcision and Presentation of Christ in the Temple — The Wise Men of the East worship the Holy Child — Flight of Joseph into Egypt — Massacre of Infants at Bethlehem — Death of Herod — Return of Joseph out of Egypt.

AUGUSTUS CÆSAR, the Roman emperor, having at this time issued an edict for a general taxation on all the nations, cities, and towns, subject to the empire, King Herod, in consequence of that decree, commanded all under his government to muster in the city of his people, or place of his descent, that an estimate might be taken of their persons and effects. Pursuant to this order, Joseph and Mary, as descendants from the line of David, departed from Nazareth, where they then resided, and came to Bethlehem, a city of Judea, the place of the nativity of David and his ancestors.

The manner and place of our Lord's birth certainly demand our highest admiration and wonder, and are a striking display of wisdom, both in the direction and accomplishment of the will of his heavenly Father. Considered in his divine nature, heaven is the habitation of his seat, and the earth is his footstool:

considered in his human nature, he is humble beneath all, being confined within the narrow limits of a manger! Though as the Son of God, he is the brightness of his Father's glory, the express image of his person, and his throne is forever and ever!—as the son of man, O wondrous condescension! he is wrapped in the meanest swaddling clothes; and, as man, he takes up his habitation with the beasts of the field. In fine, let us adore his grace and love in veiling those glories, for a time, which he enjoyed at the right hand of his Father, assuming our nature, and that in its humblest state, in order to raise us to that degree of glory and happiness, which, by our apostacy from God, we had justly forfeited; exulting with the prophet, "Sing, O heavens, and be joyful, O earth, and break forth into singing, O mountains, for the Lord hath comforted his people."

But the humble manner in which the blessed Jesus made his appearance in the world, did not long eclipse the glory of his descent; a heavenly messenger being despatched from above to apprise mankind of their Savior's incarnation. It pleased the wise Disposer of all things, by his holy angel, first to make known to some honest shepherds, who were watching their flocks by night, in the neighboring fields, the birth of the long-promised, long-expected Messiah. The radiance which shone around them terrified the astonished peasants; but, to dissipate their fears, and confirm their joys, the divine messenger interposed, and thus addressed them: "Fear not; for behold I bring you good tidings of great joy, which shall be unto all people. For unto you is born this day, in the city of David, a Saviour, which is Christ the Lord. And this shall be a sign unto you; Ye shall find the babe wrapped in swaddling clothes, lying in a manger." Luke ii: 10, &c.

The glorious news was no sooner proclaimed, than a number of the celestial choir were heard to resound the praises of the Almighty for this transcendent display of his goodness to sinful men; "And suddenly there was with the angel a multitude of the heavenly host, praising God, and saying, glory to God in the highest, and on earth peace, good-will toward men." Transported with the happy tidings of the birth of the Redeemer of Israel, the angel no sooner departed than the shepherds hastened to Bethlehem, in quest of the Babe, whom, according to the information of the sacred missionary, they found wrapt in swaddling clothes, and lying in a manger. This event, so exactly conformable to the angel's prediction, equally delighted and amazed them; nor could they conceal the purport of his mission, but published abroad all they had seen and heard.

Having viewed, with praise and wonder, their long-expected Saviour, and offered their grateful praises to God, for the manifestation of his goodness to mankind, they departed with hearts filled with love and gratitude, still glorifying the almighty Parent of universal nature.

After the expiration of eight days, from the birth of the holy infant, he was circumcised, according to the Mosaic institution; and thus, by a few drops, gave earnest of the abundance of blood which he was to shed for the purification of mankind. The blessed Redeemer passed through this ceremony, not that he stood in any necessity of conforming to the laws of any kind, being the supreme Lawgiver, with respect to his exalted nature; but, as considered in his humble state, he was born of a woman, made under the law, and came, according to his own declaration, to fulfill all righteousness, it was requisite he should conform to that custom, which characterized the Jewish nation, and was one of the principal injunctions of the Mosaic law, under which he was born; in order to fulfill all that is spoken of him in the Scriptures.

Besides, as all the promises made to Abraham were to be fulfilled in the Messiah, it was necessary he should receive the seal of circumcision, in order to prove his descent from the patriarch, concerning whom it was foretold, "In thy seed shall all the families of the earth be blessed." As a further reason for our Lord's compliance with this Jewish institution, we may urge the propriety of his finishing the former dispensation, by an exact adherence to its rules, as he was about to establish another, and much better, which could not be effected more fully, than by conforming to that sacrament, which was of divine injunction, and indispensably requisite to admission into the former.

As the same institution also required that every first-born son, without any regard to circumstances of family, should be presented to the Lord, in the temple, by delivering him into the hands of the priest, and paying five shekels, together with an offering, which, from the poorer sort, consisted of a pair of turtle doves, or two young pigeons; a ceremony in commemoration of the divine mercy in sparing the first-born of Israel, when those of Egypt, both man and beast, were destroyed; his parents having tarried at Bethlehem till the days of Mary's purification were accomplished, brought the child Jesus to Jerusalem, and there presented him in the temple to the Lord, in the manner thus described, with the offering allowed to the poorer sort of people: a repeated instance of the exact obedience of the immaculate Jesus to the ceremonial law, as well as the poverty of his parents though descended from a royal house.

During the presentation of the holy infant, there entered the temple a pious and venerable old man, named Simeon, who, with all the devout, had "waited day and night for the consolation of Irsael," and to whom it had been revealed by the Spirit of Truth, that he should not depart this mortal life, till he had seen the Lord of life and salvation.

Accordingly, it was signified to him by the Holy Ghost, at whose instance he came at the precise time into the temple, that the child there presented was the long-expected Messiah, even the Redeemer of Israel. In an ecstacy of joy he embraced the heavenly infant in his arms, and exclaimed, "Lord, now lettest thy servant depart in peace, according to thy word: for mine eyes have seen thy salvation, which thou hast prepared before the face of all people; a light to lighten the Gentiles, and the glory of thy people Israel." Luke ii: 29–32.

A certain good prophetess, called Anna, who had a long time waited for the redemption of Israel, entering the temple, at the instant in which Simeon exulted in the birth of the heavenly Infant, and finding that he was the promised Messiah, likewise joined with him in praising God, and went forth and declared the glad tidings of salvation to all the faithful in those parts.

Having, in every respect, complied with the ceremonies and rites contained in the law of Moses, Joseph and Mary, with the child Jesus, "entered in Galilee, to their city Nazareth." They did not, however, long abide there, for having adjusted their affairs, they returned again to Bethlehem, the place of our Lord's nativity.

This step appears to have been pursued in consequence of their opinion, that it was necessary, in order to his being acknowledged the Messiah, sent by God, that he should reside some time in the place of his birth. Whatever was their motive for removal, it is evident, from Scripture, that while they were in Bethlehem, with their son, certain eastern philosophers, called Magi, or wise men, on account of the appearance they had seen, went to Jerusalem, and inquired for the King of the Jews, declaring they had seen his star in their own quarter: and were come to pay him the adoration due to his dignity.

Various conjectures have been formed by the learned concerning this star, which is said to have appeared in the east; some think it was the Spirit of God, others an angel, some a comet, others a luminous appearance, &c. A modern writer thinks it was the glory that surrounded the angels, who had appeared to the shepherds of Bethlehem, on the night of the blessed Lord's nativity.

But to leave this subject, as not immediately appertaining to our purpose. The whole city of Jerusalem was alarmed at the unexpected appearance of the eastern Magi: an event which much perplexed the tyrant Herod, whose ambitious mind maintained the utmost aversion to the very thought of a rival or competitor, and consequently could not brook a report that favored the news of the birth of the King of the Jews.

Disguising, however, his sentiments, he received the Magi with seeming respect, attended to the design of their errand with affected complacency, and, to gratify their curiosity, summoned a general council, and demanded of them *where Christ should be born?* The council kept him not long in suspense; for, well remembering the prophets had particularly foretold the place of his birth, they replied to the demand of the monarch, "In Bethlehem in Judea;" and, to confirm their answer, cited prophetic authority: "And thou, Bethlehem, in the land of Judea, art not the least among the princes of Judea; for out of thee shall come a Governor, that shall rule my people Israel." Matt. ii: 6. The tyrant king, in consequence of the reply from the supreme council of the nation, directed the Magi to Bethlehem, as the place, according to ancient prophecy, designed for the honor of Christ's nativity, earnestly entreating them at the same time, immediately on their finding out the child, to send him word, that he might repair thither, and pay his adoration to him also.

But this was mere pretence, and vile hypocrisy; for, so far was Herod from entertaining any religious regard for the infant Jesus, that he vowed in his heart to destroy him as soon as he should be found; looking on him as designed for a temporal prince, who should expel him, or his descendants, from the throne of Judea, instead of a prince whose kingdom was wholly spiritual, and whose throne was not to be established upon earth, but in the heavenly Jerusalem.

Although we may have many stronger proofs of the divinity of our Saviour's mission, than his miraculous preservation from the designs of the ambitious Herod, yet this was very remarkable. The tyrant, in this case, acted with the utmost subtlety; he declined accompanying the wise men in person; nor did he even send attendants with them, who, under the guise of honoring them, might have secretly informed him of the abode of the Messiah. In short, he acted with such apparent indifference, as if he had no peculiar reason for dispatching them on the occasion.

However, the Magi, having obtained the intelligence they sought in Jerusalem, got forward, under the guidance of the same star that conducted them from their own country, but had left them on their arrival in Judea, which was the cause of their directing their course to the capital, in order to seek that information, which, by the desertion of the star, became requisite Thus it appears the design of the Almighty, in directing the eastern Magi to the capital of Judea, was, that the whole nation might be made acquainted with the cause of their journey.

It is natural and reasonable to suppose that the end of the divine wisdom, in directing these Magi to the kingdom of Judea to worship the child Jesus, was not merely to gratify the curiosity of the wise men, because the event promoted many other very important designs.

It contributed to a valuable purpose, in that the offerings of the wise men procured a subsistence for the holy family in Egypt, whither they were soon after warned to fly, in order to escape the vengeance of the enraged king; for no sooner had the wise men departed from Bethlehem, than Joseph was warned, by a heavenly messenger, of the barbarous purpose of Herod, and commanded to flee into Egypt with the young child and his mother.

Joseph, in obedience to the Almighty's command, rose that very night, and prepared to go into Egypt, "and was there until the death of Herod; that it might be fulfilled which was spoken of the Lord by the prophet, Out of Egypt have I called my Son." This prophecy, which is quoted from Hosea, seems originally to refer to the Israelites; though the evangelist's reference will be amply justified, by considering that the Egyptian captivity alludes to the subjection of the Israelites to great hardships, and their deliverance from the same by an Almighty hand.

Now, as the departure of the holy family into Egypt was in obedience to the divine command, in order to protect the holy Jesus from the incensed Herod, the application of the prophet, "Out of Egypt have I called my Son," appears very just, as well as elegant. The king of Judea long waited with the most earnest expectation, the return of the wise men, anxious to glut his resentment on the innocent Jesus; till, from their long delay, he begun to suspect a delusion, and that his designs were frustrated bv some extraordinary interposition of Providence.

At length, irritated by disappointment, he resolved to accomplish by cruelty a resolution he could not effect by art; and accordingly issued orders to a large party of soldiers to go throughout Bethlehem, and the neighboring villages, and massacre all the children whom they could find therein, from two years old and under! thinking, that the infant Jesus, whom, as a prince, he both envied and dreaded, would fall in the general slaughter. But the heavenly missionary was sheltered from above; nor was the relentless king permitted to impede the design of an Almighty Creator. However, the cities through which the soldiers carried the destructive sword exhibited such scenes of horror and distress, as could not fail to pierce every soul not entirely lost to humanity; no sound was heard but the affecting cries of parents, the groans of expiring babes, and a general imprecation of vengeance on the merciless tyrant. But he did not long survive his cruel decree, being swept from his throne by a nauseous disease, to answer for his conduct at the bar of tremendous Judge.

The tyrant Herod being cut off from the face of the earth, Joseph was warned by a heavenly messenger to return to the land of Israel. The good old man obeyed the Almighty's command, and appears to have a great desire of residing in Judea, and very probably in Bethlehem; but hearing that Herod was succeeded in his throne by his son Archelaus, and fearing that he might pursue the barbarous design of his father, he directed his course another way; but being warned again by a heavenly mission, he retired into Galilee then under the government of a mild and benevolent prince, called Antipas, and took up his habitation at Nazareth, where the particular circumstances which attended the birth of the blessed Jesus were not generally known. The evangelist affirms that Joseph, with the infant and his mother, resided in Nazareth, where the holy Jesus spent his youth—"that it might be fulfilled which was spoken by the prophets, He shall be called a Nazarene."

CHAPTER III.

State of our Lord's Childhood and Private Life — His Argument with the Jewish Doctors—Mission, Character, and Doctrine of the Baptism — Baptism of Christ, and visible Descent of the Spirit on that Solemnity.

THE precise circumstances of our Lord's childhood and life, previous to his public ministry, can not be ascertained from the writings of any of the evangelists, which can be relied on as authentic. All we can gather from those men is, that the faculties of his mind were enlarged in proportion to the growth of his body, insomuch that he arrived at the very perfection of heavenly wisdom.

As his parents were mean and poor, he had not the advantage of a finished education; and he seems to have received no other instruction, than what his parents gave him, in conformity to the Jewish laws. But supernatural abilities amply compensated for the deficiency of natural acquirements, and he gave instances, in his earliest years, of amazing penetration and consummate wisdom.

According to the Mosaic institution, his parents annually went up to Jerusalem; and, when he arrived at the age of twelve years, carried him with them to that city, in order that he might early imbibe the precepts of religion and virtue. In this place the holy Jesus tarried, without the knowledge, and, consequently, the consent of his parents, who departed with the rest that were going toward Galilee; and thinking that he was gone forward with some of their relations or acquaintances, they continued their journey, not doubting but they should overtake him on the road, or meet with him at the place where they had appointed to lodge. But on their arrival, not finding the child in the village, nor among their relations, they returned to Jerusalem, much troubled; and, after a most anxious search of three days, found him in the temple, sitting among the learned doctors, who were amazed at the wisdom of his questions, and the pertinence of his replies; which were greatly superior to what they could expect from one of his tender years, and mean education.

These doctors, or expounders of the law among the Jews, always taught the people publicly on the three great festivals; and it was on one of these public occasions that the blessed Jesus gave such manifest proofs of his wisdom and penetration, as astonished all the beholders, many of whom thought he must be something more than human.

During the obscure state of our blessed Redeemer at Nazareth, the emperor Augustus died at Campania, after a long reign of above forty years, to the general regret of the whole Roman empire. He was succeeded by Tiberius, his son, a prince of very different temper of mind from his predecessor. The emperor, in the second year of his reign, recalled Rufus from the government of Judea, and sent Valerius Gracchus to succeed him. After reigning eleven years, Gracchus was recalled, and succeeded by Pontius Pilate, a person resembling, in disposition, his master Tiberius, who was malicious, cruel, and covetous.

Soon after Pontius Pilate was appointed to the government of Judea, John the Baptist began to open his commission for preparing our Saviour's way before him, according as was appointed, by preaching "the baptism of repentance for the remission of sins." Sacred history has not informed us of the manner in which the Baptist spent the former part of his life; but, according to ancient tradition, Elizabeth, hearing of Herod's barbarous massacre of the infants of Bethlehem, fled into the wilderness, to secure the infant John from the relentless cruelty of that inhuman monster, and there nurtured him with all the tenderness of an affectionate mother. John the Baptist was about eighteen months old when his mother fled with him into the wilderness; within forty days after which, she died.

He proved very successful in his ministry, as he enforced the doctrine of repentance because the kingdom of heaven was at hand; persons of all degrees and professions flocked to him, confessed their sins, were baptized in Jordan, and submitted to whatever the prophet prescribed as necessary to obtain an inheritance in that kingdom, the approach of which he came to declare. Among the converts were many of the Pharisaical tribe, some of whom confessed their sins, and were likewise baptized in Jordan.

The conversation of the Pharisees surprised the Baptist, knowing that they maintained a high opinion of their own sanctity, for which reason it was very astonishing that they should express any desire of obtaining a remission of their sins. In short, he was much surprised to find the whole nation so affected by his threatenings, especially as he knew they expected salvation on account of their being of the seed of Abraham; a conceit which they cherished, and which they seem to have derived from a misrepresentation of the following passage: "Thus saith the Lord, who giveth the sun for a light by day, and the ordinance of the moon, and the stars, for a light by night; who divideth the sea, when the waves thereof roar; the Lord of Hosts is his name; If those ordinances depart from before me, saith the Lord, then the seed of Israel also shall cease from being a nation before me, forever. Thus saith the Lord. If the heaven above can be measured, and the foundation of the earth searched out beneath, I will also cast off the seed of Israel, for all that they have done."

But the Baptist, to curb their arrogance, called them the "offspring of vipers," instead of the children of Abraham; perhaps the Pharisees and Sadducees applied to John for baptism, thinking by that means to avoid the danger they might incur, from being the avowed enemies of the Messiah, whom they expected to come in all the pomp of royalty, and to maintain his superiority by force of arms.

Throughout the whole of the Baptist's ministration, he happily adapted his discourses to the circumstances and capacities of the various people he addressed; and took every pious means to prepare them for the reception of the promised Messiah, who was shortly to appear among them in the glorious character of Saviour and Redeemer of Israel.

Thus, by a life of inflexible virtue, discourses nervous and pathetic, exhortations sincere and fervent, and rebukes honest and courageous, the Baptist became renowned throughout the region of Judea. Such was the admiration of the people at his life and doctrine, that, from the vision of his father Zacharias in the temple, the arrival of the Magi at Jerusalem, the prophecies of Simeon, (circumstances recent in their memories,) they began to conjecture that John might be the promised Messiah, and were even ready to pronounce him the Redeemer of Israel; so, that had he aspired to worldly dignity, he might, for a time, have shone in all the grandeur of human pomp, and claimed a regard superior to the sons of men. But, pious in principle, and humble in heart, he could not arrogate honors of which he was conscious of his unworthiness; and therefore honestly undeceived his numerous followers, by assuring them that, so far from being the glorious person promised, he was only his forerunner; and that, such was his own inferiority, that he was unworthy of doing his most menial offices. "I indeed baptize you with water; but one mightier than I cometh, the latchet of whose shoes I am unworthy to loose." Luke iii: 16.

During the time of the Baptist's continuance at Bethabara, the blessed Jesus left his retirement at Nazareth, and previous to his public ministry, repaired to the banks of the river Jordan, where John was executing his commission for him, in order to be thus baptized by him. We can not impute this conduct of our Lord, to any necessity there was of his conforming to the institution of baptism; for purity needs not cleansing; it is therefore evident, that his motive was to add a sanction to that ordinance, forever after appointed to be the initiating rite of Christianity, "Go, baptize all nations," &c.

It appears that John immediately, as it were by a prophetic revelation, knew the Saviour of the world; for we find from the evangelist, that he acknowledges his superiority, and declined the office: "I have need to be baptized of thee; and comest thou to me?" Our Lord's answer, though short, is very full and expressive: "Suffer it to be so now; for thus it becometh us to fulfill all righteousness." As if he had said, Regard not the precedence at this time, but perform thy office; for it is necessary that we should, in the minutest point, conform to the divine will, by which this institution is enjoined.

This remonstrance removed the objections of John, and he baptized the immaculate Jesus in the river Jordan, in the presence of numerous spectators.

When the ceremony was performed, as he needed not the instructions usually given on the occasion, he went up straightway out of the water, and, kneeling on the bank of the river, fervently addressed his Almighty Father for an abundant effusion of his Holy Spirit, as he was now entering on his public ministry, the prelude of his important mission—the end of which was the salvation of mankind.

CHAPTER IV.

COMMENCEMENT OF OUR SAVIOUR'S MINISTRY—HIS TEMPTATION IN THE WILDERNESS—DEPUTATION OF THE SANHEDRIM TO JOHN THE BAPTIST —FIRST MIRACLE WROUGHT BY THE BLESSED JESUS.

THE great Redeemer having thus complied with the institution of baptism, and received a most convincing testimony of his heavenly Father's approbation, by the miraculous descent and effusion of the Holy Ghost upon him, while praying on the banks of Jordan, in the presence of a multitude of spectators, entered on his public ministry at the age of thirty years, according to the custom of the priests among the Jews.

It was apprehended by the people, that as he had just began his public office, he would repair to Jerusalem, the seat of power and grandeur, in order to display to the mighty and the learned his miraculous abilities and effulgent glories.

But, averse to human praise, the heavenly-minded Jesus preferred solitude to the noise and hurry of mortal life; he therefore retired into the wilderness, in order to prepare himself by fasting, meditation, prayer, and sustaining temptation, for the important work on which he was entering — the salvation of mankind.

To promote this grand design, the evangelists write, that this retirement into the wilderness was in consequence of the immediate direction of the Divine Spirit. Though solitude itself is melancholy, the blessed Jesus added to the dismal scene, by retiring on a barren spot, surrounded by high and craggy mountains, and forming a dark and gloomy chaos.

The Saviour of the world had not only been exposed to poverty and ridicule, but also to the most trying temptation of Satan; that, as the captain of our salvation has undergone the same, we ought not to faint when we are tempted, but, like him, be able to withstand the fiery darts of the devil.

It doubtless appears highly proper, in order that our blessed Lord and Master might both enter upon and prosecute his ministry with more glory to himself and advantage to mankind, that he should previously overcome the most subtle arts of that deceiver, who, under the mask of a serpent, seduced our first parents, and involved them and their posterity in one common ruin.

The peculiar devices by the old Serpent to tempt the Son of God during the time of his fasting, are not recorded in holy writ, and consequently they can not be ascertained.

But at the expiration of the forty days, when the blessed Jesus had endured the keenest hunger, the tempter, to make proof of the divinity of his mission, insolently demanded, why he bore the sensations of hunger? since, if he was the Son of God, he must have power to change the stones of that dreary wilderness into bread; and by so marvelous a transmutation, he might have the satisfaction of knowing the truth of what was said concerning him at his baptism.

But our blessed Saviour repelled his device, by citing the words of Moses, which implied, that God, whenever it seemed good in his sight, could, by extraordinary means, provide for the support of the human race. "Man shall not live by bread alone, but by every word of God." Luke iv: 4.

Satan being defeated in his effort, took him to the top of a very high mountain, and, thinking to work on him by another artifice, showed him a bright view of all the kingdoms of the world, with all their alluring glories, promising him universal empire over the whole, if he would bow down and yield him the honor of the benefaction.

But observe his accursed pride and arrogance, in promising that which is the gift of God alone — universal empire over the earth; and requiring what was due to none but the Supreme — religious homage. This blasphemy, as well as insolence, incited the blessed Jesus to exert his divine authority, and command him, in a peremptory manner, to desist; citing this special injunction from sacred writ, "Thou shalt worship the Lord thy God, and him only shalt thou serve." Thus repelled, he repeated the attempt, and, having taken our Lord to Jerusalem, placed him on the pinnacle of the temple, and, by a taunt of insolence, urged him to prove the truth of his mission, by casting himself down from thence, citing, as an encouragement for him to comply with his desire, a text from the Psalms: "If thou be the Son of God, cast thyself down; for it is written, he shall give his angels charge concerning thee, and in their hands shall they bear thee up, lest at any time thou dash thy foot against a stone." Matt. iv: 6. But our Saviour soon baffled this attempt, by another apt quotation from Scripture: "Thou shalt not tempt the Lord thy God." Matt. iv: 7. Thou shalt not provoke the Lord, either by disobeying his command, or by an impertinent curiosity to know more concerning his mind and will than he is pleased to reveal.

Thus baffled in all his arts and devices, by the wisdom and power of the Son of God, he departed from him, and an host of celestial spirits, dispatched from the regions of bliss, came and ministered refreshment to our Saviour, after his victory over the great enemy and father of mankind.

Hence, notwithstanding the ridicule of the infidel, christians may derive great encouragement to fight manfully against the flesh, the world, and the devil, under the banner of the Great Captain of their salvation, who is ever ready to supply them with spiritual armor to sustain the combat with that inveterate and subtle foe, whose devices he has experienced — being in every respect tempted like them.

During the time of our Saviour's retirement in the wilderness, his faithful harbinger, the Baptist, being assured, from the miraculous descent of the Holy Spirit, and other concurring testimonies, that Jesus was the promised and long-expected Messiah, continued publishing his mission to the multitude; so that the rulers in Jerusalem received information of the surprising events that had happened in Bethabara, beyond Jordan, before they saw the blessed Jesus, in confirmation of whose mission and doctrine they were effected. Prompted by curiosity, they despatched a deputation of priests and Levites to the Baptist, to demand of him, who he was; whether he was the Messiah, or Elias; or a prophet risen from the dead, to precede the Messiah, the powerful Prince, so earnestly expected by the whole nation of Israel?

The Baptist frankly replied, that he was not the Messiah whom they expected, nor Elias, who, as they had vainly thought, would personally appear among them, nor any other prophet risen from the dead; but, at the same time, hinted to them, that though he was not Elias himself, yet he was that person spoken of by the prophet Isaiah, and him of whom he thus prophesied, "The voice of him that crieth in the wilderness, Prepare ye the way of the Lord: make straight in the desert a highway for our God." Isa. xl: 3.

The priests and Levites, not sufficiently gratified with this reply of the Baptist, demanded of him, why he assumed the power of baptizing the people, if he was neither the Messiah, nor Elias, nor any of the ancient prophets risen from the dead? To this demand John answered, I indeed baptize, to show the necessity of repentance: but my baptism is only that of water, and wholly ineffectual of itself to the remission of sins; but that washing foretold by Zacharias, is of sovereign effect; it is not my province, but solely that of the Messiah, who is actually upon earth and among you, though ye know him not, because he hath not yet manifested himself to the world. The Messiah is so far exalted beyond me, in power and dignity, that I am not worthy to do him the meanest offices.

The day after the departure of the priests and Levites from Bethabara, our blessed Lord left the wilderness, and repaired thither himself, while John was yet baptizing and preaching the doctrine of repentance.

The Baptist, as his grand business was to direct all persons to the Messiah, for life and salvation in and through him, embraced this seasonable opportunity of pointing out to the multitude: "Behold the Lamb of God, which taketh away the sins of the world!" Lest the attending crowd should surmise that it had been previously concerted between Jesus and John, that the former should assume, and the latter give him, the appellation of Messiah, he publicly and solemnly declared, that he was, equally with them, ignorant of the pretensions of Jesus to that high character, till he saw the descent of the Holy Ghost, and heard him pronounced, in the most awful manner, the Son of God: "And John bare record, saying, I saw the Spirit descending from heaven like a dove, and it abode upon him. And I knew him not; but He that sent me to baptize with water, the same said unto me, Upon whom thou shalt see the Spirit descending, and remaining, the same is he which baptizeth with the Holy Ghost. And I saw, and bare record that this is the Son of God." John i: 32, 33, 34.

The Baptist having made this declaration, the Messiah left Bethabara, but returned the day following; and John happening to stand with two of his followers on the bank of the river Jordan, pointed to him as he passed, and, in a pious rapture, repeated what he had addressed to the multitude the preceding day: "Behold the Lamb of God!" It is hence imagined that these two disciples, or followers of the Baptist, were absent at the time of the descent of the Holy Ghost, and for that reason this method was taken of pointing out to them the venerable person of the Redeemer of the world.

Animated with an ardent desire of hearing, as well as seeing, this extraordinary person, they left John, and followed Jesus, who, conscious of their design, turned about, and, with the utmost affability, gave them an invitation to the place of his residence. The evangelist John informs us that one of these disciples was Andrew, the brother of Simon Peter; and it is conjectured, from his silence, that himself was the other; for it is remarkable, that in his writings, he has studiously concealed his own name. Be that as it may, it is abundantly evident, that the testimony of the Baptist, added to the tokens he had from the blessed Jesus, in the course of his converse with him, amply satisfied Andrew that he was indeed the promised Messiah, the Saviour and Redeemer of a lost and perishing world.

Andrew soon after found his brother Peter, and brought him to our blessed Lord, telling him that he should afterward be called Cephas, (which signifies a rock,) from his firm resolution of mind, and also be cause he should contribute toward the foundation of the Christian church.

Some time after, Jesus met with Philip, an inhabitant of the town of Bethsaida and said unto him, "Follow me." Philip immediately obeyed the divine command, having heard of the character and mission of our blessed Saviour. It is supposed that this disciple was present at the miraculous descent of the Holy Spirit on our Lord at his baptism, which being admitted, his compliance with his call is no matter of admiration.

Philip meeting with Nathanael, an inhabitant of Cana, a town in Galilee, informed him of the actual coming of the long-expected Messiah, that great Deliverer of Israel, spoken of by Moses and the ancient prophets; "Jesus of Nazareth, the son of Joseph." Nathanael was assured, from the predictions concerning the Messiah, that he was to be descended from the line of David, and born in the city of Bethlehem, and therefore discovered an amazement at his being called Jesus of Nazareth: "Can any good thing come out of Nazareth?" Can that most contemptible of places, Nazareth, be supposed to have given birth to the mighty Saviour, the Prince of Peace, especially as it was expressly foretold by the prophet, that he was to be born in Bethlehem, the city of David?

Notwithstanding the improbability of such an event, Nathanael listened to Philip, and determined on an examination of the person whom he said was the promised Messiah. Accordingly, under his direction, he repaired to the blessed Jesus, who, knowing his character, saluted him on his approach with this honorable appellation, "Behold an Israelite indeed, in whom there is no guile!"

Nathanael, amazed at our Lord's pertinent address, as he had never before seen him, asked by what means he obtained such precise knowledge of him? Our Lord replied, he had seen him under the fig-tree. Probably Nathanael had been praying under the fig-tree, and been overheard by our Lord, who, from the substance of his prayer, thus concluded his character; for when the blessed Jesus informed him that he gave him that character on account of what had passed under the fig-tree, Nathanael perceived that he knew not only what had passed at a distance, but had access to the inmost thoughts of the heart, a property not allotted to mortals, and therefore exclaimed with rapture, "Rabbi, thou art the Son of God, thou art the King of Israel."

Our Saviour then told him, he should hereafter have much stronger testimonials of the divinity of his mission, when he should be eye-witness to what the old patriarch Jacob had before seen in a vision—the angels of heaven descending and ascending, to attend the person, and execute the commands of the Son of Man: an appellation our blessed Lord assumed, not only as considering his humanity, but in order to fulfill most peremptorily that remarkable prediction of the prophet Daniel concerning him: "I saw in the night visions, and, behold, one like the Son of Man came with the clouds of heaven, and came to the Ancient of Days, and they brought him near before him. And there was given him dominion, and glory, and a kingdom, that all people, nations, and languages should serve him; his dominion is an everlasting dominion, which shall not pass away, and his kingdom that which shall not be destroyed." Dan. vii: 13, 14.

The great Redeemer, having attended the divinity of his mission by many incontestible evidences, and made five disciples, departed for Galilee, where, soon after his arrival, he was invited, with his mother and disciples, to a marriage feast at Cana, a place near Nazareth. At these nuptials there happened to be a scarcity of wine, and his mother, who interested herself in the conduct of the feast, and was therefore desirous that everything should be done with decorum, applied to her Son, hoping he would be able to remedy the defect. She had, doubtless, conceived he had the power of working miracles, and was therefore desirous that he would give proof of his ability in the presence of her friends, who were assembled at the marriage.

Addressing herself, therefore, to her Son, she told

him, "They have no wine." Our Lord gently reproved her, in these words, "Woman, what have I to do with thee? mine hour is not yet come:" that is, the time or period of my public ministry is not yet arrived; nor is it time for me to display my supernatural powers.

Notwithstanding this mild reproof, his mother still entertained an opinion that he would interest himself in behalf of her and the company, and therefore ordered the servants punctually to obey his commands.

Our blessed Lord, being assured that working a miracle would greatly tend to confirm the faith of his young disciples, exerted his divine power, by ordering the servants to fill six water pots, containing each about twenty gallons, with water; which was no sooner done, than the whole was converted into excellent wine.

He then ordered them to draw, and bear to the governor of the feast; who, being ignorant of the miracle that had been wrought, and astonished at the preference of this wine, to that which had been served up at the beginning of the feast, addressed himself to the bridegroom, in the hearing of the whole company, telling him that contrary to the usual custom, he had reserved the best wine to the last, at the same time commending so judicious a practice, as a plain proof of his approbation of his friends present at the entertainment. The bridegroom was equally surprised at the address of the governor of the feast, and the occasion of it, which was effected by the supernatural power of our blessed Lord.

This miracle, which was the first wrought by Jesus, confirmed the faith of his followers, and spread his renown through the adjacent country.

CHAPTER V.

EXPULSION OF THE PROFANERS OF THE TEMPLE—JESUS CONVERSES WITH NICODEMUS — BAPTIZES IN JUDEA— INSTRUCTS A POOR SAMARITAN — HEALS A SICK PERSON AT CAPERNAUM —RETIRES AGAIN TO NAZARETH, AND IS EXPELLED THENCE BY HIS IMPIOUS COUNTRYMEN.

OUR blessed Lord, immediately on his arrival at Jerusalem, repaired to the temple, where he was shocked at beholding a place dedicated to the solemn service of Almighty God, so prostituted to purposes of fraud and avarice, and become the resort of traders of every kind. It is evident there must have been a grand market for oxen, sheep, and doves, at such times, for Josephus tells us, that no less than two hundred and fifty-six thousand victims were offered at one passover.

Such abuse could not long escape his notice or correction, having an absolute right to chastise so flagrant a perversion of a place that, strictly speaking, was his own. 'The Lord, whom ye seek, shall suddenly come to his temple; even the Messenger of the Covenant, whom ye delight in: behold, he shall come, saith the Lord of Hosts."

CHRIST AT THE WELL.

Accordingly, the blessed Jesus, whose pious soul was vexed at their profanation of the sacred place, drove out the traders, and overset the tables of the money-changers, saying unto them that sold doves, "Take these things hence; make not my father's house a house of merchandise."

These mercenary wretches appear to have been struck at once with a consciousness of their guilt, and the severity of our Lord's reproof; as they immediately departed, without making the least resistance. But our Lord's conduct in this affair, carrying with it every token of zeal, for which the ancient prophets were so remarkable, the council assembled, and determined to inquire by what authority he attempted such a reformation, requiring, at the same time, a demonstrative proof of the divinity of his commission.

To gratify their curiosity, our Lord referred them only to the miracle of his own resurrection: "Destroy," says he, probably laying his hand on his breast, "this temple, and I will raise it up in three days." The rulers mistaking his meaning, imagined that he referred to the superb and lofty temple finished by Herod, and therefore told him such a relation was highly improbable, nor had they the least reason to think he could possibly rebuild, in three days, that magnificent structure which had been finished at immense expense, and was the labor of so many years.

Though the blessed Jesus declined compliance with the request of the mighty and noble among the inhabitants of Jerusalem, he wrought several miracles in the presence of the common people, in order to confirm the doctrines he delivered, and prove the divinity of his mission.

As there had not been any miracles wrought amongst them for a considerable time, though many were recorded in their sacred books, they beheld our blessed Lord with amazement and veneration; and numbers were satisfied that he was the long promised Messiah, "the desire of all nations," so often foretold by the ancient prophets. For wise reasons, however, he did not publicly discover that he was the Great Prophet, as he knew that the faith of numbers was yet but weak, and that consequently, many would desert his cause, when they found he was opposed by the Sanhedrim, or great council of the nation, and did not set up a worldly kingdom, as they thought the expected Messiah was to do. But the miracles wrought by the Holy Jesus did not excite the wonder and astonishment of the common and illiterate class of the people alone.

Nicodemus, a principal person among them, impartially reflecting on his wondrous works, so astonishing in their nature, so demonstrative in their proof, so salutary in their effect, so happily adapted to the confirmation of his doctrines, and so perfectly agreeable to the attributes of the Deity, as well as the predictions of the ancient prophets, concerning the Messiah, "the Sun of righteousness, who was to rise with healing in his wings," was perfectly assured that nothing less than Omnipotence itself could produce such wonders; and thence, like many others of his countrymen, concluded that Jesus was of a truth the Son, and *sent* of God, which last term is the meaning of the word *Messiah*. But scruples still arose in his mind when, on the other hand, he considered the obscurity of his birth, and the meanness of his appearance, so different from the exalted notions the people of the Jews always entertained concerning this powerful prince, who was to erect his throne in the mighty city of Jerusalem, and subject to his dominion all the states and kingdoms of the earth. To obviate, therefore, these scruples, and solve these perplexing doubts, Nicodemus resolved on an interview with the blessed Jesus; but choosing to conceal his visit from the other members of the Sanhedrim, who were greatly averse to his person and doctrine, he chose the night as most convenient for that purpose.

His salutation of the mighty Redeemer of Israel was this: "Rabbi, we know that thou art a teacher come from God: for no man can do these miracles that thou doest, except God be with him." *John* iii. 2.

Rabbi, I am sufficiently convinced that thou art immediately sent as a teacher from on high; for nothing less than power divine could enable thee to perform the miracles which thou hast wrought in the presence of multitudes. But this salutation by no means implies, that Nicodemus thought Jesus the great promised Messiah, even the Redeemer of Israel; nor could he obtain that knowledge, till it was revealed to him by the blessed Spirit of God.

We may observe, that our Saviour waiving all formality and circumlocution, which tend to no real profit, immediately preaches to this disguised Rabbi the first great doctrine of Christianity, regeneration: "Verily, verily, I say unto thee, except a man be born again, he cannot see the kingdom of God." Nicodemus, I declare unto thee, as a truth of the last importance; verily, verily, unless a man be regenerated in the spirit of his mind, have his will and affections transferred from earthly to spiritual objects, he cannot see the kingdom of God, which is holy and spiritual in its nature and enjoyments.

This was a mysterious system to the Rabbi, whose religious views extended no farther than to rites and ceremonies, and were bounded by time and space; besides, he thought the very position of our Lord an absurdity in terms. "How can a man be born when he is old? Can he enter a second time into his mother's womb, and be born?" Our Lord replies to this question, "Except a man be born of water and of the Spirit, he cannot enter into the kingdom of God." The regeneration which I preach unto you is not of a natural, but of a spiritual nature: unless a man embraces the Christian religion and doctrines, whose initiating ordinance is baptism, and become a subject of divine grace, he cannot be the subject of that glory, which consists not in earthly splendor, and the gratification of the meaner passions, but in an exemption from whatever is earthly, sensual, and devilish, and the prosecution of whatever is heavenly, holy, and spiritual. "That which is born of the flesh is flesh; and that which is born of the spirit is spirit. Marvel not that I say unto thee, ye must be born again;" wonder not at my doctrine of regeneration, which is designed to inform you, that you derive no excellence from your boasted descent from Abraham; as such you are merely earthly, subject to sins, and infirmities of every kind; as well as to show that you must undergo a spiritual mental regeneration, a renovation of the heart, which changes the whole man, and fits you for the participation of heavenly blessedness.

This important work is likewise spiritual in its operation, unseen by mortal eyes, being wrought on the mind or heart of man, by the powerful influence of the Holy Spirit, which changes his nature, and with respect to eternal things, makes him another, a new creature. "The wind bloweth where it listeth, and thou hearest the sound thereof, but canst not tell whence it cometh, and whither it goeth: so is every one that is born of the spirit."

Notwithstanding this explanation of the blessed Jesus, Nicodemus was so prepossessed with partiality toward the Jews, who, on account of their alliance to Abraham, thought they were the people of God, entitled to heaven, and consequently in no need of this new operation of the mind, called regeneration, that he again demanded, "How can these things be?" The divine instructor then reproves his dullness and misapprehension of what he had so clearly explained and propounded to him, especially as he was himself a teacher of the people, and one of the great council of the nation. "Art thou a master of Israel, and knowest not these things?" The doctrines I deliver are not fiction, and mere surmise, but founded on eternal truth, immediately revealed from God, and consistent with the will of heaven. I am witness to the same, and therefore affirm that such testimony is sufficient to render them valid. But your prejudices still prevail, nor can your belief be conquered by all the arguments I can advance. "We speak that we do know, and testify that we have seen; and ye receive not our witness."

If ye thus reject the first principles of the Christian religion, such as the necessity of regeneration, or the influence of the spirit of God upon the heart of man, how will ye believe the sublimer truths I shall hereafter deliver concerning the kingdom of God, or state of the saints in glory? If I inform you of spiritual transactions in this lower world, and ye believe not, how can ye believe if I tell you of those things which relate solely to another and heavenly state? But to confirm your belief in what I have delivered, know that my assured knowledge of these things is derived from the Father of Light, the God of Truth, by whom I am invested with gifts superior to any of the ancient prophets.

No man hath ascended the regions of immortality, and descended from thence, but "the Son of Man," consequently, no man but "the Son of Man," can, with truth and certainty, reveal the immediate will of the Father, who is in heaven. Your great lawgiver Moses, ascended not there, Mount Sinai was the summit of his elevation; whereas the Son of Man, who was in heaven, and came down from thence, with a divine commission to sinful mortals, had the most clear and convincing proofs of the will of his Almighty Father, penetrated into the designs of infinite wisdom and grace, and consequently must be higher than any prophet, being in a peculiar sense, the prophet of the most high God, or Angel of the presence.

This divine preacher, who spake as no man ever spake, likewise labors to eradicate the favorite principle of the Jews: I mean, that of confining all blessings, temporal and eternal, to their own nation and people, as well as to show the vanity of their expecting the appearance of the Messiah, in pomp and magnificence.

To effect this glorious design, he lays open to the Rabbi, that it was agreeable both to the doctrines of Moses, as well as the will of God, that the Redeemer, in this state of mortality, should be exposed to poverty and .distress of every kind: that his conquests were not to be of a temporal nature, over the hearts and wills of mankind; that his throne was not to be established in the earthly, but heavenly Jerusalem; previous to which he was to shed his blood, as, by virtue of the same, all of every nation and kingdom throughout the earth might pass into the heavenly world, and there, forever, provided they relied on his merits, and conformed their lives to the doctrines he preached, enjoy that summit of bliss, which, through his sufferings, was provided for them, by God himself, to all eternity.

This is the sum and substance of Christianity; this is the sum and substance of what our blessed Lord preached to Nicodemus, that great ruler and teacher of the Jews; a sermon comprehending the whole of what need be taught, notwithstanding religion is at this day rent to pieces by sectaries; each of whom invent some new-fangled doctrine, suggested by ignorance, presumption, or both united.

That God Almighty, the Father, out of his unsupplicated, unmerited grace and mercy to the sinful race of men, sent his only begotten Son to purchase eternal life, through the effusion of his own blood, for all of every nation and kingdom throughout the earth, who should believe in him; that is, who should believe in the divinity of his mission, the efficacy of his atonement, and, in consequence of that faith, conform, as far as the infirmities of sinful nature will permit, to the rules of his Gospel. "Only let your conversation be as becometh the Gospel of Christ:" condemnation justly passed on all transgressors of the law of God, (which are all mankind) can alone be averted according to the divine institution, the propriety of which it is the height of impiety and presumption to call in question; by faith in the blessed Jesus, such a faith as we have just explained. "He that believeth on him is not condemned; but he that believeth not is condemned already, because he hath not believed in the name of the only begotten Son of God."

It appears from the future conduct of Nicodemus, that instead of supposing Jesus to be only "a teacher come from God," he was fully convinced that he was the "Messiah, the Redeemer of Israel:" for he afterwards constantly espoused his cause in the great council of the nation; and when his countrymen put him to an ignominious death, he, together with Joseph of Arimathea, conveyed him to burial, when all others had forsaken him.

The time of the passover at Jerusalem being expired, Jesus, together with his disciples, withdrew into the remote parts of Judea, where he continued a considerable time, preaching the kingdom of God, and baptizing the new converts. John the Baptist being also, at the same time, baptizing in the river Enon, a dispute arose between his disciples and certain Jews concerning the preference of the baptism of Jesus.

Being unable to decide the point, they referred it to the opinion of John; on which the pious Baptist immediately declared, that he was only the harbinger of the great Messiah, who baptized not only with water but with the Holy Spirit; adding, that his own ministry was on the decline, as the beauty of the morning star, the harbinger of the sun, decreases, when that fountain of life but dawns in the chambers of the east.

The Baptist likewise mentioned to his disciples and hearers many circumstances tending to prove the divinity of the mission of the holy Jesus, and the important design of his incarnation.—"He that believeth on the Son hath eternal life, but he that believeth not the Son shall not see life; but the wrath of God abideth on him."

The Baptist, having publicly preached the great doctrine of salvation, through faith in Jesus, departed from the wilderness of Judea, where he had continued a considerable time, and went into Galilee, often repairing to the court of Herod, who esteemed, or affected to esteem, both his preaching and person. But John being faithful in his ministry, could not fail to remonstrate on the injustice and impiety of a known practice of Herod, which was, his cohabiting with Herodias, his brother Philip's wife; and thereby incurring the displeasure of that ambitious woman, he was, at her instance, cast into prison, and there reserved for future destruction.

While these things happened in Galilee, our blessed Lord continued preaching in the wilderness, whither great numbers resorted, attracted by curiosity to see the miracles which fame reported he daily wrought. The success of his ministry exciting the envy of the hypocritical tribe of Pharisees, our blessed Lord thought proper to retire into Galilee, in order to promote the design of his mission in those parts.

In the course of his journey, being weary of traveling in so warm a country, and excessively thirsty, he sat down in Samaria by a celebrated well, given by the old patriarch Jacob to his son Joseph, while his disciples were gone to the city to procure provisions.

While the humble Jesus was sitting by the well-side, a woman, a native of the country, came with her pitcher to fetch water; and our Lord requested of her to give him to drink. The appearance of Jesus astonished the woman, because she knew him to be a Jew, and the Samaritans were held in the utmost contempt by those people, who, indeed, arrogated a preference to all nations upon earth. But though she knew him to be a Jew, she knew not that he was the Son of God, full of grace and truth, divested of human prejudices, and the very essence of humility and every virtue. As the design of his mission and incarnation was to promote the real happiness of mankind, he embraced every opportunity of enforcing his salutary doctrines; and therefore, though his thirst was extreme, he delayed its gratification, in order to inform this woman, though of an infamous character, of the means by which she might obtain living water, or, in other words, eternal life. As the best method to effect this purpose, he gave her to understand, that had she known the character of the supplicant, she would have eagerly satisfied his desire, and been rewarded by a gift the most invaluable—even living water, issuing from the well of eternal salvation.

The woman taking his words in the common acceptation, imagining that he suggested his power of supplying her with water flowing from a perpetual spring, which, in that parched climate, appeared impossible, demanded of him if he was vested with a power superior to their father Jacob, who dug this well, drank out of it with his family, and left it for the benefit of posterity.

The Saviour and friend of mankind, still benign in his purpose toward this poor sinner, replied, "That all who drank of the water of Jacob's well would thirst again, being but a temporary allay of a desire incident to human nature; whereas, those who drank of the water which he was ready to dispense, should never thirst; because that water flowed from the inexhaustible Fountain of Divine Grace, and could not be drained but with immensity itself."

Though this great Preacher of Israel, by a simple and natural allegory, displayed the power of divine grace, the woman, ignorant of the allusion and meaning of the blessed Jesus, desired of him that water, that she might not thirst in future, nor have occasion to come to Jacob's well daily for water.

To show her the nature of sin, and thereby create in her soul desires after the water of life, the blessed Jesus, by some pertinent questions and replies, evinced his knowledge of her infamous course of life, and by that means convinced her that he acted under an influence more than human. To evade, however, the present subject of discourse, which filled her with a degree of awe and fear, she proposed for discussion a case long warmly contested between the Jews and Samaritans: Whether Mount Gerizim, or the city of Jerusalem, was destined by God as the place peculiarly set apart for religious worship? Our blessed Lord replied to this insignificant question, that it was not the place, but the manner, in which adoration was offered to the Father of Spirits, that rendered such worship acceptable; observing that "God is a spirit, and they that worship him must worship him in spirit and in truth." John iv: 24.

In consequence of this reply to her, which apparently referred to things spiritual and eternal, she informed the blessed Jesus of her expectation of the arrival of the promised Messiah, who should punctually inform them concerning these points, so long and undecisively contested.

Our Lord, embracing the opportunity of preaching himself to this poor woman, as the Saviour of sinners, replied without hesitation, "I that speak unto thee, am he."

While Jesus continued talking with the woman, his disciples returned, and approached him at the very time when he told the woman that he was the Messiah. Though they were astonished at his condescension in conversing with an inhabitant of Samaria, and even of instructing her in the doctrines of religion, none presumed to ask him why he conversed with one who was an enemy to the Jews, and the worship in the temple of Jerusalem. But the woman, hearing Jesus call himself the Messiah, left the pitcher, and ran into the city, to publish the glad tidings, That the great Deliverer of mankind was then sitting by the well of Jacob, and had told her all the secret transactions of her life. This report astonished the Samaritans, and, at the same time, roused their curiosity to see a person foretold by Moses and the prophets, and of whose appearance there was then so universal an expectation.

The disciples, on their return, set before their Master the provisions they had purchased; but he, wholly absorbed in meditation, refused the refreshment so highly requisite, telling them that he had "meat to eat that they knew not of." This unexpected answer surprised his disciples, who, understanding his words in their natural sense, asked one another, whether any person had, during their absence, supplied him with provisions. But Jesus soon explained the mystery, by telling them that he did not mean natural, but spiritual food; that to execute the commission he had received from his Father, was far better to him than meat or drink; and the satisfaction he was going to receive from the conversion of the Samaritans, much greater than any sensual enjoyments.

Many of the Samaritans were now near Jesus, who, lifting up his eyes, and seeing the ways crowded with people coming to him from the city, stretched out his benevolent hands toward them, and addressed his disciples in the following manner: "Say not ye there are yet four months, and then cometh harvest? Behold, I say unto you, lift up your eyes, and look on the fields, for they are already white unto harvest."—John iv: 35. Behold yonder multitudes, how they are thronging to hear the word, which has only a few minutes been sown in their hearts! It is not, therefore, always necessary to wait with patience for the effect, which sometimes immediately follows the cause. To gather this spiritual harvest, and finish the work of him that sent me, is my proper food; adding, for the encouragement of his disciples, as you have labored with me in this harvest, so shall you participate in the great recompense of eternal rewards: "He that reapeth receiveth wages, and gathereth fruit unto life eternal; that both he that soweth, and he that reapeth, may rejoice together." John iv: 36.

Many of the people had been so affected at the words of the woman, that they were fully persuaded Jesus could be no other than the great Messiah; accordingly, their first request was, that he would deign to take up his residence in their city. The compassionate Redeemer of the human race so far complied, as to stay with them two days—an interval which he spent in preaching to them the kingdom of God: so that the greatest part of the city embraced the doctrine of the gospel, and, at his departure, said unto the woman, "Now we believe, not because of thy saying; for we have heard him ourselves, and know that this is indeed the Christ, the Saviour of the world." John iv: 42.

Having accomplished his gracious design in Samaria, Jesus continued his journey to Galilee, to exercise his ministry, and preach there the kingdom of God; telling his disciples, that the time was now accomplished which had been predetermined by Omnipotence for erecting the happy kingdom of the Prince of Peace.

Our Lord had performed several miracles at Jerusalem during the passover, at which the inhabitants of Galilee were present. His preaching was, therefore, at first attended with great success; for they listened attentively to his doctrine, and received it with particular kindness and courtesy—especially the people of Cana, where he had turned the water into wine.

During his residence in that city, a nobleman of Capernaum came to him, requesting, with great humility and reverence, that he would come down and heal his son, who was at the point of death. Our blessed Saviour readily complied with the latter part of his request; but to remove a prejudice they had conceived, that it was necessary to be personally present in order to restore the sick person to health, he refused to go down to Capernaum, dismissing the father with this assurance, that his son was restored to health: "Go thy way; thy son liveth." John iv: 50. The nobleman obeyed the word of Jesus, and immediately departed for his own house; but before his arrival, he was met by his servants, with the joyful news that his son was recovered. On this the father inquired at what time they perceived an alteration for the better; and from their answer was satisfied, that immediately after the words were spoken by the blessed Jesus, the fever left him, and he was recovered in a miraculous manner. This amazing instance of his power and goodness abundantly convinced the nobleman and his family, that Jesus was the true Messiah, the great prophet so long promised to the world.

After some stay in the city and neighborhood of Cana, Jesus went to Nazareth, where he had spent the greater part of his youth, and, as his constant custom was, went to the synagogue on the Sabbath day, and read that celebrated prediction of the Messiah in the prophet Isaiah; "The spirit of the Lord is upon me, because he hath anointed me to preach the gospel to the poor; he hath sent me to heal the broken-hearted, to preach deliverance to the captives, and recovering of sight to the blind, to set at libert them that are bruised, to preach the acceptable year of the Lord. Luke iv: 18, 19.

It should be remembered, that our blessed Saviour read this passage in the original Hebrew, which was then a dead language; and, as he had never been taught letters, could do it only by inspiration from above. But he did more; he explained the passage with such strength of reason, and beauty of expression, that the inhabitants of Nazareth, who well knew he had never been initiated into the rudiments of learning, heard him with astonishment. But as he performed no miracle in their city, they were offended at him. Perhaps they thought the place of his residence should have been his peculiar care; and, as he could, with a single word, heal the sick at a distance, not a single person in Nazareth should have been afflicted with any kind of disease. That they really entertained sentiments of this kind, seems plain from our Saviour's own words: "Ye will surely say to me, Physician, heal thyself: whatever we have heard done in Capernaum, do also here in thy country; evidently alluding to the great and benevolent miracle he had wrought on the nobleman's son.

But the holy Jesus, by enumerating the miracles Elijah had done in behalf of the widow of Sarepta, who was a heathen, and the inhabitants of an idolatrous city in the time of famine, when many widows in Israel perished with hunger, and of Naaman the Syrian, who was cured of his leprosy by the prophet Elisha, when numbers of Jews, afflicted with the same loathsome disease, were suffered to continue in their uncleanliness, sufficiently proved that the prophets had, on some extraordinary occasions, wrought miracles in favor of those whom the Israelites, from a fond conceit of their being the peculiar favorites of heaven, judged unworthy of such marks of particular favor. The council was so incensed at this reply, that forgetting the sanctity of the Sabbath, they hurried him through the streets, "to the brow of the hill whereon their city was built," intending to cast him headlong down the precipice. But the Son of God defeated their cruel intentions, by miraculously confounding their sight, and withdrawing from the fury of these wretched people.

CHAPTER VI.

OUR LORD PROCEEDS TO CAPERNAUM—ADDS TO THE NUMBER OF HIS FOLLOWERS—PROCLAIMS THE GOSPEL IN GALILEE—PREACHES TO A NUMEROUS AUDIENCE HIS WELL-KNOWN AND EXCELLENT DISCOURSE UPON THE MOUNT.

THE holy Jesus, aggrieved by the cruel Nazarenes, departed from them, and visited Capernaum, the capital of Galilee, (on the borders of the Lake of Gennesaret,) which was a place highly convenient for his design; for, besides the numerous inhabitants of that city, the trading towns on the lake were crowded with strangers, who, after hearing the doctrine of the gospel preached by the great Redeemer of mankind, would not fail to spread, in their respective countries, the happy tidings of salvation.

While Jesus tarried at Capernaum, he usually taught in the synagogues on the Sabbath day, preaching with such energy of power, as greatly astonished the whole congregation. He did not, however, constantly confine himself to that city; the adjacent country was often blessed with his presence, and cheered with the heavenly words of his mouth.

In one of the neighboring villages, he called Simon and Andrew, who were following their occupation of fishing on the lake, to accompany him. These disciples, who had before been acquainted with him, readily obeyed the heavenly mandate, and followed the Saviour of the world. Soon after, he saw James and John, who were also fishing on the lake, and called them also. Nor did they hesitate to follow the great Redeemer of mankind; and, from their ready compliance, there is reason to believe that they, as well as Simon and Andrew, were acquainted with Jesus at Jordan, unless, we suppose, which is far from being improbable, that their readiness proceeded from the secret energy of his power upon their minds. But, however this be, the four disciples accompanied our blessed Saviour to Capernaum, and soon after to different parts of Galilee.

How long our Lord was on this journey can not be determined; all the evangelists have mentioned is, that he wrought a great number of miracles on diseased persons; and that the fame of these wonderful works drew people from Galilee, Jerusalem, Judea, and beyond Jordan. Nor was the knowledge of these miracles concealed from the heathen, particularly the inhabitants of Syria; for they also brought their sick to Galilee to be healed by him. Consequently, the time our blessed Saviour spent in these tours, must have been considerable, though the evangelists have said very little concerning it.

But whatever time was spent in these benevolent actions, the prodigious multitudes which flocked to him from every quarter, moved his compassion toward those who were bewildered in the darkness of ignorance, and determined him to preach to them "the words of eternal life."

For this blessed purpose, he ascended a mountain in that neighborhood; and placing himself on an eminence, from whence he could be heard by throngs of people attending him, he inculcated, in an amazingly pathetic manner, the most important points of religion. But, alas! they were coldly received, because many of them were directly opposite to the standing precepts delivered by the scribes and Pharisees. Surely, these people, who had seen the blessed Jesus perform so many benevolent actions to the poor, the diseased, and the maimed, might have entertained a more favorable opinion of his doctrine, and known that so compassionate and powerful a person must have been actuated by the spirit of God, and, consequently, that the doctrine he taught was really divine.

He opened his excellent sermon with the doctrine of happiness, a subject which the teachers of wisdom have always considered as the principal object in morals, and employed their utmost abilities to convey a clear idea of it to their disciples, but differed very remarkably with regard to the particulars in which it consisted. The Jews were, in general, persuaded that the enjoyments of sense were the sovereign good. Riches, conquest, liberty, mirth, women, fame, revenge, and other things of the same kind, afforded them such pleasures, that they wished for no better in the Messiah's kingdon, which they all considered as a secular one; and that a "golden," instead of a "scepter of righteousness," would have been the "scepter of his kingdom." Nay, some of the disciples themselves retained, for a time, tho like kind of notion, till they were convinced of their mistake, by the spirit, word, and conduct of their divine Master.

Having shown in what true happiness consisted, our Saviour addressed himself to his disciples, and explained their duty, as the teachers appointed to conduct others in the paths that lead to eternal felicity; and excited them to diligence in dispensing the salutary influences of their doctrine and example, that their hearers might honor and praise the great Creator of heaven and earth, who had been so kind to the children of men. As his definition of happiness was very different from what the Jews were accustomed to hear from the scribes and Pharisees, he thought proper to declare, that he was not come to destroy the moral precepts contained in the law and the prophets, but to fulfill or confirm them.

Nothing is so steadfast as the eternal truths of morality: the heavens may pass away, and the whole frame of nature be dissolved, but the rules of righteousness shall remain immutable and immortal. And, therefore, he ordered his disciples, on the severest penalties, to enforce, both by preaching and example, the strict observation of all the moral precepts contained in the sacred writings, and that in a much greater latitude than they were taken by the teachers of Israel; and, in consideration of the frailties of human nature, taught them that excellent form of prayer, which has been used by Christians of most denominations to this very day: "Our Father," &c.

If earthly parents are called fathers, the Almighty has the best title from every creature, and particularly from men, being the father of their spirits, the maker of their bodies, and the continual preserver of both

Father is the most magnificent title invented by poets and philosophers, in honor of their gods; it conveys the most lively idea possible to the human breast. As it is used by mankind in general, it marks the essential character of the true God; namely, that he is the first cause of all things, or the author of our being, and, at the same time, conveys a strong idea of the tender love he bears to his creatures, whom he nourishes with an affection, and protects with a watchfulness, infinitely superior to that of an earthly parent. The name of father also teaches us, that we owe our being to God, points out his goodness and mercy in upholding us, and expresses his power in giving us the things we ask. Nor is this all: we are likewise taught to give our Maker the title of father, that our sense of the tender relation in which he stands to us may be confirmed; our faith in his power and goodness strengthened; our hopes of obtaining what we ask in prayer cherished; and our desire of obeying and imitating him quickened; for the light of nature teaches us, that it is disgraceful in children to degenerate from their parents, and that they can not commit a greater crime than to disobey the commands of an indulgent father.

Lastly, we are commanded to call him father in the plural number, (and that even in our secret addresses to the throne of grace,) to put us in mind that we are all brethren, the children of one common parent; and that we ought to love one another with sincerity, as we pray not for ourselves only, but for all the human race.

"Who art in heaven." The words do not suppose the presence of God confined; he is present every where; about our paths, about our bed, and narrowly inspecteth every action of the sons of men. But they express his majesty and power, and distinguish him from those we call fathers upon earth, and from false gods, which are not in heaven, the happy mansion of bliss and felicity; where the Almighty, who is essentially present in every part of the universe, gives more especial manifestation of his presence to such of his creatures as he hath exalted to share with him in the eternal felicities of the heavenly Jerusalem.

"Hallowed be thy name." By the name of God, the Hebrews understood God himself, his attributes, and his works; and, therefore, the meaning of the petition is, May thy existence be universally believed, thy presence loved and imitated, thy works admired, thy supremacy over all things acknowledged, thy providence reverenced and confided in! May all the sons of men think so highly of his divine majesty, of his attributes, of his works! and may we so express our veneration for God, that his glory may be manifested in every corner of the world!

"Thy kingdom come." Let the kingdom of the Messiah be extended to the utmost parts of the earth, that all the children of men "may become one fold, under one shepherd — Jesus Christ the righteous."

"Thy will be done on earth as it is in heaven." May thy will, O thou great Father of the universe, be made known to us by the light of thy glorious Gospel, that we may be enabled to imitate the angels of light, by giving as sincere, universal, and constant obedience to thy divine commands, as the imperfections of human nature will permit.

"Give us this day our daily bread." Give us, from time to time, such wholesome and proper food, that we may be enabled to worship thee with cheerfulness and vigor.

"And forgive us our debts, as we forgive our debtors." The Almighty, as supreme governor of the universe, has a right to support his government, by punishing those who transgress his laws. The suffering of punishment, therefore, is a debt which sinners owe to the divine justice; so, that when we ask God, in prayer, to forgive our debts, we beg that he would be mercifully pleased to remit the punishment of all our sins, and that, laying aside his displeasure, he would receive us into favor, and bless us with life eternal. In this petition, therefore, we confess our sins, and express the sense we have of their guilt; namely, that they deserve death; and surely, nothing can be more proper than such a confession in our addresses to God; because humility and a sense of our unworthiness, when we ask favors of the Almighty, whether spiritual or temporal, have a tendency to augment the goodness of God in bestowing them upon us.

The terms of this petition are worthy our notice: "Forgive us only as we forgive." We must forgive others, if we hope ourselves to be forgiven; and are permitted to crave from God, such forgiveness only as we grant to others; so, that if we do not forgive even our enemies, we seriously and solemnly implore the Almighty to condemn us to the punishment of eternal death. How remarkably careful, therefore, should men be to purge their hearts from all rancor and malice, before they enter the temple of the Almighty, to offer up their prayers to the throne of grace!

"And lead us not into temptation,. but deliver us

from evil." That is, do not lead us into such temptations as are too hard for human nature; "but deliver us," by some means, from the evil, either by removing the temptation, or increasing our strength to resist it. This petition teaches us to preserve a sense of our own inability to repel and overcome the solicitations of the world; and of the necessity there is of our receiving assistance from above, both to regulate our passions, and enable us to prosecute a religious life.

"For thine is the kingdom, and the power, and the glory, forever." Because the government of the universe is thine forever, and thou alone possessest the power of creating and upholding all things; and because the glory of thine infinite perfections remains eternally with thee, therefore all men ought to hallow thy name, submit themselves to thy government, and perform thy will; and, in an humble sense of their dependence, seek from thee the supply of their wants, the pardon of their sins, and the kind protection of thy providence.

This is emphatically called the Lord's Prayer, because delivered by the Son of God himself; and, therefore, we should do well to understand it thoroughly, that when we enter the temple of the Lord, and address him in solemn prayer, we may have hopes that he will grant our petitions. And, above all, not to harbor in our breasts the least envy or malice against any who have offended us; for it is only on a supposition that we have forgiven others, that we may have the least reason to hope for obtaining forgiveness from the great Creator.

The divine Preacher proceeded to discover the great duty of fasting, in which he directed them not to follow the hypocrites, in disfiguring their faces, and clothing themselves in the melancholy weeds of sorrow, but to be chiefly solicitous to appear before God as one that truly fasteth. Then will the Almighty, who constantly surrounds us, and is acquainted even with the most secret thoughts of our hearts, openly bestow upon us the rewards of a true penitent — mortification, contrition, and humility he can discern, without the external appearance of sorrow and repentance. It must, however, be remembered, that our blessed Saviour is here speaking of private fasting, and to this alone his directions are to be applied; for when we are called upon to mourn over public sins or calamities, it ought to be performed in the most public manner.

Heavenly-mindedness was the next virtue inculcated by the blessed Jesus; and this he recommended with a peculiar earnestness, because the Jewish doctors were, in general, strangers to this grace, in which he was desirous his followers should be clothed, as being the most excellent ornament for a teacher of righteousness. This virtue is strenuously recommended by our blessed Saviour, by showing the deformity of its opposite, covetousness, which has only perishable things for its object. "Lay not up for yourselves treasures upon earth, where moth and rust doth corrupt, and where thieves break through and steal. But lay up for yourselves treasures in heaven, where neither moth nor rust doth corrupt, and where thieves do not break through and steal. For where your treasure is, there will your heart be also." Matt. vi: 19 – 21.

More solid happiness will accrue from depositing your treasures in heaven, than in laying them up on earth, where they are subject to a thousand disasters, and even, at best, can remain only for a short series of years; whereas, those laid up in heaven are permanent, and will lead to a "crown of glory that fadeth not away, eternal in the heavens." Nor let any man be so foolish as to think he can place his heart on the happiness of a future life, when his treasures are deposited in this vale of misery; for wherever are laid up the goods which his soul desireth, there his heart and affections will also remain. If, therefore, ye are desirous of sharing in the joys of eternity, you must lay up your treasures in the "mansions of my Father's kingdom."

Lest they should imagine it was possible to be both heavenly-minded and covetous at the same time, he assured them that this was full as absurd as to imagine that a person could, at the same time, serve and divide his affections equally between two masters of opposite characters; for either he will hate the one, and love the other, or else he will hold to the one, and despise the other: "Ye cannot serve God and Mammon." Matt. vi: 24.

To strengthen this doctrine, he added a few plain evident instances of the power, perfection, and extent of God's providence, in which his tender care for the least and weakest of his creatures shines with a remarkable luster, demonstrating the wise and parental attention of the Deity to all the creatures of his hand. He desired them to observe the birds of the air, the lilies, and even the grass of the field—leading his most illiterate hearers to form a more elevated and extensive idea of the divine government, than the philosophers had attained; who, though they allowed, in general, that the world was governed by God, had very confused notions of his providence with regard to every individual creature and action. He taught them that the

Almighty Father of the whole is the guardian and protector of the universe; that every action is subject to his will, and nothing left to the blind determination of chance.

Having enforced these heavenly precepts, he exhorted them to place an humble dependence on the Spirit, to strive to practice the precepts of religion, however difficult the task might appear. "Enter ye in at the straight gate; for wide is the gate, and broad is the way that leadeth to destruction, and many there be which go in thereat. Because straight is the gate, and narrow is the way which leadeth unto life, and few there be that find it." Matt. vii: 13, 14. How straight indeed is the gate, and narrow is the way that leadeth to life. In the way nothing is to be found that flatters the flesh, but many things that have a tendency to mortify it — poverty, fasting, watching, injuries, chastity, sobriety. And with regard to the gate, it receives none that are puffed up with the glory of this life, none that are indulging in luxury; it does not admit those that love riches, or are encumbered with the goods of this world. None can pass through it but those who renounce all worldly lust, and are resolved to forsake all sin. There is, however, no reason for us to despair of entering through this heavenly portal; if we sincerely endeavor, the assistance of the Holy Spirit will be freely given us, and we shall safely pass through the "straight gate," and pursue our journey with ease along the "narrow path," till we arrive at the blissful mansion of the heavenly Canaan.

But lest evil-minded men, under the mask of piety and religion, should endeavor to draw them from the paths of righteousness, our blessed Saviour cautioned his disciples to beware of such persons, and carefully make the strictest scrutiny into their lives and doctrines.

Our Lord closed his sermon with the parable of the houses built on different foundations; intimating, that the bare knowledge, or the simple hearing, of the divinest lessons of the truth ever delivered, nay, even the belief of these instructions, without the practice of them, is of no manner of importance. Religion alone is the foundation which can so firmly establish us, that we can not be shaken by all the tempests of afflictions, temptations, and persecutions of the present age. It is this foundation alone, which, like a flinty rock, on the eternal basis of the mountains, can support us in the day of trial. This alone can enable us to frustrate the attempts of men and devils, and patiently endure all the troubles of mortality.

CHAPTER VII.

OUR BLESSED LORD CURES THE LEPROSY AND PALSY — CASTS OUT A DEVIL — SUCCORS THE MOTHER-IN-LAW OF PETER; AND AFTERWARD PURSUES HIS JOURNEY THROUGH THE COUNTRY OF GALILEE.

THE great Preacher of Israel, having finished his excellent discourse, came down from the mountain, surrounded by a multitude of people, who had listened with astonishment to the doctrines he delivered, which were soon confirmed by divers miracles. A leper met him in his way to Capernaum, and being, doubtless, acquainted with the wondrous works he had already performed, threw himself, with great humility, before the Son of God, using this remarkable expression, "Lord, if thou wilt, thou canst make me clean."

The species of leprosy common among the Jews, and the other eastern nations, was equally nauseous and infectious; but this was so far from preventing the blessed Jesus from approaching so loathsome an object, that it increased his pity — he even touched him; but instead of being polluted himself, the leper was instantly cleansed, and he departed glorifying God.

The evangelist adds, that Jesus forbade him to tell any person what had been done, but repair immediately to the priest, and offer the gift commanded by Moses.

HRIST HEALING THE MAN SICK WITH PALSY.

Having performed the cure on the leper, our blessed Lord proceeded to Capernaum; but as he entered the city, he was met by a Roman centurion, who represented to him, in the most pathetic manner, the deplorable condition of his servant, who was grievously afflicted with a palsy. The compassionate Redeemer of the world listened attentively to his complaint, and immediately told him he would come and heal him. The centurion thought this a great condescension to one who was not of the seed of Jacob, and therefore told him, that he did not mean he should give himself the trouble of going to his house, as this was an honor he had not the least reason to expect, he being confident that his word alone would be sufficient — diseases and devils being as much subject to his commands, as his soldiers were to him.

Our Lord was amazed at these words; not that he was ignorant of the centurion's faith, or the basis on which it was built: he well knew the thoughts of his heart long before he uttered his request, but he was filled with admiration at the exalted idea the Roman officer had conceived of his power; and to make his faith the more conspicuous, he gave it the praise it so justly deserved: "Verily I say unto you, I have not found so great faith, no, not in Israel." Matt. viii: 10.

This centurion, doubtless, relied upon the miracle Jesus had before wrought upon the nobleman's son; but the excellency and peculiarity of it consisted in applying the most grand ideas of superior power to Jesus, who, according to outward appearance, was only one of the sons of men.

This exalted faith induced the blessed Jesus to declare the gracious intentions of his Almighty Father with regard to the Gentiles; namely, that he would as readily accept their faith as that of the Jews, and place them with Abraham, Isaac, and Jacob in the kingdom of heaven; while those who boasted of being the offspring of these great patriarchs, but fell far short of the heathen in faith, should be excluded from the blissful seats of Paradise. "And I say unto you, that many shall come from the east and the west, and shall sit down with Abraham, and Isaac, and Jacob, in the kingdom of heaven. But the children of the kingdom shall be cast out into outer darkness: there shall be weeping and gnashing of teeth." Matt. viii: 11, 12.

Having thus addressed the multitude, the blessed Jesus turned himself to the centurion, and said, "Go thy way, and as thou hast believed, so be it done unto thee." Though the idea thou conceived of my power is just, though remarkably great, as a reward for thy faith I grant the petition thou hast asked of me. "And," the evangelist adds, "his servant was healed in the self-same hour." Matt. viii: 13.

On the succeeding Sabbath, our Saviour went into the Jewish synagogue at Capernaum, and taught the people, delivering his instructions in so graceful and elegant a manner, that they were all astonished; and, to increase their admiration, one of the congregation, possessed with an unclean spirit, cried out in a terrible manner, "Let us alone; what have we to do with thee, thou Jesus of Nazareth? Art thou come to destroy us? I know thee who thou art, the Holy One of God." Mark i: 24.

But the blessed Jesus, who wanted the testimony of no such confessors, commanded him to keep silence, and immediately come out of the man, which command the evil spirit instantly obeyed, to the great surprise and astonishment of all the spectators.

The enemies of the gospel have always endeavored to depreciate our Saviour's miracles, pretending that no more is meant by a person possessed of the devil, than that he was afflicted with some loathsome disease, and that because sepulchres were considered as polluted places, and, therefore, whenever any melancholy person frequented them, they were said to be possessed with unclean spirits.

To this objection, namely, that the demoniacs were in reality nothing more than persons afflicted with some loathsome disease, we reply, it is evidently false, the evangelist having taken care to be very particular on this head. "They brought unto him all sick people that were taken with divers diseases, and those which were possessed with devils, and those which were lunatic, and those that had the palsy, and he healed them." Matt. iv: 24. "He gave to the apostles power over unclean spirits, to cast them out, and to heal all manner of sickness and all manner of disease." Matt. x: 1. And, accordingly, "he healed many that were sick of divers diseases, and cast out many devils." Mark i: 34.

But the vast concourse of people that now gathered round him in Capernaum began to be troublesome, and he retired into a desert, whither the multitude soon followed him, and entreated him never to depart from them. But as this request was inconsistent with the design of his mission, he, for the first time, refused their request, and "preached in the synagogues of Galilee." Luke iv: 44.

CHAPTER VIII.

JESUS CONFIRMS HIS MISSION BY PRODUCING A MIRACULOUS DRAUGHT OF FISHES — CURING THE LEPROSY A SECOND TIME — APPEASING THE BOISTEROUS WAVES — CASTING DEVILS OUT OF DIVERS PERSONS GRIEVOUSLY POSSESSED.

OUR blessed Lord, having spread his glorious doctrine throughout Galilee, returned to Capernaum, followed by such numbers of people, that he found it necessary to step into Peter's ship, from whence he taught the multitude, who stood on the shore listening with great attention to his doctrine.

Having concluded his discourse, he turned himself to Simon Peter, desiring him to launch out further from the shore, and let down his net. On which, the disciple told him of the unsuccessful pains they had taken during the whole night, but added, that he would, in obedience to his command, make one trial more. Nor had he any cause to repent; for the net was no sooner in the lake, than they found it so full of large fishes that it was in danger of breaking.

This success, after such fruitless toil, astonished Peter, who, falling down at the feet of Jesus, cried out, "Depart from me, for I am a sinful man, O Lord." He was conscious of the many sins he had been guilty of, and therefore afraid of being in the company of so divine a person, lest some offence might have exposed him to more than ordinary chastisement.

But the benevolent Redeemer of mankind removed his fears by telling him, that from thenceforth the employment for him and his companions should be far more noble, they should catch men; that is, they should turn them from the crooked paths of iniquity to the straight road leading to the heavenly mansions.

In one of the cities through which he passed, he found "a man full of leprosy," who, seeing Jesus, fell on his face, and besought him, saying, "Lord, if thou wilt, thou canst make me clean."

It was the custom in Judea for the priest to banish from society those who were afflicted with a contagious leprosy. The disease of this person, therefore, was of a less pestilential kind, as he was suffered to enjoy the conversation of men. His case, however, excited the pity of the compassionate Jesus, who immediately cleansed him, ordered him to repair to Jerusalem, and after showing himself to the priest, offer the gifts commanded by Moses, giving him the same admonition he had done to others, namely, not to tell any man what had been done for him. But the blessing he had received was so great and unexpected, that instead of concealing, he published every where the great things Jesus had done for him, which brought such crowds to the Son of God, that he was obliged to retire from Capernaum into the wilderness, to refresh his body with rest, and his spirit with prayer and meditation.

The generality of commentators suppose that this leper, and the other mentioned in the previous chapter, are one and the same person; but this is a mistake. The former was cured in the fields, the latter in the city. After cleansing the first, Jesus went to Capernaum, and healed the centurion's servant; but after curing the latter he retired into the wilderness, to shun the prodigious crowds, which soon gathered round him, from the leper's publishing every where the miracle Jesus had wrought for him.

Our blessed Lord, finding all his endeavors to conceal himself in the desert would be in vain, ordered his disciples to accompany him to the other side of the lake, upon which, a certain scribe, who happened to be present, declared he would follow him; but Jesus, who well knew that his desire was only to gain the profits and advantages of an earthly kingdom, which he supposed the Messiah would establish, told him, if he intended nothing more by following him than to improve his worldly fortune, he would find himself wretchedly mistaken. "The foxes have holes," said the blessed Jesus to this teacher of Israel, "and the birds of the air have nests, but the Son of Man hath not where to lay his head." Matt. viii: 20.

The disciples having prepared the ship, took on board their Master, and departed for the other side of the lake, attended by many boats full of people, who were desirous of hearing his heavenly discourses, and of being spectators of his astonishing works. But Jesus, being fatigued with the labors of the day, sat himself down at the stern of the ship, and fell asleep.

The weather, which had till now been calm and serene, suddenly changed. A terrible storm came on, and the rising waves dashed impetuously against the ship, threatening every moment to bury them all in the bowels of the deep. The darkness of night increased the horrors of the tempest. Now they were carried on the top of the mountainous waves, and seemed to touch the skies; then plunged to the bottom of the deep, while the foaming billows roared horridly above them. In vain the disciples exerted their utmost strength, the storm continued to increase, and baffled all the efforts of human exertion; the waves broke over the ship, the waters rushed in, and she began to sink. All hope of escaping had vanished, despair seized every individual, and they were on the brink of perishing, when they ran to Jesus, crying out, "Master, Master, we perish!" Their vehement cries roused him from his sleep. He raised his hand, so often employed in acts of mercy and benevolence, and, with a stern and awful voice, rebuked the boisterous element. The raging sea instantly obeyed his command. The aerial torrent stopped short in its impetuous course, and became as silent as the grave, while the mountainous waves sunk at once into their beds, and the surface of the deep became as smooth as polished marble.

Soon after the storm was allayed, they arrived in the country of Gadara, and, on their landing, two men, possessed with devils, came from the tombs to meet Jesus. One of them, who was more furious than the other, had been often bound with chains and fetters, but to no purpose, being always broken with great fury, so that no man attempted further to restrain him. Being therefore at liberty, he shunned the society of men, wandering day and night in deserted places among the sepulchres or caverns where the dead were deposited, crying and making the most dismal complaints, and cutting himself with stones.

The disciples were terrified at the approach of these furious mortals; but Jesus soon dissipated their fears, commanding, while the men were at a distance, the devils to come out of them. The heavenly mandate was no sooner given, than they fell on their faces, crying out "What have I to do with thee, Jesus, thou Son of the Most High God?" Mark v: 7 "Art thou come hither to torment us before the time?" Matt. viii: 29. "I adjure thee, by God, that thou torment me not!" Mark v: 7. The apostate spirits well knew the power of the Son of God, and trembled lest he should immediately cast them into the torments prepared for them, and not suffer them to continue roving through the earth till the day of judgment, when they should be condemned to eternal punishment in the sight of the whole creation.

Jesus, being willing that the torments suffered by these miserable men, should be known before he healed them, asked one of the devils his name, who answered "Legion, for we are many," (Mark v: 9,) begging, at the same time, that he would not command them to repair into the deep, or bottomless pit, but suffer them to enter a herd of swine feeding at a distance.

How subtle are the wiles of the devil! The power of the Son of God he knew was not to be resisted; but he could not help envying the benevolent miracles he had wrought for the sons of men, and was therefore willing to prevent, as much, as possible, their good effects on the miserable people of this country. This was the true reason why he begged leave to enter the herd of swine—he knew he could destroy them—and this he hoped would render our blessed Saviour odious to the wicked inhabitants of Gadara.

Though Jesus well knew his crafty design, yet he permitted the devils to enter the swine, that his disciples, and others who were with him, might be fully convinced these unhappy persons were really possessed by apostate spirits, and, at the same time, give them a terrible instance of their power, when free from all restraint.

The divine permission was no sooner granted, than the spectators beheld, at a distance, the torments of these poor creatures, with what amazing rapidity they ran to the confines of the lake, leaped from the precipices into the sea, and perished in the waters; while the persons who, a moment before, were raving and cutting themselves in the most shocking manner, became at once meek and composed, having recovered entirely the exercise of their reason.

The keepers of the herd, terrified at this astonishing miracle, ran into the city, publishing, in every part, the cure of the men possessed with the devils, and the destruction of the swine.

This surprising report threw the inhabitants into the greatest consternation: they left the city, to be spectators of so wonderful an event; but when they saw the men who had been possessed sitting at the feet of Jesus, decently clothed, and in their right minds, their fear was increased. For, knowing they had trespassed in keeping the swine, (which was contrary to the law of Moses,) they dreaded a more severe punishment; and, being ignorant of the goodness of Jesus, though he had given them so remarkable a proof of it in the cure of these wretched mortals, they besought him that he would leave their country.

There prevailed a custom among the heathen, when

any illustrious hero had delivered his country from its enemies, or from any other great evil, to erect proud columns to his memory; his statue was seen in every place; altars blazed to his glory; they honored him with the high appellation of Saviour; and thought nothing, not even divine honors, too great to confer upon him. But when Christ had removed a monster from the Gadarenes, more formidable and fearful than any in heathen history, even a legion of devils, and rendered the way, by which no man could pass before, secure from danger, instead of being received by them as a Saviour and as the Son of God, with the acclamations and hosannas of the people, he was besought to depart out of their coasts. Stupid people! they had, indeed, lost their herd of swine, but surely the valuable gift they had received, in two of their countrymen and fellow creatures being delivered from the tyranny of Satan, was better than the cattle on a thousand hills, and merited, at least, their thanks and acknowledgments.

The stupid request of the Gadarenes was, however, complied with by the blessed Jesus, who, entering the ship, returned to the country from whence he came, leaving them a valuable pledge of his love, and us a noble pattern of perseverance in well-doing, even when our kindnesses are condemned or requited with injuries.

RAISING JAIRUS' DAUGHTER FROM THE DEAD.

CHAPTER IX.

Our Lord proceeds in acts of Mercy and Benevolence — Adds Matthew to the number of Disciples — Casts out an evil Spirit—Passes again through Galilee — Selects Twelve from among his Disciples, as his constant Followers and Companions and addresses the Multitude in an excellent Discourse.

THE arrival of our Saviour and his disciples at Capernaum, a city of Galilee, was no sooner published, than such throngs of people were gathered together, that the house could not contain them, nor even the court before it. He, however, preached the words of eternal life to the listening audience, among whom were many Pharisees and doctors of the law, who, from the fame of his miracles, were come from all quarters to hear him.

He not only addressed them in the most nervous and pathetic manner, in order to inculcate the doctrines he delivered, but also performed such astonishing miracles as ought to have removed all their scruples with regard to the truth of his mission.

Among other instances he gave of his divine power, was that of restoring a man to perfect health, who had long been afflicted with the palsy, and was reduced by that terrible disease to the most melancholy condition, being unable to move any member of his body, but seemed rather an emaciated carcase than a man. This miserable object was brought on his bed by four persons, who, being unable to enter by the door, on account of the multitude, carried him to the top of the house, which, like the other roofs in that country, was flat, and had a battlement round, according to the direction given by Moses, Deut. xxii: 8.

On these roofs there was a kind of trap-door, by which they came out of the houses upon the roofs, where they spent a considerable part of the day. It was also common to have a flight of stairs from the garden to the roof, and by these the persons seemed to have carried the sick of the palsy, but finding the door fastened, forced it open, and uncovered the roof, and through the opening let down, by ropes, the sick of the palsy, lying on his bed, into the midst of the company, before Jesus; who, seeing the faith of the friends of this afflicted person, had compassion on him, and spake aloud, "Son, be of good cheer; thy sins are forgiven thee."

The scribes, taking offence at this saying, cried out, This man speaketh blasphemy; for he appropriates that to himself, which is solely the province of Omnipotence. "Who can forgive sins, but God only?" They were ignorant that the person who uttered such gracious words was the Son of God, and, consequently, had the power of forgiving the sins of the human race.

But our Lord, who had recourse to the most secret recesses of the heart, and was willing to show them that he was really endued with the Spirit of God, said to them, "Wherefore think ye evil in your hearts? For whether it is easier to say to the sick of the palsy.

Thy sins be forgiven thee; or to say, Arise, and take up thy bed and walk?" These were questions beyond the abilities of the haughty scribes to answer, and they held their peace. The blessed Jesus then added, that the miracle he was going to perform would sufficiently demonstrate that he had not usurped what did not, in the strictest manner, belong to him. And, turning himself from those bigoted teachers of Israel toward the sick of the palsy, he said unto him, "Arise, take up thy bed, and go unto thine house." Matt. ix: 6.

Nor was this divine mandate any sooner given, than the man was restored to his former health and strength, and, to the astonishment of all present, rose, took up his bed, and departed to his own house, glorifying God. And all the people, when they saw this great work, expressed the highest degree of surprise, mixed with admiration, for the great honor the Almighty had conferred on human nature.—"They glorified God, who had given such power unto men." But with regard to the scribes and Pharisees, though they must have been confounded at this miracle, yet they still continued in their unbelief; an instance, which should awaken in us the most serious thoughts, as it abundantly demonstrates, that the palsy of the soul is a much more deplorable disease than the palsy of the body.

The blessed Jesus having wrought this miracle, repaired to the sea-side, and taught a multitude of people. What the subject of his sermon was, the evangelists have not told us; but it was, doubtless, like the rest, calculated to promote the eternal welfare of mankind.

His discourse being ended, he returned to the city, and in his way, saw Matthew or Levi, the son of

Alpheus, a rich publican, sitting in his office, where the customs were levied, at the port of Capernaum, whom he ordered to follow him. Matthew immediately obeyed the summons, and followed the Saviour of the world, to pursue a far more honorable and important employment — being afterward both an apostle and evangelist.

Some little time after his call, he made a splendid entertainment for his master, inviting all the publicans he knew, hoping that, by hearing the heavenly conversation of Christ, they might also repent, and embrace the doctrines of the gospel.

The self-righteous scribes and Pharisees, who considered all men as sinners, except themselves, especially the publicans, were highly offended that one who called himself a prophet, should so far demean himself, as to be seen in the company of such men; and asked his disciples, with an air of insolence, in the hearing of all the guests, how their Master could sit down at the same table with publicans and sinners?

Our Lord replied to this artful question, that the sick only had need of a physician, and desired them to reflect seriously on the prophet Hosea's declaration: "I will have mercy, and not sacrifice." The turning sinners into the path of righteousness, which is the highest act of benevolence, is far more acceptable to the Almighty, than all the ceremonies of the law of Moses so highly magnified by your fraternity, who, on many occasions, observe them at the expense of charity; adding, I am not come to call the righteous, but sinners, to repentance. The chief object of my attension is the conversion of sinners.

This answer, however satisfactory to an unprejudiced

person, was far from being so to the scribes and Pharisees, who, joining with some of John's disciples then present, returned to Matthew's house, and demanded of Jesus, why his disciples wholly neglected to fast, a duty often performed both by the rulers of Israel, and the disciples of John? To this the blessed Jesus replied, It is not a proper season for the friends of the bridegroom to fast and afflict themselves, while they enjoy his company; "but the days will come, when the bridegroom shall be taken away from them, and then they shall fast." The various calamities and afflictions that shall attend them, after the departure of their Master, shall cause them to fast, which they shall repeat as often as the circumstances of distress and danger, with which they will be surrounded, shall require; and added, that to have obliged his disciples to observe the precepts of frequent abstinence, at a time when he was employing them to preach the gospel, by which all the legal ceremonies of the law were to be abolished, would have been as absurd as to sew a new piece of cloth upon a rotten garment, which would only make the rent worse; or to put new wine into old leathern bottles, which, on the first fermentation of the liquor, would burst—indicating, that infant virtue must not immediately be put to the greatest trials, lest it be destroyed by the severity of the exercise.

During this controversy between our Lord and the haughty scribes and Pharisees in Matthew's house, Jairus, a ruler of the synagogue, came running to him, in all the agonies of grief, and in the presence of the whole company, fell on the ground before him, beseeching that he would come and heal his daughter, who lay at the point of death.

When did the beneficent Jesus deny his gracious assistance to those who implored it of him? He immediately arose, and followed the ruler toward his house, surrounded by a great multitude of people, who were desirous of seeing so great a miracle.

But as he passed through the street, a woman, who had, for twelve years, been afflicted with an issue or flux of blood, and had spent her whole substance on physicians to no purpose, "came behind him, and touched the hem of his garment; for she said within herself, If I may but touch his clothes, I shall be well." Nor was she deceived; for no sooner had she touched the border of the garment of the Son of God, than her issue of blood dried up; and she felt, by the return of her health and strength, and other agreeable sensations that accompany such sudden changes from painful diseases to perfect health, that the cure was absolutely complete.

But this transaction could not be concealed: the blessed Jesus knew the whole, and her secret thoughts, before she put them into practice; and, pleased with the opinion this woman had entertained both of his power and goodness, would not, by any means, suffer it to pass unapplauded. Accordingly, he turned himself about, and asked, "Who touched me?" He well knew the person; but asked this question for the fuller manifestation of the woman's faith, and that he might have an opportunity of instructing and comforting her.

His disciples, being ignorant of what had passed, were surprised at the question; Thou seest," said they to their Master, "the multitude thronging and pressing thee, and sayest thou, Who touched me?" They could not distinguish between the spiritual and corporeal touch, nor knew that such efficacious virtue had gone out of their Master. Jesus, however, persisted in knowing who it was that had done the thing; and the woman, finding it in vain to conceal her action any longer, came to him trembling, and told him all. Perhaps the uncleanness of her distemper was the reason of her fear, thinking he would be offended, even at her touching the hem of his garment. But the divine Physician, far from being angry, spoke to her in the kindest manner, and commended her faith, on which account he had consented to heal her plague: "Daughter, be of good comfort; thy faith hath made thee whole." Matt. ix: 22.

Such a miraculous incident must, doubtless, have greatly strengthened the ruler's faith; for, behold, a virtue, little inferior to that of raising the dead, issues from the border of Christ's garment, and heals a disease, which, for the space of twelve years, had baffled all the skill of the healing art, and defied the power of medicine. Indeed, the faith of this ruler had great need of the strongest confirmation; for news was brought him, that his daughter was even now dead, and therefore it was needless for him to give any further trouble to Jesus — not in the least suspecting he had power to recall the departed spirit, and to reanimate the breathless body.

This message was a terrible blow to the affectionate parent. His only daughter, who, a few days before, was in the bloom of youth, was now a pale and lifeless corpse; and with her all his joys and comforts were fled. But Jesus, commiserating his grief, desired him to be comforted, promising that his daughter should be restored.

On his coming to the ruler's house, he found it full of mourners, who made terrible lamentations — a sufficient demonstration that the damsel was really dead; and, accordingly, when our blessed Saviour desired the mourners to cease their funeral ceremonies, as the maid was not dead, but sleeping, they laughed him to scorn.

It is necessary to remark, in this place, that the Jews, when they spoke of a person's death, styled it sleep, to intimate their belief that his spirit existed in the happy scenes of paradise, and their hopes of a future resurrection to life eternal. But the blessed Jesus used the word with remarkable propriety, to signify that though she was now locked in the cold embrace of death, yet he was going to release her from the power of the king of terrors, with the same ease as a person is awaked from sleep. Thus our blessed Saviour, in the very manner of performing a miracle, modestly declined the honor that would undoubtedly result from a work so greatly superior to all the powers of men.

Having thus briefly addressed the mourners, he entered the chamber where the damsel was lying; but suffered none to follow him, except Peter, James, and John, together with the father and mother of the damsel. Probably his reason for suffering these only to be spectators of so stupendous a work, was, that they might have an opportunity of examining the whole transaction in the most careful manner, and be thence enabled, afterward, to report it upon the fullest conviction, and with every circumstance of credibility.

The blessed Jesus now approached the body, took her by the hand, and, with a gentle voice, said,

"Maid, arise." The heavenly command was instantly obeyed; the damsel arose, as from a sleep, and with all the appearance of health and vigor, for Jesus commanded to give her something to eat — a plain proof that she did not appear in a weak and languishing condition of a person worn out with disease, or even like one who had fainted away — a circumstance that abundantly proves the greatness and perfection of the miracle. It is, therefore, no wonder, that her parents should be astonished at so stupendous a work, the fame of which was soon spread through all the neighboring country, though Jesus, who was, in every sense above praise, and therefore never courted it, had strictly charged them that they should tell no man what was done.

These instances of power did the blessed Jesus display, to convince the world, that those who die in him are not dead; and that he hath the keys of life and death. Those also of the present age, who believe that the soul sleeps with the body till the resurrection, will do well to consider the expression of the evangelist, "Her spirit came again," (Luke viii: 55,) which sufficiently shows that the soul exists separately, when the body is laid in the chambers of the grave.

Our blessed Saviour, having performed this benevolent miracle, left the ruler's house, and was followed through the streets by two blind men, imploring assistance: nor did they implore in vain; the Redeemer of mankind was, and still is, always ready to grant the petitions of those who apply to him for relief. Accordingly, he was no sooner entered into a house, to avoid the thronging multitude, than he touched their eyes, and said, "According to your faith, be it unto you,"

(Matt. ix: 29,) and immediately the invaluable gift of sight was bestowed upon them.

The blind men were so overjoyed at beholding the light, that though our Saviour charged them to keep the miracle a secret, they published his fame in every part of the country, being unwilling to conceal what, in gratitude for so great a mercy, they thought themselves obliged to divulge.

The men, who had thus miraculously received their sight, being departed, the multitude brought to him a dumb man possessed with a devil. So moving a sight could not fail of attracting a compassionate regard from the Saviour of the world, who, being never weary of well-doing, immediately cast out the apostate spirit; on which the dumb man recovered the use of his speech, and spoke in a very rational manner to the multitude, who, with one voice, declared, that such wondrous works were never wrought by any of the old prophets: "It was never so seen in Israel." Matt. ix: 33. These works did not remove the prejudice of the Pharisees, who, being unable to deny the miracles, insinuated that he did it by a power received from Beelzebub, the prince of the devils. A poor pretence indeed! and did not escape the animadversion it deserved, from the Saviour of the world, as we shall see in a succeeding chapter. Well might the prophet Isaiah cry out in a prophetic ecstacy, "Who hath believed our report? and to whom is the arm of the Lord revealed?"

But all their calumnies could not provoke the meek and merciful Jesus to cease from performing these compassionate offices for the children of men. On the contrary, he exerted himself still more and more to promote the prosperity of the whole human race.

Accordingly, he left Capernaum, and traveled through the country in search of miserable objects, on which he might confer happiness and peace, visiting "all the cities and villages, teaching in their synagogues, and preaching the gospel of the kingdom, and healing every sickness, and every disease, among the people." Matt. ix: 35.

On his return from this tour to Capernaum, he was attended by a great number of people, who expressed a more than common desire to hear the doctrine of the gospel—an incident abundantly sufficient to engage the attention of this divine teacher, who was ever careful to cultivate the latent seeds of virtue, and cherish the least appearance of piety and religion.

It was not this desire of the people alone, that excited his compassion toward them; he well knew they were wholly destitute of spiritual teachers; for the scribes and pharisees, who ought to have instructed them, were blind, perverse, and lazy guides, who, instead of seeking the glory of the Almighty, made it their whole business to support and augment their own. They magnified the ritual ceremonies and traditions, but took no care to inspire the people with a love of virtue; "to do justice, love mercy, and walk humbly with their God," were no parts of their doctrine. The small appearance of religion they entertained was wholly hypocritical; and the disputes carried on with so much bitterness between the factions of the Pharisees and Sadducees, distracted the minds of the people.

The inhabitants of Judea were truly in a deplorable state, which called loudly for the compassion of the Son of God, who always regarded the descendants of Jacob with the most tender affection. He saw the sheep of

Israel scattered on the barren wastes of error and superstition, without a shepherd to lead them to the heavenly pastures of the law and the prophets. He saw, he commiserated their distress, and resolved to provide some remedy for it. Accordingly, he directed his apostles to intercede with the Almighty, who, by his servants, the prophets, had sown the seeds of piety and virtue in the minds of the Jews, that he would not suffer the rich harvest to be lost for want of laborers. "The harvest," said the blessed Jesus to his disciples, "truly is plenteous, but the laborers are few. Pray ye, therefore, the Lord of the harvest, that he will send forth laborers into his harvest." Matt. iv: 37, 38.

To these gracious acts he added the most powerful of all intercessions to the throne of grace—his own prevailing prayer—and, accordingly, ascended to the top of a mountain, and there spent the night in making the most powerful petitions in behalf of the lost sheep of Israel to his heavenly Father.

Having spent the night in this pious exercise, he lost no time in putting his beneficent intentions in execution; for no sooner had darkness withdrawn her sable veil, and the blushing rays of the morn adorned the chambers of the east, than the benevolent Redeemer of mankind called his disciples to him, and chose twelve, whom he named apostles, to be with him, and that he might send them forth to preach. He ordered them to be with him, that they might learn from his own mouth the doctrines they were to preach to the whole world; that they might see his glory, and the transcendent glory of the virtues which adorned his human life; that they might be witnesses of all the wondrous works he should perform, during his residence in this vale of misery, and by which his mission from the courts of heaven was to be fully demonstrated.

These twelve persons, thus qualified, were to supply the people with that spiritual food they so greatly wanted, both while their Master continued here below, and after his ascension to the right hand of power.

Having ordained them to their respective offices, he sent them out by two and two, into the most distant parts of Judea, to preach the glad tidings of the gospel, and prepare the way for their Master, the great Shepherd of Israel. And, that nothing might be wanting to render their preaching acceptable to the people, and confirm the important doctrines they delivered, he invested them with full power to cure all diseases, cast out devils, and even to raise the dead.

After appointing the twelve apostles, he came down from the mountain, and was joyfully received by the multitudes of people who were waiting for him in the plain, and pressed to touch him — well knowing, that if they could only touch the hem of his garment, they should be healed of whatever distemper they were afflicted with — a sufficient reason why they were continually waiting for him, and were willing to accompany him, even to the remotest corners of the wilderness.

The preaching and miracles of our Lord were at tended to, not by the low and vulgar only, but persons of the first rank and character came from distant parts of the country to converse with him, hear his doctrine, and be spectators of his wonderful works. It therefore evidently appears, that persons of all ranks were desirous of following him; and their desire could be founded on nothing but the truth of his doctrines and miracles.

After healing all the sick among the multitude, he turned toward his disciples, and delivered a divine discourse, something like that he had before preached to them on the mountain: but in the former he only pronounced blessings, whereas, in the latter, he added curses also; and in this principally it differs from that recorded by St. Matthew. We shall, therefore, only select a few passages from the sermon now delivered, as we have given a larger paraphrase on the other.

"Woe unto you that are rich! for ye have received your consolation." Luke vii: 24. Riches, considered in themselves, by no means render us the objects of the Almighty's hatred, unless accompanied by those vices which too often flow from an opulent fortune, as luxury, covetousness, and the like. The woe therefore, is here denounced against those only who are contaminated with these vices; for those who make a proper use of their wealth, and possess the virtues which should accompany affluence, have no share in the malediction.

"Woe unto you that are full! for ye shall hunger." The pain ye shall suffer in a future life shall be sharp and excruciating. The opportunities you have neglected of doing good to your afflicted brethren in this life, shall then be remembered with the most poignant grief, and bewailed with the most bitter lamentations.

"Woe unto you that laugh now! for ye shall mourn and weep." This malediction of our blessed Saviour is not inconsistent with the apostle's precept, which commands Christians always to rejoice. Neither is the mirth, against which the woe is here denounced, to be understood of that constant cheerfulness of temper which arises in the breasts of true Christians, from the comfortable and cheerful doctrine with which they are enlightened by the gospel, the assurance they have of reconciliation with God, and the hope they have of everlasting life, and the pleasure they enjoy in the practice of the duties of religion; but it relates to that turbulent carnal mirth, that excessive levity and vanity of spirit, which arises not from any solid foundation, but from sensual pleasures, or those vain amusements of life, in which the giddy and gay contrive to spend their time—that sort of mirth which dissipates thought, leaves no time for consideration, and gives them an utter aversion to all serious reflections. Persons who constantly indulge themselves in this kind of mirth, shall weep and mourn eternally, when they are excluded from the joys of heaven, and banished forever from the presence of God, by the light of whose countenance all the righteous are enlivened, and made transcendently happy.

"Woe unto you when all men shall speak well of you! for so did their fathers to the false prophets." Woe unto you, if, by propagating such doctrines as encourage men in sin, you shall gain to yourselves the applause and flattery of the generality of men; for thus, in old times, did the false prophets and deceivers, who, accommodating their doctrines to the lusts and passions of men gained their applause, but incurred the wrath and displeasure of a just and all-seeing God.

CHAPTER X.

CONTINUATION OF OUR LORD'S GLORIOUS DOCTRINES — BENEFICENT ACTS AND ASTONISHING MIRACLES WROUGHT IN CONFIRMATION OF THE DIVINITY OF HIS MISSION, AND THE EXTENDING OF HIS HEAVENLY KINGDOM

THE divine Preacher having closed this excellent sermon, he repaired to Capernaum, and was met by certain messengers from a centurion, desiring him to come and heal a servant who was dear to him, and ready to die.

This centurion, from the account given of him by the evangelist, seems to have been a proselyte to the Jewish religion, as he was a lover of the sons of Jacob, and had erected for them a place of worship; and accordingly the inhabitants of Capernaum strongly espoused his cause on this occasion, saying, "that he was worthy for whom he should do this. For he loveth our nation, and he hath built us a synagogue." Luke vii: 4, 5.

There was not the least danger that this petition would be rejected by the blessed Jesus, who sought all occasions of doing good to the children of men. Accordingly, he very readily accompanied the messengers; but, before he came to the house, he was met by some of the centurion's friends, who expressed the high idea that officer entertained of his power, and desired that he would not take the trouble of coming to his house, as a word was abundantly sufficient to perform the cure. At this message, Jesus turned himself about, and said to the multitude, "I say unto you, I have not found so great faith, no, not in Israel." Luke vii: 9.

The persons having delivered their message, returned to the house, and found the servant, who had been sick, perfectly recovered.

Having thus miraculously healed the centurion's servant, he repaired to Peter's house to eat bread; but the multitude came again together, and surrounded the house in a tumultuous manner, demanding, in all probability, that he would heal their sick; and it was not without difficulty they were dispersed by his friends.

The multitude being dispersed, Jesus called unto him the twelve apostles he had before chosen, and conferred on them the power of working miracles, in confirmation of the doctrines they were appointed to preach, and delivered them such instructions as he thought necessary to enable them to discharge the duties of this important commission.

"Go," said their heavenly Master, "and preach, saying, the kingdom of heaven is at hand." Publish in every corner of Judea, the glad tidings of the gospel, and the near approach of the Messiah's kingdom — not a temporal, but a spiritual, empire — consisting of righteousness and peace.

To inure them to those hardships and dangers which were to attend them in their preaching, after the death of their Master, our Lord forbade them to provide anything for their journey — teaching them to rely wholly on the providence of God for support in every distress, and to have recourse to his protection in every danger.

Our Lord's disciples had, perhaps, flattered themselves with the pleasing expectation, that the glad tidings they were going to publish, and the miraculous cures they were enabled to perform, would procure them an honorable reception wherever they came. Their Master, however, told them the event would not, in any manner, answer their expectations; but that they were every where to be despised, persecuted, delivered into the hands of the rulers, and punished as wicked men. But, at the same time, he promised them the aid of the Almighty, and gave them instructions how to behave in every particular. He added, that those who rejected their message should be treated with severity by the great Judge of all the earth; but those who received them kindly, and gave even a cup of cold water to the least of his disciples, for their Master's sake, should not fail of receiving a large reward.

Having received this commission, the apostles visited all parts of Palestine, where the Jews inhabited, preaching the doctrine of repentance, working miracles for its confirmation, and particularly healing the sick, while our blessed Lord continued the course of his ministry in Galilee.

The apostles being returned from their tour, Jesus went to Nain, a town situated near Endor, about two miles south of Mount Tabor, attended by many of his disciples, and a great multitude of people.

On their coming to the entrance of the city, a melancholy scene presented itself to the eyes of Jesus and his followers: "Behold, there was a dead man carried out, the only son of his mother, and she was a widow." Luke vii: 12. Who would not have imagined, that God had indeed "forgotten to be gracious, and, in his anger, shut up his tender mercies" from this poor widow, suffering under the heaviest load, and laboring under the most oppressive burden of distress? Deprived of her son, her only son, in the flower of his youth, when he might have repaid his mother's toils, and been to her in the place of a husband—of that husband she had long since lost, and whose loss was supportable only through the comfort of this child, the surviving image of his departed father, the balm of her grief, the hope of her afflicted soul—who now shall administer consolation to this solitary widow, to this lonely parent, bereaved of her husband, deprived of her child? What misery can be more complicated? What can be more natural than that she should "refuse to be comforted," that she should "go down to the grave with mourning," and visit the chambers of death, the residence of the beloved remains of her husband and her son, with sorrow?

Toward this receptacle of mortality, that dreary waste of forgetfulness, the mournful funeral was now, with slow and solemn pomp, advancing, when the compassionate Redeemer of mankind met the melancholy procession, composed of a long train of her weeping neighbors and relations, who pitied her distress, sympathized with her in this great affliction, and were melted with compassion at her deplorable circumstances: but sighs and tears were all they had to offer; relief could not be expected from a human being; their commiseration, though grateful to her oppressed soul, could neither restore the husband nor the son; submission and patience were the only lessons they could preach, or this afflicted daughter of Israel learn.

But though man was unable to relieve the distresses of this disconsolate widow, the Saviour of the world, who beheld the melancholy procession, was both able and willing to do it. There was no need of a powerful solicitor to implore assistance from the Son of God; his own compassion was abundantly sufficient. When the Lord saw her, he had compassion on her: he both sought the patient, and offered the cure unexpectedly. "Weep not," said the blessed Jesus to this afflicted woman. Alas! it had been wholly in vain to bid her refrain from tears, who had lost her only child, the sole comfort of her age, without ministering the balm of comfort to heal her broken spirit. This our Redeemer well knew; and, therefore, immediately advancing toward the corpse, "he touched the bier." The pomp of the funeral was instantly stopped, silence closed every mouth, and expectation filled the breast of every spectator. But this deep suspense did not long continue; that glorious voice, which shall one day call our dead bodies from the grave, filled their ears with these remarkable words, "Young man, I say unto thee, arise." Nor was this powerful command uttered without its effect. "He spake, and it was done;" he called with authority, and immediately "he that was dead, sat up, and began to speak. And he restored him to his mother." He did not show him around to the multitude, but, by a singular act of modesty and humanity, delivered him to his late afflicted, now astonished and rejoicing mother, to intimate, that in compassion to her great distress, he had wrought this stupendous miracle.

A holy and awful fear fell on all who heard and saw this astonishing event; "and they glorified God, saying, that a great prophet is risen up amongst us, and that God hath visited his people."

Here it must be observed, that as this miracle is liable to no objection, it therefore abundantly proves, that the power of the blessed Jesus was truly and absolutely divine. He met this funeral procession by accident. It was composed of the greatest part of the inhabitants of the city, who bewailed the disconsolate state of the afflicted widow, and therefore well knew that the youth was really dead. The powerful word, which called the breathless body to life, was delivered in an audible voice, before all the company, and even at the very gate of the city, the place of public resort.

This miracle, with others amply attested, abundantly evinces the truth of our Saviour's mission, and that he was indeed the Son of God, the Redeemer of mankind.

CHAPTER XI.

THE CHARACTER OF JOHN THE BAPTIST CLEARED AND JUSTIFIED BY THE BLESSED JESUS — HE VISITS SIMON THE PHARISEE — DISPLAY OF OUR LORD'S HUMILITY AND CONDESCENSION.

WE have taken notice, in a foregoing chapter, that Herod, incensed at the honest freedom of the Baptist, in reproving his adulterous commerce with Herodias, his brother Philip's wife, had cast him into prison; and in this he still continued, though his disciples were suffered to visit and converse with him. In one of these visits, they had given him an account of our Saviour's having elected twelve apostles to preach the gospel, and of his miracles, particularly of his raising to life the daughter of Jairus, and the son of the widow of Nain. On hearing these wonderful relations, the Baptist dispatched two of his disciples to Jesus, to ask him this important question, "Art thou he that should come, or do look we for another?"

Accordingly, the disciples of John came to Jesus, and proposed the question of their master, at the very time when he "cured many of their infirmities and plagues, and of evil spirits; and to many that were blind he gave sight." Jesus, therefore, instead of directly answering their question, bade them return and inform their master what they had seen: "Go,' said he, "and show John again those things which ye do hear and see: the blind receive their sight, and the lame walk; the lepers are cleansed, and the deaf hear; the dead are raised up, and the poor have the gospel preached to them." Matt. xi: 4, 5. Go, tell your master, that the very miracles the prophet Isaiah so long since foretold should be wrought by the Messiah, you have yourselves seen performed.

It appears, from the Scriptures, that the Baptist, through the whole course of his ministry, had borne constant and ample testimony to our Saviour's divine mission, that he exhorted those who came to him to rest their faith not on himself, but on "him that should come after him," and that, as soon as he was acquainted who Jesus was, by a visible descent of the Holy Ghost, and a voice from heaven, he made it his business to dispose the Jews in general, and his own disciples in particular, to receive and reverence him, by testifying every where that he was the "Son of God, the Lamb of God, who came down from heaven, and spake the words of God, and to whom God had given the Spirit not by measure." It seems that the scribes and Pharisees, seeing their pretended mortifications eclipsed by the real austerity of the Baptist, affirmed, that his living in the deserts, his shunning the company of men, the coarseness of his clothing, the abstemiousness of his diet, and the other severities he practiced, were the effects of his being possessed by an apostate spirit, or of a religious melancholy. "For John came neither eating nor drinking, and they say, he hath a devil." Matt. xi: 18.

On the other hand, they would not listen to the

heavenly doctrines preached by Christ, because he did not separate himself from society—attributing his free manner of living to a certain looseness of disposition, though they well knew that he observed the strictest temperance himself, and never encouraged the vices of others, either by dissimulation or example. "The Son of Man came eating and drinking; and they say, Behold a man, gluttonous, and a wine-bibber, a friend of publicans and sinners; but Wisdom is justified of her children." Matt xi: 19.

He next proceeded to upbraid the several cities where his most wonderful works had been performed. For though they had heard him preach many awakening sermons, and seen him perform such astonishing miracles, as would have converted Tyre, Sidon, and Sodom, cities infamous for their impiety, contempt of religion, pride, luxury, and debauchery, yet, so great was their obstinacy, that they persisted in their wickedness, notwithstanding all he had done to convert them from the evil of their ways. "Woe unto thee, Chorazin! woe unto thee, Bethsaida! for if the mighty works which were done in you had been done in Tyre and Sidon, they would have repented long ago in sackcloth and ashes. But I say unto you, It shall be more tolerable for Tyre and Sidon, at the day of judgment, than for you. And thou, Capernaum, which art exalted unto heaven, shall be brought down to hell; for if the mighty works which have been done in thee had been done in Sodom, it would have remained unto this day. But I say unto you, That it shall be more tolerable for the land of Sodom, in the day of judgment, than for thee." Matt. xi: 21, &c.

Having denounced these judgments on the cities

which had neglected to profit by his mighty works, he concluded his discourse with these heavenly words: "Come unto me, all ye that labor, and are heavy laden, and I will give you rest. Take my yoke upon you, and learn of me; for I am meek and lowly in heart: and ye shall find rest unto your souls. For my yoke is easy, and my burden is light." Matt. xi: 28, &c

Having concluded this public address, one of the Pharisees (named Simon) desired he would "eat with him:" the blessed Jesus accepted the invitation, accompanied him to his house, and sat down to meat.

He had not continued long at the table before a woman, who had lately left the paths of vice for those of virtue, placed herself behind him, and, from a deep conviction of her former crimes, and the obligations she owed the Saviour of mankind for bringing her to a sense of them, shed such quantities of tears, that they trickled down on his feet. But observing that her tears had wet the feet of her beloved Instructor, she wiped them with the hairs of her head, kissed them with the most ardent affection, and anointed them with precious ointment she had brought for the purpose.

It was a custom, among the inhabitants of the east, to pour fragrant oils on the heads of such guests as they intended particularly to honor, while they sat at meat; and probably the woman's original intention was to anoint Jesus in the usual manner. But being exceedingly humble on account of her former crimes, she could not presume to take that freedom with him, and therefore poured it on his feet, to express at once the greatness of her love, and the profoundness of her humility. The Pharisee, who had attentively observed the woman, concluded from thence, that our Saviour could not be a prophet. "This man," said the Pharisee to himself, "if he were a prophet, would have known who and what manner of woman this is that toucheth him; for she is a sinner." Luke vii: 39.

But though Simon spoke this only in his heart, his thoughts were not concealed from the great Redeemer of mankind, who, to convince him that he was a prophet, and that he knew not only the character of men, but even the secret thoughts of their hearts, immediately conversed with him on the very subject he had been revolving in his mind. He did not, indeed, expose him before the company, by relating what he had said in secret; but, with remarkable delicacy, pointed out to Simon alone the unreasonableness of his thoughts. "Simon," said the blessed Jesus, "I have somewhat to say unto thee. There was a certain creditor which had two debtors; the one owed five hundred pence, and the other fifty. And when they had nothing to pay, he frankly forgave them both. Tell me, therefore, which of them will love him most? Simon answered and said, I suppose that he to whom he forgave most. And he said unto him, Thou hast rightly judged." And then immediately he applied this parable to the subject of the woman, on which the Pharisee had so unjustly reasoned with himself. "Simon," continued our Saviour, "seest thou this woman? I entered into thine house, thou gavest me no water for my feet: but she hath washed my feet with tears, and wiped them with the hairs of her head. Thou gavest me no kiss: but this woman since the time I came in, hath not ceased to kiss my feet. My head with oil thou didst not anoint: but this woman hath anointed my feet with ointment." Luke vii: 40-46.

This woman's kind services were in no danger of losing their reward from the blessed Jesus, who possessed the softer and finer feelings of human nature in their utmost perfection. Accordingly, he added, in pursuance of so kind an invitation he had before made to weary and heavy-laden sinners, "Wherefore I say unto thee, her sins, which are many, are forgiven; for she loved much: but to whom little is for given, the same loveth little." Luke vii: 47.

The blessed Jesus having thus commended the conduct of the woman to the company, and rebuked, with great delicacy, the unjust suspicions of Simon, turned himself to the woman, and, in the kindest manner, assured her that "her sins were forgiven." But the power he assumed in forgiving sins, greatly offended the Jews, who, not being acquainted with his divinity, considered his speech as derogatory to the honor of the Almighty. Jesus, however contemned their malicious murmurs, and repeated his assurance, telling the woman, that her faith had saved her, and bade her depart in peace.

The next day Jesus traveled from Capernaum to different parts of Galilee, going "throughout every city and village, preaching and showing the glad tidings of the kingdom of God." Luke viii: 1. That is, he declared to the people the welcome tidings of the Almighty's being willing to be reconciled to the children of men, on condition of their repentance and embracing the gospel of the grace of God. Leaving Galilee, he repaired to Jerusalem to keep the passover, being the second feast of that kind since his public ministry. In this journey he was accompanied by certain pious women, "who ministered to him of their substance."

CHAPTER XII.

Miraculous Cure effected at the Pool of Bethesda — Reproof of the Superstition of the Jews, in condemning the performance of necessary Works on the Sabbath-day — After doing many acts of Mercy and wonder, our blessed Lord is visited by his Mother and his Brethren, and makes a spiritual Reflection on that Incident.

OUR Lord had no sooner entered the ancient city of Jerusalem, so long famous for being the dwelling-place of the Most High, than he repaired to the public bath or pool, called, in the Hebrew tongue, "Bethesda," that is, "the house of mercy," on account of miracles wrought there, by the salutary effects of the water, at certain seasons. This bath was surrounded by five porches, or cloisters, in which those who frequented the place were sheltered both from the heat and cold; and were particularly serviceable to the diseased and infirm, who crowded thither to find relief in their afflictions.

These porches were now filled with a "great multitude of impotent folk, of blind, halt, withered, waiting for the moving of the water. For an angel went down at a certain season into the pool, and troubled the water: whosoever then first after the troubling of the water stepped in, was made whole of whatsoever disease he had." John v: 3, 4.

Among these objects of pity was one who had labored under his infirmity no less than thirty and eight years. The length and greatness of this man's afflictions, which were well known to the Son of God, were sufficient to excite his tender compassion, and make him the happy object to demonstrate that his power of healing was infinitely superior to the sanative virtue of the waters; while the rest were suffered to remain in their afflictions.

Had not our Lord at this time restored any of them to health, he would not have acted contrary to the general account which the evangelists give of his goodness on other occasions; namely, "that he healed all who came to him." For such diseased persons who left their habitations, through a persuasion of his power and kindness, were proper objects of mercy; whereas the sick in the cloisters of Bethesda were no more so than the other sick throughout the whole country, whom he could have cured with a single word of his mouth, had he been pleased to have uttered it.

Our compassionate Lord now approached the man whom he had singled out as the person on whom to manifest his power: he asked him, whether he was desirous of being made whole?—a question which must have induced the man to declare publicly his melancholy case, in the hearing of the multitude, and consequently, rendered the miracle more conspicuous. And as this was done on the Sabbath-day, our blessed Saviour seems to have wrought it to rouse the sons of Jacob from their lethargy, and convince the inhabitants of Jerusalem, that the long-expected

Messiah was now come, and had actually visited his people.

This distressed mortal, beholding Jesus with a sorrowful countenance, and understanding that he meant his being healed by the sanative virtue of the waters, answered, "Sir, I have no man, when the water is troubled, to put me into the pool: but while I am coming, another steppeth down before me."—John v: 7. But the compassionate Redeemer of mankind soon convinced him that he was not to owe his cure to the salutary nature of the waters, but to the unbounded power of the Son of God; and accordingly said to him, "Rise, take up thy bed, and walk." No sooner was the heavenly mandate uttered, than the impotent man, to the astonishment of the multitude, "was made whole, and took up his bed and walked." John v: 9.

This great and miraculous cure could not fail of having a great effect on the spectators; and his carrying his bed on the Sabbath-day—which the Jews considered as a profanation of that day of rest—tended greatly to spread the fame of the miracle over the whole city. Nor did the man scruple to obey the commands of his kind physician; he well knew that the person who had the power of working such miracles must be a great prophet, and, consequently, that his injunction could not be sinful. He, therefore, thought that he gave a sufficient answer to those Jews, who told him it was not lawful to carry his bed on the Sabbath-day, to say, "He that made me whole, the same said unto me, take up thy bed and walk." John v: 11. He that restored my strength in an instant, and removed, with a single word, a disease that had many years afflicted me, commanded me, at the same time, to take up my bed and walk; and surely a person endued with such power from on high, would not have ordered me to do anything but what is truly right.

The votaries of infidelity should remember, that this signal miracle was performed in an instant, and even when the patient did not expect any such favor, nor even know the person to whom he owed it. No one, therefore, can pretend that imagination had any share in performing it. In short, the narrative of this miracle of mercy sufficiently proves, that the person who did it was really divine.

The Jews had long-expected the Messiah; but they had expected him to appear as a temporal prince, who would not only restore the former luster of the throne of David, but infinitely augment it, and even place it over all the kingdoms of the earth. And hence, they were unwilling to acknowledge Jesus for their Messiah, notwithstanding the proofs of his mission were undeniable, because they must, in so doing, have abandoned all their grand ideas of a temporal kingdom. Our blessed Saviour, therefore, desired them to consult their own Scriptures, particularly the writings of the prophets, where they would find the character of the Messiah displayed, and be fully convinced they were all fulfilled in his person.

He also gave them to understand, that the proofs of his mission were as full and clear as possible, being supported by the actions of his life, which, in all things, agreed with his doctrines; for he never sought the applause of men, or assumed secular power, but was always innocent and humble, though he well knew that these virtues made him appear little in the eyes of those who had no idea of a spiritual kingdom, but expected that the Messiah would appear in all the pomp of secular authority.

In short, the fatal infidelity of the Jewish doctors was principally owing to their pride. They had long filled the minds of the people with grand ideas of the glory and power of the Messiah's kingdom; they had represented him as a potent prince, who was to appear at once adorned with all the ensigns of power; and therefore to have ascribed that august character to a mere teacher of righteousness, destitute even of the ordinary advantages of birth, fortune, and erudition, would have been so plain a confession of their ignorance of the Scriptures, as must have exposed them to the ridicule and contempt of the whole people.

Our blessed Saviour added, that he himself should not only be their accuser to the God of Jacob for their infidelity, but Moses, their great legislator, in whom they trusted, would join in that unwelcome office; for, by denying him to be the Messiah, they denied the writings of that prophet. "For had ye," added he, "believed Moses, ye would have believed me; for he wrote of me. But if ye believe not his writings, how shall ye believe my words?" John v: 46, 47.

Thus did the blessed Jesus assert himself to be the Son of God, the great Judge of the whole earth, and the Messiah promised by the prophets; and, at the same time, gave them such convincing proofs of his being sent from God, that nothing could be said against them.

Convincing as these proofs were, yet they did not in the least abate the malice of the scribes and Pharisees;

for the very next Sabbath, upon his disciples plucking a few ears of corn as they passed through the fields, and eating the grain after rubbing it out in their hands, they again exclaimed against this violation of the Sabbath. But our blessed Saviour soon convinced them of their error, by showing, both from the example of David, and the constant practice of their own priests, who never omitted the necessary works of the temple on the Sabbath-day, that works of necessity were often permitted, even though they broke a ritual command; that acts of mercy were the most acceptable services to God, of any whatever; that it was inverting the order of things, to suppose that "man was made for the Sabbath, and not the Sabbath for the benefit of man:" adding, that if the service of the temple should be said to claim a particular dispensation from the law of the Sabbath, he and his disciples, whose business of promoting the salvation of mankind was of equal importance, might justly claim the same exemption; as they were carrying on a much nobler work than they who attended on the service of the temple. Thus did our blessed Saviour prove, that works of mercy should not be left undone, though attended with the violation of some of the most sacred institutions of the ceremonial law.

Soon after this dispute with the scribes and Pharisees, our blessed Saviour entered one of the synagogues of Jerusalem on the Sabbath-day, and found there a man whose right hand was withered.

The Pharisees, who observed the compassionate Jesus advance toward the man, did not doubt but he would heal him; and therefore watched him attentively, that they might have something to accuse him with the people. Their malice had arrived to that monstrous pitch, that they determined to injure his reputation, by representing him as a Sabbath-breaker, if he dared to heal the man, while they themselves were profaning it by an action which would have polluted any day; namely, of seeking an opportunity of destroying a person who had never injured them, but done many good actions for the sons of Jacob, and was continually laboring for their eternal welfare.

The Saviour of the world was not unapprised of these malicious intentions. He knew their designs, and defied their impotent power, by informing them of the benevolent action he designed—though he well knew they would exert every art they were masters of, in order to put him to death.

Therefore, when our Saviour ordered the man to show himself to the whole congregation, in order to excite their pity, these hypocritical teachers declared, in the strongest terms, the unlawfulness of his performing even such beneficent actions on the Sabbath: "Is it lawful to heal on the Sabbath-day?" They did, not, however, ask this question with an intention to hinder him from performing the miracle. No, they had a very different intention than that of accusing him. For they hoped he would have declared openly that such actions were lawful; or, at least, make no reply to their demands, which they would have construed into an acknowledgement of what they asserted.

Nor did our Lord fail to expose their malice and superstition; and accordingly asked them, "Is it lawful on the Sabbath-day to do good, or to do evil? to save life, or to destroy it?" Luke vi: 9. Is it not more lawful for me, on the Sabbath-day, to save men's lives, than for you to seek my death without the least provocation? This severe rebuke would admit of no answer, and therefore they held their peace, pretending not to understand his meaning. He therefore made use of an argument, which stupidity itself could not fail understanding, and which all the art of these hypocritical sophists was unable to answer. "What man," said the blessed Jesus, "shall there be among you that shall have one sheep, and if it fall into a pit on the Sabbath-day, will he not lay hold on it and lift it out? How much then is a man better than a sheep? Wherefore it is lawful to do well on the Sabbath-day." Matt. xii: 11, 12.

The former question they pretended not to understand, and therefore held their peace; but this argument effectually silenced them, though they were determined not to be convinced. This unconquerable obstinacy grieved the spirit of the meek, the benevolent Jesus, who beheld them with anger, that, if possible, an impression might be made, either on them or the spectators.

But, at the same time that he testified his displeasure toward the Pharisees, he uttered words of comfort to the lame man, bidding him stretch his hand; and he no sooner obeyed the divine command, than it was restored whole as the other.

This astonishing work, performed in the midst of a congregation, many of whom, doubtless, knew the man while he labored under this infirmity, and in the presence of his most inveterate enemies, must certainly have had a great effect on the minds of the people, especially as they saw it had effectually silenced the Pharisees, who had nothing to offer, either against the miracle itself, or the reasoning and power of him who had performed it.

But though these whited sepulchres, as our blessed Saviour justly termed them, were silenced by his arguments, and astonished at his miracles, yet they were so far from abandoning their malicious intentions, that they joined their inveterate enemies, the Herodians, or Sadducees, in order to consult how they might destroy him—well knowing, that if he continued his preaching, and working of miracles, the people would wholly follow him, and their own power soon become contemptible. Jesus, however, thought proper to prevent their malicious designs, by retiring into Galilee, and there pursuing his benevolent purposes.

This retreat could not, however, conceal him from the multitude, who flocked to him from all quarters, bringing with them the sick and maimed, who were healed, and sent away in peace.

Soon after this, as Jesus was disputing with the Pharisees, he was informed that his mother and brethren, or kinsmen, were without, desiring to speak to him: upon which the blessed Jesus stretched out his hands toward his disciples, and said, "Behold my mother and my brethren! For whosoever shall do the will of my Father which is in heaven, the same is my brother, and sister, and mother." Matt. xii: 49, 50. This glorious truth should be stamped on the minds of all believers, as it shows that every one, of what nation or kindred soever, who is brought into subjection to the will of God, is allied to the blessed Jesus, and entitled to the salvation of God.

CHAPTER XIII.

OUR LORD DELIVERS MANY REMARKABLE PARABLES, AND EXPLAINS SEVERAL OF THEM—HE RETURNS TO NAZARETH, AND COMMISSIONS THE TWELVE APOSTLES, WHOM HE HAD BEFORE SELECTED AS HIS CONSTANT ATTENDANTS AND FOLLOWERS, TO DISPERSE AND PREACH THE GOSPEL OF THE KINGDOM OF GOD IN DIVERS PLACES—CIRCUMSTANCES OF THE DEATH OF JOHN THE BAPTIST.

THE miraculous power of our blessed Lord, both in performing the most astonishing acts, and confuting the most learned of the Pharisaical tribe, who endeavored to oppose his mission and doctrine, brought together so great a multitude, that he repaired to the sea-side; and, for the better instruction of the people, entered into a ship, and the whole multitude stood on shore. Being thus conveniently seated, he delivered many precepts of the utmost importance, beginning with the parable of the sower, who cast his seed on different kinds of soil, the products of which were answerable to the nature of the ground—some yielding a large increase, others nothing at all. By this striking similitude, the blessed Jesus represented the different kinds of hearers, and the different manner in which they were affected by the truth of religion. Some wholly suppressed the doctrines delivered; in others they produced the fruit of righteousness in a different proportion. And surely a more proper parable could not have been delivered, when such multitudes came to hear his discourses, and so few practiced the precepts, or profited by the heavenly doctrines they contained.

The parable being finished, his disciples asked, why he taught the people in parables? to which he answered, "Because it is given unto you to know the mysteries of the kingdom of heaven, but to them it is not given. For whosoever hath, to him shall be given, and he shall have more abundance; but whosoever hath not, from him shall be taken away, even that he hath. Therefore speak I to them in parables: because they seeing, see not; and hearing they hear not, neither do they understand." Matt. xiii: 11, &c. As if he had said, You, my beloved disciples, who are of a humble, docile temper, and are willing to use means and resort to me for instruction and the explanation of the truths I deliver, to you it shall be no disadvantage, that they are delivered in parables. Besides, my discourses are plain and intelligible to all unprejudiced minds: truth will shine through the veil in which it is arrayed, and the shadow will guide you to the substance. But these proud, these self-conceited Pharisees, who are so blinded by their own prejudices that they will neither hear nor understand a thing plainly delivered, to them I preach in parables, and hide the great truths of the gospel under such metaphorical robes as will ever conceal them from persons of their own temper. They have, therefore, brought upon themselves this blindness, that in seeing they see not, and this willful deafness, that in hearing they hear not, neither do they understand.

The blessed Jesus added, that there was no reason for their being surprised at what he had told them, as it had long before been predicted by the prophet Isaiah: "By hearing ye shall hear, and shall not understand; and seeing ye shall see, and shall not perceive. For this people's heart is waxed gross, and their ears are dull of hearing, and their eyes have they closed; lest any time they should see with their eyes, and hear with their ears, and should understand with their heart, and should be converted, and I should heal them." Matt. xiii: 14, 15. There is some variation in the words, as quoted by the evangelist and those found in Isaiah; but the import of both is the same, and may be paraphrased in the following manner: The sons of Jacob shall, indeed, hear the doctrines of the gospel, but not understand them; and see the miracles by which these doctrines are confirmed, without perceiving them to be wrought by the finger of God: not because the evidences produced by the Messiah are insufficient, but because the corrruption of their hearts will not suffer them to examine and weigh these evidences; for the sins of this people have hardened their hearts; their pride and vanity have shut their ears; and their hypocrisy and bigoted adherence to tradition and forced interpretations of the law and the prophets, have closed their eyes, lest the brilliant rays of truth should strike their sight with irresistible force, and the powerful voice of divine Wisdom force their attention, and command their assent — being unwilling to be directed to the paths of righteousness, which lead to the heavenly Canaan.

Such are the reasons given by our blessed Saviour for his teaching the people by parables; and to enhance the great privilege his disciples enjoyed, he added, that many patriarchs and prophets of old had earnestly desired to see and hear these things which they now saw and heard, but were denied that favor — God having, till then, showed them to his most eminent saints in shadows only, and as they lay brooding in the womb of futurity.

Our Lord having, by these means, excited the desire of his disciples, proceeded to explain to them the parable of the sower. Having ended the interpretation of the parable of the sower, he continued his discourse to his disciples, explaining to them, by the similitude of a lighted lamp, the use they were to make of all the excellent instructions they had and should receive from him.

Having explained these parables to his disciples, he turned himself to the multitude on shore, and, in his usual endearing manner, delivered the parable of the enemy sowing tares among the wheat.

The next parable he spake to the multitude was that of the mustard-seed, which, though very small when sown, becomes, in Palestine and other parts of the east, a full-spreading tree — intimating to his audience, under this similitude, that notwithstanding the gospel would at first appear contemptible, from the ignominy flowing from the crucifixion of its Author, the strictness of its precepts, the weakness of the persons by whom it was preached, and the small number and mean condition of those who received it, yet, being founded on truth itself, it would increase to an astonishing magnitude, filling the whole earth, and affording a spiritual nourishment to all persons of all nations, who should enjoy all the privileges of the Messiah's kingdom equally with the Jews.

Our blessed Saviour concluded his discourse to the multitude with the parable of the leaven, to intimate the influence of the doctrine of the gospel on the minds of particular persons. "The kingdom of heaven is like unto leaven, which a woman took and hid in three measures of meal, till the whole was leavened." Matt xiii: 33.

While Jesus was thus employed in his heavenly Father's business, his mother and brethren came a second time, desiring to see him. In all probability, they feared that the continued fatigue of preaching would injure his health; and were therefore desirous of taking him with them, that he might refresh himself. But the blessed Jesus, who was never weary of doing good, answered his indulgent parent, as before: "My mother and my brethren are these which hear the word of God, and do it." Luke viii: 21.

Night approaching, Jesus dismissed the multitude, and returned to the house, in Capernaum, where he abode, and there explained to his disciples the parable of the tares in the field. The husbandman, said our blessed Saviour, is the Son of Man; the field, the Christian church, planted in different parts of the world; the wheat, are those that believe in Christ, who obey the precepts of the gospel, and are supported by the influences of the Holy Spirit; and the tares, the bad professors, seduced into the paths of vice, by the temptations of the devil. Our blessed Lord therefore, by this parable, represented the mixed nature of the church on earth, the dismal end of the hypocrites, and those who forget God; for these may deceive, for a time, by assuming the robes of virtue and religion, yet they will not fail, sooner or later, to betray themselves, and show that they are only wolves in sheep's clothing. At the same time, however sincerely we may wish to see the church freed from her corrupted members, we must not extirpate them by force, lest, being deceived by outward appearances, we also destroy the wheat, or sound members. We must leave this distinction to that awful day, when the great Messiah will descend to judgment; for then a final separation will be made: the wicked cast into torments, that will never have an end; but the righteous received into life eternal, where they "shall shine forth as the sun, in the kingdom of their Father." Matt. xiii: 43.

Our Lord, on this occasion, delivered the parable of the treasure hid in the field, and of the pearl of great price. The former was designed to teach us that some meet with the gospel as it were by accident, and without seeking after it, agreeable to the prediction of the prophet, "That God is found of them that seek him not." But, with regard to the latter, it was designed to intimate that men sometimes take the utmost pains to become acquainted with the great truths of the gospel. And surely the similitudes, both of the treasure and pearl, are very naturally used to signify the gospel; the former, as it enriches all who possess it; and the latter, because it is more precious than rubies.

But that the disciples might expect that the Christian church would consist of a mixed multitude of people, the good blended with the bad, in such a manner that it would be difficult to separate them, he compared it to a net cast into the sea, which gathered fish of every kind, good and bad, which were separated when the net was drawn to land: that is, at the last great day of accounts, when the righteous will be conveyed to life eternal, and the wicked cast into everlasting misery.

Our blessed Saviour, having finished these parables, asked his disciples if they understood them? and upon their answering in the affirmative, he added, that every teacher of the gospel ought to resemble a person whose house was completely furnished, and brought "forth out of his treasure things new and old."

Soon after, Jesus left Capernaum, and repaired to Nazareth, where he had been brought up, and preached in the synagogue the glad tidings of the kingdom of God; but his townsmen, though astonished at his doctrine, could not overcome the prejudices they had conceived against him, on account of the meanness of his family, and thence refused to own him for the Messiah. Our Saviour, finding them the same incorrigible persons as when he visited them before, departed from them, and taught in the neighboring villages. They, in common with all the Jews, were strangers to the true character of the Messiah, whom they considered as a temporal prince; and therefore could not bear that a person so mean as Jesus appeared to be, should perform works peculiar to that idol of their vanity, a glorious, triumphant, secular Messiah.

While our Lord resided in the neighborhood of Nazareth, he sent out his disciples to preach in different parts of Galilee, and to proclaim the glad tidings, that God was then going to establish the kingdom of the Messiah, wherein he would be worshiped in spirit and in truth. And, in order that they might confirm the doctrines they delivered, and prove that they had received their commission from the Son of God, they were endowed with the power of working miracles

How long they continued their preaching can not be known, but it is reasonable to think they spent a considerable time in it, preaching in several parts of Judea.

The miracles which the apostles wrought, raised the expectations of men higher than ever: the people were astonished to see the disciples of Jesus perform so many miracles; and thence concluded, that our Saviour must be greater than any of the old prophets, who could not transmit the power they enjoyed to others. This extraordinary circumstance could not fail of spreading his fame through all the country; it even reached the ears of Herod the Tetrarch, who, fearing a per son of such extraordinary abilities, was very uneasy; which some of his courtiers observing, endeavored to remove, telling him that one of the old prophets was risen from the dead; but this did not satisfy him, and he declared that he believed it was John the Baptist risen from the dead. "And he said unto his servants, This is John the Baptist; he is risen from the dead, and therefore mighty works do show forth themselves in him." Matt. xiv: 2.

The evangelists having, on this account, mentioned John the Baptist, inform us that Herod had put him to death; but when this happened is uncertain.

It has already been observed, that Herod had cast John into prison for his boldness in reproving him for the unlawful affinity in which he lived with his brother's wife. The sacred writers have not told us how long he continued in prison; but it is plain, from his two disciples, who came from him to our Saviour, that his followers did not forsake him in his melancholy condition. Nay, Herod himself both respected and feared him, knowing that he was highly and deservedly beloved by the people; he consulted him often, and in many things followed his advice. But Herodias, his brother's wife, (with whom he lived in so shameful a manner,) being continually uneasy, lest Herod should be prevailed upon to set him at liberty, sought all opportunities to destroy him; and, at last, an incident happened, which enabled her to accomplish her intentions.

The king having, on his birth-day, made a great feast for his friends, she sent her daughter Salome, whom she had by Philip, her lawful husband, into the saloon, to dance before the king and his guests. Her performance was remarkably elegant, and so charmed Herod, that he promised, with an oath, to give her whatsoever she asked.

Having obtained so extraordinary a promise, she ran to her mother, desiring to know what she should ask; and was instructed by that wicked woman, to require the head of John the Baptist. Her mother's desire, doubtless, surprised Salome, as she could not possibly see the use of asking what could be of no service to her. But Herodias would take no denial, peremptorily insisting on her demanding the head of the Baptist. Accordingly, she returned to Herod, saying, "I will that thou give me, by and by, in a charger, the head of John the Baptist."

So cruel a request thrilled every breast; the gayety of the king was vanished; he was vexed and confounded. But being unwilling to appear either rash, fickle, or false, before a company of the first persons of his kingdom for rank and character, he commanded the head to be given her—not one of the guests having the courage to speak a single word in behalf of an innocent man, or attempt to divert Herod from his mad purpose, though he gave them an opportunity of doing it, by signifying to them that he performed his oath merely out of regard to the company. Thus Herod, through a misplaced regard to his oath and his guests, committed a most unjust and cruel action; an action that will forever brand his memory with dishonor, and render his very name detestable to the latest posterity.

Soon after the command was given, the head of that venerable prophet, whose rebukes had struck Herod with awe in the loosest moments, and whose exhortations had often excited him to virtuous actions, was brought, pale and bloody, in a charger, and given to the daughter of Herodias, in the presence of all the guests.

The young lady eagerly received the bloody present, and carried it to her mother, who enjoyed the whole pleasure of revenge, and feasted her eyes with the sight of her enemy's head, now silent and harmless. But she could not silence the name of the Baptist; it became louder, filling the earth and heavens, and publishing to every people and nation this woman's baseness and adultery.

Thus fell that great and good man, John the Baptist, who was proclaimed by our blessed Saviour himself, to be "more than a prophet." Josephus tells us, that his whole crime consisted in exhorting the Jews to the love and practice of virtue; and in the first place to piety, justice, and regeneration, or newness of life; not by the bare abstinence from this or that particular sin, but by an habitual purity of mind and body.

It may not be improper, on this occasion, to hint,

that the history of this birth-day, transmitted to posterity in the Scriptures, stands a perpetual beacon, to warn the great, the gay, and the young, to beware of dissolute mirth. Admonished by so fatal an example, they should be careful to maintain, in the midst of their jollity, an habitual recollection of spirit, lest reason, at any time, enervated by the pleasures of sense, should slacken the rein of wisdom, or let it drop, though only for a moment; because their headstrong passions, ever impatient of control, may catch the opportunity, and rush with them into follies, or crimes whose consequences will be unspeakably, perhaps eternally bitter.

CHAPTER XIV.

Our Lord adds to the confirmation of his Mission and Doctrine by working a Miracle in the Wilderness of Bethsaida—The People, struck with the Power and Grace of the blessed Jesus, propose to raise him to the earthly dignity of King—Peter, by means of his blessed Master, performs a miracle in walking upon the Sea.

THE disciples were so alarmed at the cruel fate of the Baptist, whose memory they highly revered, that they returned from their mission, and assisted in performing the last offices to the body of their old master—many of the apostles having been originally the disciples of John. As soon as the pious rites were over, they repaired to Jesus, and told him all that had happened.

Their compassionate Master, on hearing this melancholy news, retired with them by the sea into a desert place, belonging to Bethsaida, that by retirement, meditation, and prayer, they might be refreshed and recruited for their spiritual labors; and, at the same time, leave an example to us, that we should often retire from the noise and hurry of the world, and offer up the most fervent prayers to our heavenly Father.

MIRACLE OF THE LOAVES AND FISHES.

But the multitude attended so closely, that their departure was not long concealed; and great numbers of people repaired to the place where they supposed Jesus and his disciples had secluded themselves. Struck with the greatness of his miracles on those that were sick, and anxious to hear more instruction from the mouth of so divine a teacher, no difficulties were too great for them to surmount, nor any place too retired for them to penetrate, in search of their admired preacher.

Nor was the beneficent Saviour of the world regardless of their pious esteem. He saw them, and was "moved with compassion" toward them, because they were as sheep not having a shepherd; multitudes of people without a pastor; a large harvest without laborers—motives abundantly sufficient to excite compassion in the Son of God.

The situation of these numerous throngs of people scattered abroad, without a guide, without a guardian; a flock of defenceless sheep, without a single shepherd to defend them from the jaws of the infernal wolf, was truly deplorable: the blessed Jesus, therefore, that "good shepherd who came to lay down his life for the sheep," was moved with pity toward them; the same pity which brought him from the courts of heaven, for the sake of his lost and wandering sheep in the desert, now brought him to this multitude of people, whom he instructed in the doctrines of eternal life, and with his usual goodness, healed all the sick among them.

Intently devoted to teaching and healing of the people, our blessed Saviour did not perceive the day to wear away, and that the greatest part of it was already spent; but his disciples, too anxious about the things of this world, thought proper to advise him of it — as if the Son of God wanted any directions from man. The day, said his disciples, is now far advanced, and the place a solitary desert, where neither food nor lodging can be procured; it would, therefore, be convenient to dismiss the people, that they may repair to the towns or villages on the borders of the wilderness, and provide themselves with food and lodgings; for they have nothing to eat.

But our Lord prevented that trouble, by telling them there was no necessity for sending the people away to procure victuals for themselves, as they might satisfy the hunger of the multitude, by giving them to eat; and, at the same time, to prove what opinion his disciples entertained of his power, addressed himself to Philip, who was well acquainted with the country, and said, "Whence shall we buy bread, that these may eat?"

Philip, astonished at the seeming impossibility of procuring a supply for so great a multitude, with the small sum of money which he knew was their all, and forgetting the extent of his Master's power, answered, "Two hundred pennyworth of bread is not sufficient for them, that every one of them may take a little." John vi: 7.

Our blessed Saviour might now have put the same question to Philip that he did on another occasion: "Have I been so long time with you, and yet hast thou not known me, Philip?" John xiv: 9. Hast thou beheld so many miracles, and art still ignorant that I can supply food, not only for this people, but for all the sons of men, and for the "cattle upon a thousand hills?"

But he contented himself with answering, "Give ye them to eat." The twelve, not yet comprehending the design of their Master, repeated the objection of Philip; but added, that they were willing to expend their whole stock, in order to procure as large a supply as possible. "Shall we go," said they, "and buy two hundred pennyworth of bread, that they may eat?"

But this was by no means the design of their great Master, who, instead of making a direct answer to their question, asked them, "How many loaves have ye?" How much provision can be found among this multitude? Go, and see.

The disciples obeyed the command of their Master; and Andrew soon returned, to inform him that the whole stock amounted to no more than five barley loaves, and two small fishes—a quantity so inconsiderable, that it scarcely deserved notice. "What are they," said the disciples, "among so many? What, indeed, would they have been among such a multitude of people, if they had not been distributed by the creating hand of the son of God?

Jesus, notwithstanding the smallness of the number, ordered them to be brought to him; and immediately commanded the multitude to sit down on the grass, with which the place abounded, directing his disciples, at the same time, to range them in regular order, by hundreds and fifties in a company, each company forming a square, containing an hundred in rank and fifty in file, that the number might be more easily ascertained, and the people more regularly served.

The multitude being seated, Jesus took the loaves and fishes into his hands, in sight of all the people, that they might be convinced of the small quantity of provisions that were then before them, and that they could only expect to be fed by his supernatural power. But that hand, which had constantly sustained nature, could now easily multiply these five loaves and two fishes; for, as the Psalmist elegantly observes, "He openeth his hand, and filleth all things living with plentiousness." Accordingly, he looked up to heaven, returned thanks to God, the liberal giver of all good things, for his infinite beneficence in furnishing food for all flesh, and for the power he had conferred on him of relieving mankind by his miracles, particularly for that he was about to work. This done, he blessed them; and so peculiarly efficacious was his blessing, that these five barley loaves and two fishes were multiplied into a quantity sufficient to supply the wants of five thousand men, besides women and children, who, on the most favorable supposition, must amount to an equal number. "And Jesus took the loaves; and when he had given thanks, he distributed to the disciples, and the disciples to them that were set down; and likewise of the fishes, as much as they would." John vi: 11.

Thus did the compassionate and powerful Redeemer feed at least ten thousand people with five barley loaves and two small fishes, giving a magnificent proof both of his power and goodness. For, after all had eaten to satisfy, they took up twelve baskets full of the broken pieces, a much larger quantity than was at first set before our Lord to divide.

The people, when they had seen the Saviour of the world perform so stupendous a miracle, were astonished above measure, and, in the height of their transport, purposed to take Jesus by force, and make him a king, concluding, that he must then assume the title of tne Messiah, whose coming they had so long earnestly expected, and under whose reign they hoped to enjoy all kinds of temporal felicity.

But our Lord, well knowing the intentions of the multitude, and the inclinations of his disciples to second them, ordered the latter to repair immediately to their boat, and sail to Bethsaida, while he sent away the multitude. They would, it seems, gladly have detained the people, with whom they fully agreed in sentiments; and even lingered till he constrained them to get into the boat, so fully were they still possessed of the opinion, that their master was to take the reins of government, and become a powerful prince over the house of Jacob.

The people suffered the disciples to depart without the least remorse, as they saw that Jesus did not go with them.

Perhaps they imagined he was sending away, to provide such things as they had need of. Nor did they refuse to disperse when he commanded them, purposing to return in the morning, as we find they actually did.

Having thus sent the disciples and the multitude away, Jesus himself repaired to the summit of a mountain, spending the evening in heavenly contemplation and ardent prayers to his Almighty Father.

But the disciples, meeting with a contrary wind, could not continue their course to Bethsaida, which lay about two leagues to the northward of the desert mountain where the multitude were miraculously fed. They, however, did all in their power to land as near that city as possible, but were tossed up and down all the night by the tempest; so that in the fourth watch, or between three and six o'clock in the morning, they were not above a league from the shore.

Their divine Master beheld, from the mountain, their distressed situation; but they were ignorant of his presence, though he was coming to their relief. Such was the state of the disciples; they were tossed by boisterous waves, and opposed in their course by the rapid current of the wind, so that all hopes of reaching the place intended were vanished; when, behold, their heavenly Master, to assist them in this distressful situation, comes to them, walking on the foaming surface of the sea. Their Lord's approach filled them with astonishment; they took him for an apostate spirit, and shrieked for fear. Their terrors were, however, soon removed: their great and affectionate Master talked to them, with the sound of whose voice they were perfectly acquainted. "Be of good cheer," said the blessed Jesus, "it is I, be not afraid."

Peter, a man of warm and forward temper, beholding Jesus walking on the sea, was exceedingly amazed, and conceived the strongest desire of being enabled to perform so wonderful an action.

Accordingly, without the least reflection, he immediately begged that his Master would bid him come to him on the water. He did not doubt but that Jesus would gratify his request, as it sufficiently intimated that he would readily undertake anything, however difficult, at the command of his Saviour. But it appeared, that his faith was too weak to support him to that height of obedience to which he would have willingly soared. To convince this forward disciple of the weakness of his faith, and render him more diffident of his own strength, our blessed Saviour granted his request. He ordered him to come to him upon the water.

Peter joyfully obeyed his divine Master; he left the boat, and walked on the surface of the sea. But the wind increasing, made a dreadful noise, and the boisterous waves at the same time threatened to overwhelm him. His faith now staggered; his presence of mind forsook him; he forgot that his Saviour was at hand; and, in proportion as his faith decreased, the waters yielded, and he sunk. In this extremity he looked around for his Master, and, on the very brink of being swallowed up, cried, "Lord, save me!" His cry was not disregarded by his compassionate Saviour: "he stretched forth his hand and caught him, and said unto him, O thou of little faith, wherefore didst thou doubt?"

Peter was convinced, before he left the ship, that it was Jesus who was coming to them on the water: nor did he even doubt it when he was sinking, because he then implored his assistance. But when he found the storm increase, and the billows rage more terribly than before, his fears suggested that either his Master would be unable or unwilling to support him amid the frightful blasts of the tempest.

This miracle alarmed the disciples, for, though they had so lately seen the miracle of the five loaves, they did not seem to have formed a proper idea of his power; but being persuaded that he could be no other than the expected Messiah, they "came and worshiped him, saying, Of a truth thou art the Son of God." Matt. xiv.: 33.

Our Saviour seems to have confirmed this miracle

by working another; for the evangelists tell us, that he had no sooner entered the ship, and hushed the violence of the storm, than they arrived at the place whither they were going. "Then they willingly received him into the ship; and immediately the ship was at the land, whither they went." John vi: 21.

When our Lord disembarked, the inhabitants of the neighboring country ran to him, bringing with them all those that were sick—and they were all healed. It must be remembered, that though Jesus ordinarily resided in the neighborhood of Capernaum, yet he had been absent ever since his visiting Nazareth; and therefore it is natural to think, that the inhabitants, on his return, would not omit the opportunity of bringing their sick in such prodigious crowds, that it seems our Saviour did not pay particular attention to each of them, and this was the reason of their beseeching him "that they might only touch the hem of his garment: and as many as touched were made perfectly whole." Matt. xiv: 36.

The virtue of that power by which he wrought these miracles, lay not in his garments, for then the soldiers who seized them at his crucifixion might have wrought the same miracles; but it was because Jesus willed it to be so. It was now the acceptable time, the day of salvation, foretold by Isaiah, and Christ's power was sufficient to remove any distemper whatsoever.

CHAPTER XV.

Pharisaical Superstition severely reprimanded —The great Redeemer continues to display his Power and Benevolence in the relief of several Objects of Affliction—Guards his Disciples against the prevailing Errors and Fallacies of the Scribes and Pharisees —Proceeds on the Works of his heavenly Father.

THE season of the grand passover approaching, Jesus went up to Jerusalem, to attend that solemnity. But the Jews being offended at his discourse in the synagogue of Capernaum, made an attempt upon his life. Our Lord, therefore, finding it impossible to remain at Jerusalem in safety, departed from that city, and retired into Galilee.

The Pharisees were sensible they could not perpetrate their malicious designs upon him on that occasion; they therefore followed him, hoping to find something by which they might accuse him; and at length ventured to attack him for permitting his disciples to eat with unwashed hands, because, in so doing, they transgressed the tradition of the elders.

Moses had, indeed, required external cleanness as a part of their religion, but it was only to signify how careful the servants of the Almighty should be to purify themselves from all uncleanness, both of flesh and spirit. These ceremonial institutions were, in process of time, prodigiously multiplied, and the Pharisees, who pretended to observe every tittle of the law, considered it as a notorious offence to eat bread with unwashed hands, though, at the same time, they suffered the more weighty precepts of the law to be neglected and forgotten.

To expose the absurdity of such superstitious customs, our Saviour applied to them the words of the prophet Isaiah: "This people honoreth me with their lips, but their heart is far from me." Adding, that all their worship was vain, and displeasing to the Almighty, while they praised themselves, and imposed upon others the frivolous precepts of man's invention, and at the same time neglected the eternal rules of righteousness; and to remove all objections that might be brought against this imputation of gross profaneness in the Pharisees, he supported it by a very remarkable instance. God, said the Saviour of the world, hath commanded children to honor their parents, and to maintain them when reduced to poverty by sickness, age, or misfortunes; promising life to such as obey this precept, and threatening death to those who disregard it. But, notwithstanding the peremptory commandment of Omnipotence, you teach that it is more sacred in children to enrich the temple, than to nourish their parents, although reduced to the utmost necessity; pretending, that what is offered to the great Parent of the universe, is much better bestowed, than what is given to the support of our earthly parents; making the honor of God absolutely different from the happiness of his creatures. Nay, ye teach that it is no breach of the commandment for a man to suffer his parents to perish, provided he has given what ought to nourish them to the temple at Jerusalem. Thus have ye concealed, under the cloak of piety, the most horrid, the most unnatural crime, any person can commit.

Having thus reproved the Pharisees, he called the multitude to him, and desired them to reflect on the absurdity of the precepts inculcated by the scribes. These hypocrites, said he, solicitous about trifles, neglect the great duties of morality, which are of eternal obligation. They shudder with horror at unwashed hands, but are perfectly easy under the guilt of a polluted conscience, though they must be sensible, that "not that which goeth into the mouth, defileth the man; but that which cometh out of the mouth, this defileth a man." Matt. xv: 11.

The haughty Pharisees were highly offended at his speaking in a degrading manner of their traditions. And the apostles, who would gladly have reconciled their Master and the Pharisees, insinuated to Jesus that he ought to have acted in another manner. To which our Saviour answered, "Every plant, which my heavenly Father hath not planted, shall be rooted up." Matt. xv: 13. As if he had said, You have no cause to fear their anger, as both they and their doctrine shall perish together, for neither of them came from God: adding, "Let them alone: they be blind leaders of the blind. And if the blind lead the blind, both shall fall into the ditch." Matt. xv: 14.

His disciples, not fully comprehending this doctrine, desired their Master to explain it. This our Saviour complied with, and showed them, that meats being of a corporeal nature, could not defile the mind of man, nor render him polluted in the sight of the Almighty, unless they were used to excess, or in opposition to the commandment of God; and even then the pollution arose from the man, and not from the meat. But, on the contrary, that which proceedeth out of the mouth of a man, comes from his heart and really polluteth his mind.

These doctrines of truth could not fail of irritating the Pharisees, as they tended to strip them of the mask with which they concealed their deformity, and rendered themselves so venerable in the eyes of the vulgar; and therefore their plots were leveled against his reputation and life.

Jesus, to avoid their malice, retired to the very borders of Palestine, to the coast of those two celebrated Gentile cities, Tyre and Sidon, proposing there to conceal himself for a time; but he could not be hid. It was as impossible for the Son of righteousness to be concealed where he came with his healing wings and message of peace, as it is for the sun in the firmament, when he riseth in all his glory: "As a bridegroom cometh out of his chamber, and as a giant rejoiceth to run his course." For a certain woman of Canaan, having heard of him, determined to implore his assistance. She was, indeed, one of the most abject sort of Gentiles, a Canaanite, one of that detested race with which the Jews would have no dealings, nor even conversation; but notwithstanding all these discouraging circumstances, she threw herself, as an humble petitioner, on the benevolent mercies of the Son of God. Strong necessity urged her on; and insuperable distress caused her to be importunate. Alas! unhappy parent! her only daughter, her beloved child had an unclean spirit and was grievously vexed with a devil. When her case was so urgent, and her woes so poignant, who can wonder that she was importunate and would take no refusal from this divine Person, whom, she knew, was able to deliver her? Accordingly, she came; she fell at his feet; she besought him; she cried, saying, "Have mercy upon me, O Lord, thou Son of David, have mercy." I plead no merits; as a worthless, suffering wretch, I entreat only the bowels of thy mercy; I entreat it, for I believe thee to be the Son of David, the promised Messiah, the much-desired Saviour of the world; have mercy on me, for the case of my child and her distresses are my own: "My daughter is grievously vexed with a devil." Matt. xv: 22.

Is it not, at the first view, astonishing that such a petitioner should be apparently rejected, and that by a bountiful Redeemer, who kindly invited all that were heavy laden to come to him? who promised never to cast out any that would come, and whose business it was "to go about doing good?"

We, however, find that he answered this woman not a word; he did not, in appearance, take the least notice, either of her or her distress. But this silence did not intimidate her; she still cried, she still besought, she still importunately pressed her petition, so that the very disciples were moved with her cries, and became her advocates. They themselves, though Jews, besought their master to dismiss this petitioner, to grant her request, and send her away.

But Jesus soon silenced them by an answer agreeable to their own prejudices: "I am not sent," said he, "but unto the lost sheep of the house of Israel." To this the disciples readily assented; and as they had a high opinion of the Jews' prerogative, were so well satisfied with the answer, that we hear them pleading no more for this lost, this miserable Gentile.

But this soothed not her griefs: it was her own cause; and what is immediately our own concern animates us to the most zealous application. Somewhat encouraged that she was the subject of discourse, she ventured to approach the Saviour of the world, though she well knew that the law actually forbade such an intercourse; yet she came, she worshiped "this Son of David," she confessed again his divinity, and prayed, saying, "Lord help me!"

The compassionate Saviour now condescended to speak to her, but with words seemingly sufficient to have discouraged every farther attempt; nay, to have filled her with bitter dislike to his person, though she had conceived such high and noble notions of his mercy and favor; "It is not meet," said he, "to take the children's bread, and cast it to the dogs." Matt. xv: 26. It is not justice to deprive the Jews, who are the children of the covenant, the descendants of Abraham, of any part of those blessings which I came into the world to bestow, especially on you, who are aliens and strangers from the commonwealth of Israel.

This answer, though seemingly severe, could not shake her humility, nor overcome her patience; she meekly answered, "Truth Lord; yet the dogs eat of the crumbs which fall from their master's table." Matt. xv: 27. Let me enjoy that kindness which the dogs of any family are not denied; from the plenty of miraculous cures, which thou bestowest on the Jews, drop this one to me, who am a poor distressed heathen; for they will suffer no greater loss by it, than the children of a family do by the crumbs which are cast to the dogs. Our Lord, having put the woman's faith to very severe trial, and well knowing that she possessed a just notion of his power and goodness, as well as of her own unworthiness, wrought, with pleasure, the cure she solicited in behalf of her daughter; and, at the same time, gave her faith the praise it so justly deserved; "O woman, great is thy faith: be it unto thee even as thou wilt. And her daughter was made whole from that very hour." Matt. xv: 28.

After performing this miracle, Jesus returned to the sea of Galilee, through the region of Decapolis. In this country, a man was brought to him who was deaf, and had an impediment in his speech. Objects in distress were always treated with benevolence by the holy Jesus; but, as the people now thronged about him, in expectation that he would soon establish his kingdom, he thought proper to take the man, with his relations, aside from the multitude; after which, he put his fingers in his ears, and touched his tongue, that the deaf man, who could not be instructed by language might know from whence all his benefits flowed. He then "looked up to heaven, he sighed, and saith unto him, Ephphatha, that is, Be opened. And straightway his ears were opened, and the string of his tongue was loosed, and he spake plain. And he charged them that they should tell no man." Mark vii: 34, 35, 36.

But, notwithstanding they were enjoined to secrecy, the man, or his relations, published it in every part of the country, doubtless thinking they could not be too lavish in the praises of so great a benefactor, especially as the modesty with which he had performed the cure, abundantly demonstrated that his sole view was the benefit of the human race.

CHAPTER XVI.

The blessed Jesus delegates a special Power to Peter, one of his Disciples — Pronounces the final Judgment of the World; and is afterward Transfigured upon the Mount.

JESUS having displayed his power and goodness in restoring the blind man to his sight, departed from Bethsaida, and returned into the territory of Cesarea Philippi, where, being desirous of proving, in some measure, the faith of the apostles, he asked them, saying, "Whom do men say that I, the Son of Man, am? And they said, Some say thou art John the Baptist; some Elias; and others, Jeremias, or one of the prophets." Matt. xvi: 13, 14.

The people in general mistook the character of our Saviour, because he did not assume that outward pomp and grandeur with which they supposed the Messiah would be adorned. Jesus was therefore desirous of hearing what idea his disciples formed of his character, as they had long enjoyed the benefit of his doctrine and miracles; and accordingly asked them, what they themselves understood him to be? To this question Simon Peter replied, "Thou art the Christ, the Son of the living God."

Our Saviour acknowledged the title; telling Peter that God alone had revealed the secret to him. And, in allusion to his surname, Peter, which signifies a rock, our Saviour promised, that upon himself, as the foundation, or upon the confession which Peter had just made, of his being "the Christ, the Son of the living God," he would build his church, and that he should have a principal hand in establishing the Messiah's kingdom, never to be destroyed. "Other foundation can no man lay." 1 Cor. iii: 11. On him may our souls rest, and the fiercest tempest shall rage in vain! "And I say also unto thee, That thou art Peter; and upon this rock will I build my church; and the gates of hell shall not prevail against it. And I will give unto thee the keys of the kingdom of heaven: and whatsoever thou shalt bind on earth, shall be bound in heaven; and whatsoever thou shalt loose on earth, shall be loosed in heaven." Matt. xvi: 18, 19.

Having delegated this power to Peter, our Saviour strictly forbade his disciples to tell any man that he was the Messiah; because it had been foretold by the prophets, that he should be rejected by the rulers of Israel as a false Christ, and suffer the pains of death. "Then charged he his disciples, that they should tell no man that he was Jesus the Christ." Matt. xvi: 20. Circumstances which could not fail of giving his followers great offence, as they did not yet understand the true nature of his kingdom; and therefore he thought proper to let every man form a judgment of his mission from his doctrine and miracles.

The foregoing discourses had doubtless filled the apostles with lofty imaginations, and therefore our Saviour thought proper to acquaint them with his sufferings, in order to check any fond expectation of temporal power. Peter, however, was greatly displeased to hear his Master talk of dying at Jerusalem, when he had just before acknowledged the title of Messiah. Accordingly, he rebuked him for the expression, which he was so bold as to think unguarded. But Jesus, turning himself about, said to Peter, "Get thee behind me Satan: thou art an offence to me: for thou savorest not the things that be of God, but those that be of men." Matt. xvi: 23.

Peter's conduct, in this respect, arising from an immoderate attachment to sensual objects, our Saviour thought proper to declare publicly, that all who intended to share with him in the glory of the heavenly Canaan, must deny themselves; that is, they must be always ready to renounce every worldly pleasure, and even life itself, when the cause of religion required it: he also told them, that in this world they must expect to meet with troubles and disappointments, and that whoever intended to be his disciple, must "take up his cross, and follow him."

Thus did the blessed Jesus fully explain to his disciples the true nature of his kingdom; and, at the same time, intimated, that though they had already undergone many afflictions, yet they must expect still more and greater, which they must sustain with equal fortitude, following their Master in the footsteps of his afflictions. This duty, however hard, was absolutely necessary; because, by losing their temporal life, they would gain that which was eternal: "For whosoever shall save his life, shall lose it; but whosoever will lose his life for my sake, the same shall save it." Luke ix: 24. "For what is a man profited if he should gain the whole world, and lose his own soul? Or what shall a man give in exchange for his soul?" Matt. xvi: 26.

To add to the weight of this argument, and to enforce the necessity of self denial, our Saviour particularly declared, that a day was fixed for distributing rewards and punishments to all the human race; and that he himself was appointed by the Father as universal Judge; so that his enemies could not flatter themselves with the hope of escaping the punishment they deserved, nor his friends be afraid of losing their eternal reward. "Whosoever therefore shall be ashamed of me, and my words, in this adulterous and sinful generation, of him also shall the Son of Man be ashamed, when he cometh in the glory of his Father, with the holy angels." Mark viii: 38.

About eight days after this discourse, our blessed Saviour being with the multitude in the country of Cesarea Philippi, left them in the plain, and accompanied by Peter, James, and John, ascended an exceedingly high mountain.

In this solitude, while Jesus was praying with these three disciples, he was transfigured; his face became radiant and dazzling, it shone like the sun in his meridian clearness. At the same time, his garment acquired a snowy whiteness, far beyond anything human art could produce; a whiteness, bright as the light, and sweetly refulgent, but in a degree inferior to the radiance of his countenance.

Thus, as it were, for an instant, the son of God during his state of humiliation, suffered the glory of his divinity to shine through the veil of human nature with which it was covered; and to heighten the grandeur and solemnity of the scene, Moses, the great lawgiver of Israel, and Elijah, a zealous defender of the law, appeared in the beauties of immortality—the robes in which the inhabitants of the heavenly Canaan are adored. The disciples, it seems, did not see the beginning of this transfiguration: happening to fall asleep at the time of prayer, they lost that pleasure, together with a great part of the conversation which these two prophets held with the only begotten Son of God.

They, however, understood that the subject was his meritorious sufferings and death, by which he was to redeem the world; a subject that had, a few days before, given great offence to his disciples, particularly to Peter. At beholding the illustrious sight, the disciples were greatly amazed; but the forwardness of Peter's disposition prompting him to say something, he uttered he knew not what: "Master," said he, "it is good for us to be here: and let us make three tabernacles; one for thee, and one for Moses, and one for Elias." Mark ix: 5.

This disciple imagined that Jesus had now assumed his proper dignity, that Elias was come according to Malachi's prediction, and the Messiah's kingdom was at length begun. Accordingly, he thought it was necessary to provide some accommodation for his Master and his august assistants, intending, perhaps to bring the rest of the disciples, with the multitude, from the plain below, to behold his matchless glory. This, he thought, was much better for his Master, than to be put to death at Jerusalem, concerning which, Jesus had been talking with the messengers from heaven, and the design of which Peter could not comprehend.

But "while he yet spake, behold, a bright cloud overshadowed them: and, behold, a voice out of the cloud, which said, This is my beloved Son, in whom I am well pleased; hear ye him." Matt. xvii: 5.

When the three disciples heard the voice, which, like the roaring thunder, burst from the cloud, and was such as mortals were unaccustomed to hear, they fell on their faces, and continued in that posture till Jesus approached, raised them up, and dispelled their fears, saying unto them, "Arise, and be not afraid. And when they had lifted up their eyes, they saw no man save Jesus only." Matt. xvii: 7, 8.

Jesus, having continued all night with his three disciples, on the mountain, returned to the plain early in the morning, charging them to conceal what they had seen, till after he was risen from the dead. He well knew that the world, and even his own disciples, were not yet able to comprehend the design of his transfiguration; and that if it had been published before his resurrection, it might have appeared incredible; because nothing but afflictions and persecutions had hitherto attended him. "He was truly a man of sorrows, and acquainted with grief."

CHAPTER XVII.

Our Saviour relieves a Youth tortured with a Dumb Spirit — Conforms cheerfully to the custom of the country, by paying the Tribute—Reproves the Pride of his Disciples, and delivers some excellent moral Precepts.

WHEN our Lord approached the descent of the mountain, accompanied by his three disciples, he saw a great multitude surrounding the nine who continued in the plain, and the scribes disputing with them. The people, seeing Jesus coming down from the mountain, ran to him, and saluted him with particular reverence. After which, Jesus asked the scribes, what was the subject of their debate with his disciples? To which one of the multitude answered, "Master, I have brought unto thee my son, which hath a dumb spirit: and wheresoever he taketh him, he teareth him; and he foameth and gnasheth with his teeth, and pineth away: and I spake to thy disciples that they should cast him out; and they could not." Mark ix: 17, 18.

This answer being made by one of the multitude, and not by the scribes, to whom the question was directed, indicates that they had been disputing with the disciples on their not being able to cure this afflicted youth:

perhaps their making this unsuccessful attempt had given the scribes occasion to boast that a devil was at length found, which neither they nor their Master could conquer. This seems to be indicated by the manner in which our Saviour addressed himself to these arrogant rulers. "O faithless generation!" says he, "how long shall I be with you? how long shall I suffer you?" Must I always bear with your infidelity? After speaking in this manner to the scribes, he turned himself to the father of the young man, and said, "Bring thy son hither." But no sooner was he brought in sight of his deliverer, than the evil spirit attacked him, as it were, with double fury: "The spirit tare him; and he fell on the ground, and wallowed foaming." Mark ix: 20.

Jesus could easily have prevented this attack; but he permitted it that the minds of the spectators might be impressed with a more lively idea of this youth's distress. And, for the same reason, probably, it was, that he asked the father how long he had been in this deplorable condition! To which the afflicted parent answered, "Of a child: and ofttimes it hath cast him into the fire, and into the waters, to destroy him: but if thou canst do anything, have compassion on us, and help us." Mark ix: 21, 22.

The inability of our Lord's disciples to cast out this spirit, had greatly discouraged the afflicted father; and the exquisite torture of his son, and the remembrance of its long continuance, so dispirited him, that he began to fear this possession was even too great for the power of Jesus himself, as the scribes had probably before affirmed; and therefore could not help expressing his doubts and fears. But, Jesus, to make him sensible of his mistake, said to him, "If thou canst believe, all things are possible to him that believeth." On which, the father cried out, with tears, "Lord, I believe; help thou mine unbelief." The vehement manner in which he spake causing the crowd to gather from every quarter, Jesus rebuked the foul spirit, saying unto him, "Thou dumb and deaf spirit, I charge thee, come out of him, and enter no more into him." Mark ix: 25.

No sooner was the powerful exit pronounced, than the spirit, with a hideous howling, and convulsing the suffering patient in the most deplorable manner, came out, leaving the youth senseless, and without motion; till Jesus, taking him by the hand, restored him to life, and delivered him perfectly recovered to his father.

The nine disciples, during this whole transaction, remained silent. They were, doubtless, mortified to think that they had lost, by some fault of their own, the power of working miracles, lately conferred upon them by their Master; and, for this reason, were afraid to speak to him in the presence of the multitude. But when they came into the house, they desired Jesus to inform them why they had failed in their attempt to heal that remarkable youth? To which Jesus answered, "Because of your unbelief." But to encourage them, he described the efficacy of the faith of miracles. "If ye have faith as a grain of mustard-seed, ye shall say unto this mountain, Remove hence to yonder place, and it shall remove; and nothing shall be impossible unto you." Matt. xvii: 20. Nothing shall be too great for you to accomplish, when the glory of God and the good of the church are concerned, provided you have a proper degree of faith; even yonder mountain, which bids defiance to the storm, and smiles at the attacks of its mingled horrors, shall, at your command, leave its firm basis, and remove to another place.

The expulsion of the dumb spirit seems to have astonished the disciples more than any other miracle they had seen their Master perform; so that our Saviour found it necessary to moderate their high admiration of his works, by again predicting his own death, and retiring, for a time, into the unfrequented parts of Galilee.

After a short tour through the desert part of Galilee, Jesus returned into Capernaum, the place of his general residence. Soon after his arrival, the tax-gatherers came to Peter, and asked him, whether his Master would pay the tribute? That disciple, it seems, had promised that Jesus would satisfy their demand; but, on a more mature consideration, feared to ask him concerning his paying taxes, on any pretence whatever.

Jesus was, however, no stranger to what had happened, and the fear of Peter to ask him; and therefore turned his discourse to this subject, by saying unto him, "What thinkest thou, Simon? of whom do the kings of the earth take custom or tribute? of their own children, or of strangers? Peter saith unto him, Of strangers. Jesus saith unto him, Then are the children free;" insinuating, that, as he was himself the Son of the great King, to whom heaven, earth, and the sea belong, he had no right to pay tribute to any monarch whatever, because he held nothing by a derived right. Or, if we suppose this contribution was made for the service and reparation of the temple, he meant, that as he was the Son of that omnipotent Being to whom the tribute was paid, he could have justly excused himself. But the blessed Jesus was always careful not to give offence; and therefore sent Peter to the lake, with a line and hook, telling him, that in the mouth of the first fish that came up, he should find a piece of money equal to the sum demanded of them both. "Notwithstanding, lest we should offend them, go thou to the sea, and cast a hook, and take up the fish that first cometh up; and when thou hast opened his mouth, thou shalt find a piece of money; that take, and give unto them, for me and thee." Matt. xvii: 27.

Our Lord took this extraordinary method of paying the tribute-money in this manner, because the miracle was of such a kind as could not fail to demonstrate that he was the Son of the great Monarch worshiped in the temple and who rules the universe. In the very manner, therefore, of paying this tribute, he showed Peter that he was free from all taxes; and, at the same time, gave this useful lesson to his followers, that when their property is affected only in a small degree, it is better to recede a little from their just right, than to offend their brethren, or disturb the state, by obstinately insisting on it.

CHAPTER XVIII.

OUR BLESSED LORD ATTENDS, FOR THE FOURTH TIME, THE CELEBRATION OF THE PASSOVER AT JERUSALEM — ADDRESSES THE MULTITUDE AT THE SOLEMN FEAST OF TABERNACLES — EXEMPTS THE WOMAN TAKEN IN ADULTERY FROM THE PUNISHMENT ANNEXED BY THE JEWS TO THAT CRIME — ESCAPES FROM THE SNARES LAID FOR HIM BY THE INVETERATE SCRIBES AND PHARISEES.

THE great Redeemer, having promoted his Father's work in Galilee, departed into Judea, passing through the country beyond Jordan, that the Jews who inhabited those distant parts might enjoy the unspeakable benefits of his discourses and miracles. After sowing the seeds of eternal life, and publishing the glad tidings of salvation in those remote countries, he repaired to Jerusalem to celebrate the fourth passover; but the malignity of the scribes and Pharisees was so great, that he staid but a short time in the capital; and then returned into Galilee, where the multitude again resorted to him, and he again instructed them in the paths that lead to everlasting life.

The feast of the tabernacles now drew on, at which all the males of the Jewish nation, capable of traveling, repaired to Jerusalem, and dwelt in the tabernacles,

H

or booths made of the boughs of trees, in commemoration of their fathers having had no other habitation, during their forty years' sojourning in the wilderness. To this feast some of the kinsmen of the blessed Jesus desired he would accompany them, and there show himself openly to the whole nation of the Jews. They did not themselves believe that he was the great Prophet so long expected, and therefore condemned the method he pursued in his public ministry as altogether absurd.

They could not conceive what reason he had for spending so much of his time in the deserts and remote corners of the kingdom, while he professed so public a character as that of the Redeemer of Israel. Jerusalem, the seat of power, was in their opinion the more proper place for him to deliver his doctrines, and work his miracles in the most public manner possible, before the great and learned men of the nation, whose decision in his favor would have great weight in increasing the number of his disciples, and inducing the whole nation to own him for the Messiah. "Depart hence, and go into Judea, that thy disciples also may see the works that thou doest. For there is no man that doeth anything in secret, and he himself seeketh to be known openly. If thou do these things, show thyself to the world. For neither did his brethren believe in him." John vii: 3–5.

Our Lord well knew the rancorous prejudice of the inhabitants of Jerusalem, and therefore did not think proper to reside among them any longer than was absolutely necessary. They had more than once attempted his life, and therefore very little hope remained that they would embrace his doctrine; but, on the contrary, there was great reason to think they would destroy him, if possible, before he had finished the work for which he assumed the veil of human nature, and resided among the sons of men. "My time," said the blessed Jesus to these unbelieving relations, "is not yet come: but your time is always ready. The world can not hate you; but me it hateth, because I testify of it, that the works thereof are evil. Go ye up unto this feast: I go not up yet unto this feast; for my time is not yet full come." John vii: 6–8. As if he had said, It is not proper for me to go before the feast begins; but you may repair to the capital whenever you please; the Jews are your friends, you have done nothing to displease them; but the purity of the doctrine I have preached to them, and the freedom with which I have reproved their hypocrisy and other enormous crimes, have provoked their malice to the utmost height, and therefore, as the time of my sufferings is not yet come, it is not prudent for me to go so soon to Jerusalem.

There was also another reason why our blessed Saviour refused to accompany these relations to the feast of tabernacles; the roads were crowded with people, and these gathering around him, and accompanying him to Jerusalem, would, doubtless, have given fresh offence to his enemies, and have, in a great measure, prevented his miracles and doctrines from having the desired effect. He therefore chose to continue in Galilee, till the crowd were all gone up to Jerusalem, when he followed, as it were in secret, neither preaching nor working miracles by the way, so that no crowd attended him to the feast.

As Jesus did not go up openly to Jerusalem, so neither did he, on his arrival, repair to the temple, and there preach openly to the people. This gave occasion to several disputes among the Jews with regard to his character. Some affirmed that he was a true prophet; and that his absenting himself from the feast could only be owing to accident; while others as confidently asserted, that he only deceived the people, and paid no regard to the institutions they had received from heaven.

But about the middle of the feast, Jesus appeared openly in the temple, and taught the people, delivering his doctrines with such strength of reasoning and elegance of expression, that his very enemies were astonished, knowing that he had never enjoyed the advantage of a learned education. "Now about the midst of the feast, Jesus went up into the temple, and taught. And the Jews marveled, saying, How knoweth this man letters, having never learned?" John vii: 14, 15.

To which the Redeemer of mankind replied, My doctrine was not produced by human wisdom, the sages of the world were not my instructors; I received it from heaven; it is the doctrine of the Almighty, whose messenger I am; "My doctrine is not mine, but his that sent me." John vii: 16. Nor can he who is desirous of practicing the doctrines I deliver, if he will lay aside his prejudices, and sincerely desire to be taught of God, be at a loss to know from whom my doctrines are derived; because he will easily discern whether they are comformable to the will of man or of God. It is not difficult to discover an impostor, because all his precepts tend to advance his own interest, and gratify his pride. Whereas all the doctrines delivered by a true prophet have no other end than the glory of God, however contrary they may prove to himself. "He that speaketh of himself seeketh his own glory: but he that seeketh his glory that sent him, the same is true, and no unrighteousness is in him." John vii: 18.

The scribes and Pharisees were highly provoked at this attachment of the common people to Jesus; and accordingly, on the last and great day of the feast, they met in council, and sent several officers to apprehend him, and bring him before them. Jesus, during these transactions in the council, continued in the temple, teaching the people. My ministry, said he to the multitude, is drawing near its period; and therefore you should, during the short time it has to last, be very careful to improve every opportunity of hearing the word; you should listen with the greatest attention to every discourse, that your minds may be stored with the truths of the Almighty, before I return to my Father; for, after my departure, you shall earnestly wish for the same opportunities of seeing me, and hearing my instructions, but shall never obtain them. "Yet a little while am I with you, and then I go unto him that sent me. Ye shall seek me, and shall not find me: and where I am thither ye can not come." John vii: 33, 34.

The Jews, who did not understand that our blessed Saviour alluded to his own death, resurrection, and ascension to the right hand of the Majesty on high, whither their sins would not permit them to follow him, wondered at this doctrine, and imagined that he intended to leave Judea, and preach to their brethren dispersed among the Gentiles. But this supposition was not sufficient; because if he did go and preach among the Gentiles, they thought it was not impossible for them to follow him thither: "Then said the Jews among themselves, Whither will he go, that we shall not find him? will he go unto the dispersed among the Gentiles, and teach the Gentiles? What manner of saying is this that he said, Ye shall seek me, and shall not find me: and where I am, thither ye can not come?" John vii: 35, 36.

While the divine Teacher was thus instructing the people in the temple, the water from Siloam was brought in, according to the appointment of the prophets Haggai and Zechariah, part of which they drank with loud acclamations in commemoration of the mercy showed to their fathers, who were relieved by a stream which miraculously flowed from a rock, and refreshed a whole nation, then ready to perish with thirst in a dreary and sandy waste; and the other part they poured out as a drink-offering to the Almighty, accompanying it with their prayers, for the former or latter rain to fall in its season; the whole congregation singing the following passage: "With joy shall ye draw water out of the wells of salvation." Isaiah xii: 3.

It was the custom of the blessed Jesus to deliver moral instructions, in allusion to many occurrences that happened; and accordingly, he took this opportunity of inviting, in the most affectionate manner, all who were desirous of knowledge or happiness, to come to him and drink, alluding to the ceremony they were then performing. And, to encourage all such as were desirous of believing in him, he promised them the gifts of the Holy Spirit, which he represented under the similitude of a river flowing out of their belly: "In the last day, that great day of the feast, Jesus stood and cried, saying, if any man thirst, let him come unto me, and drink. He that believeth on me, as the Scriptures hath said, out of his belly shall flow rivers of living water." John vii: 37, 38.

During this discourse to the people, the officers from the council came to apprehend him; but hearing that the topic he was discussing was a singular one, and he seemed to deliver his discourse with remarkable fervor, their curiosity induced them to listen some time before they laid hands on him. But the eloquent manner in which he delivered his subject appeased their rage; the sweetness of his pronunciation, and the plainness and perspicuity of his discourse, elucidated the beauties of truth, and caused them to shine before the understanding with their native luster. Accordingly, his very enemies, who were come from the council on purpose to apprehend him, were astonished; the greatness of the subject, made, as it were, visible by the divine speaker, filled their understandings; the warmth and tenderness with which he delivered himself, penetrated their hearts; they felt new and uncommon emotions, and, being overwhelmed with the greatness of their admiration, were fixed in silence and astonishment; they condemned themselves for having undertaken the office, and soon returned to the rulers of Israel without performing it.

If our Lord had pleaded for his life before the officers of the council who were sent to apprehend him, the success of his eloquence, even in that case, had been truly wonderful; but, in the case before us, it surely was superior to all praise, for, in a discourse addressed to others, and even on a spiritual subject, it disarmed a band of inveterate enemies, and made them his friends.

Nor were the officers the only persons affected by this discourse; for many of them declared he must be one of the old prophets, and others, that he was none other than the Messiah himself. Some, however, led away with the common mistake, that he was born at Nazareth, asked, with disdain, if the Messiah was to come out of Galilee? and whether they would acknowledge a Galilean for the Messiah, when the Scriptures absolutely declared that he was to be born in Bethlehem, the native town of his father David? "Many of the people, therefore, when they heard this saying, said, Of a truth, this is the Prophet. Others said, This is the Christ. But some said, Shall Christ come out of Galilee? Hath not the Scriptures said, That Christ cometh of the seed of David, and out of the town of Bethlehem, where David was?" John vii: 40–42.

Such were the dissensions on this subject, that some of his enemies, knowing that the officers were sent to apprehend him, threatened to lay hands on him; but the Almighty would not suffer them to execute their wicked design: "And some of them would have taken him; but no man laid hands on him." John vii: 44.

The officers now returned to the council, and were asked why they had not brought Jesus of Nazareth? To whom the officers answered, "Never man spake like this man." This reply enraged the council, who reviled them for presuming to entertain a favorable opinion of one whom they had pronounced an impostor. It is strange, said they, that you, who are not ignorant of our sentiments concerning this person, should entertain a favorable idea of him. Have any persons of rank, or any celebrated for their knowledge of the laws, believed on him? Are not his followers the lower orders of the people, who are totally ignorant of all the prophecies concerning the Messiah? The officers made no answer to the railing accusations of their master; but Nicodemus, a member of the council, arraigned their conduct in a very poignant manner: "Does our law?" says he, "condemn any man before he has been heard?" They had before condemned their officers for being ignorant of the law, when it appeared they were themselves far more ignorant, in pretending to condemn a person before they had proved him guilty. They were acting directly contrary to the fundamental principles of the law of equity, at the time they boasted of their profound knowledge of its precepts.

Incensed at this reprimand of Nicodemus, they asked him, with an air of disdain and surprise, if he was also one of those mean persons who had joined together to support the pretences of a Galilean, though the Scriptures had plainly said, that Bethlehem was the place of the Messiah's nativity: adding, that if he refused to listen to them, he should soon be convinced that the great prophet mentioned by Moses was not to be born in Galilee. "Art thou also of Galilee? Search and look; for out of Galilee ariseth no prophet." John vii: 52.

Having made this reply to Nicodemus, the council broke up, and Jesus, who knew their malicious intentions, retired to the Mount of Olives, where he spent the night with his disciples.

Our blessed Lord, early the following morning, returned to the temple, and again taught the people. The scribes and Pharisees now determined to render him odious to the multitude, or obnoxious to the Roman governor; and therefore placed before him a woman who had been taken in the act of adultery, desiring his opinion what punishment she ought to suffer. "This woman," said they to Jesus, "was taken in adultery, in the very act. Now Moses in the law commanded us, that such should be stoned; but what sayest thou?" John viii: 4, 5.

Had our Lord disapproved the sentence of the law, they would, doubtless, have represented him to the multitude as a person who contradicted Moses, and favored adultery; which could not have failed of rendering him odious to the people. On the other hand, had he ordered her to be stoned, it would have afforded a plausible pretence for accusing him to the Roman governor, as a person who stirred up the people to rebellion—the Romans having now taken the power of life and death into their own hands.

But Jesus, who well knew their malicious intentions, made no answer; but "stooped down, and with his finger wrote on the ground, as though he heard them not." John viii: 6. They, however, still continued pressing him to give an answer; and, at last, Jesus, in allusion to the law, which ordered that the hands of the witnesses, by whose testimony an adulterer was convicted, should be the first upon him, said, "He that is without sin among you, let him first cast a stone at her." Let those who are remarkably zealous for having justice executed upon others, at least take care to purify themselves from all heinous crimes.

This reply had its desired effect. The hypocritical scribes and Pharisees were convicted of sin by their own consciences, so that they immediately retired, fearing Jesus would have made their particular sins public. "And they which heard it, being convicted by their own conscience, went out one by one, beginning at the eldest, even unto the last." John viii: 9. The woman's accusers being all retired, Jesus told her, that as no man had pronounced sentence of death upon her, neither would he pronounce it; but advised her to be very careful, for the future, to avoid the temptations which had induced her to commit so black a crime.

The wisdom, knowledge, and power of our blessed Saviour, were eminently displayed on this occasion: his wisdom, in defending himself against the malicious attempts of his enemies; his knowledge, in discovering the secrets of their hearts; and his power, in making use of their own consciences to render their artful intentions abortive. It was, therefore, with remarkable propriety, that the great Redeemer of mankind now called himself the "light of the world;" as if he had said, I am the spiritual sun, that dispels the darkness of ignorance and superstition, in which the minds of men are immersed, and discovers the path that leads to eternal life; nor shall any who follow me ever be involved in darkness. "I am the light of the world: he that followeth me shall not walk in darkness, but shall have the light of life." John viii: 12.

This assertion of our Lord highly provoked the Pharisees, who told him he must be a deceiver, because he boasted of himself. To which the great Redeemer of mankind replied, You are not to imagine that I called myself the light of the world from a principle of pride and falsehood: that title justly belongs to me; nor would you yourselves refuse to acknowledge it, did you know from what authority I received my commission, and to whom, when I have executed it, I must return. But of these things ye are totally ignorant, and therefore judge according to outward appearance, and condemn me because I do not destroy those who oppose me, as you vainly think the Messiah will do those who shall refuse to submit to his authority. But the design of the Messiah's coming is very different from your mistaken notions; he is not come to destroy, but to save, the children of men. "Though I bear record of myself, yet my record is true: for I know whence I came, and whither I go; but ye can not tell whence I come, and whither I go. Ye judge after the flesh; I judge no man." John viii: 14, 15. He added, that if he should condemn any person for unbelief, the condemnation would be just, because his mission was true, being confirmed by his own testimony and that of his Almighty Father, the God of Jacob, by whose authority, and agreeable to whose will, all his sentences would be passed: "And yet if I judge, my judgment is true: for I am not alone, but I and the Father that sent me." John viii: 16.

Having thus asserted the divinity of his mission, and shown that his judgment was just, he proceeded to inform them that his Father himself bare witness to the truth of his mission. You can not, said he, justly complain, even if I should punish you for your unbelief, because you are, by your own laws, commanded to believe the testimony of two witnesses, that my mission evidently is true. For the actions of my life, which are perfectly agreeable to the character of a messenger from heaven, bear sufficient witness of me: and the Father, by the miracles he has enabled me to perform, beareth witness of me: ye are, therefore, altogether culpable in objecting to my mission. "It is also written in your law, that the testimony of two men is true. I am one that beareth witness of myself, and the Father that sent me beareth witness of me." John viii: 17, 18.

The Jews then asked him, Where is thy Father, the other witness to whom thou appealest? Jesus replied, Your conduct sufficiently demonstrates that ye are strangers both to me and my Father; for had ye known who I am, ye must have also known who it is I call my Father: had ye been convinced that I am the Messiah, ye must also have been convinced that the Father is no other than that omnipotent Being, who created and upholds all things by the word of his power. "Then said they unto him, Where is thy Father? Jesus answered, Ye neither know me, nor my Father: if ye had known me, ye should have known my Father also." John viii: 19.

This discourse, the evangelist tells us, was held in the treasury, a court of the temple, where the chests were placed for receiving the offerings of all those who came to worship in the temple, and therefore must have been a place of great resort, being frequented by all, even the priests and rulers. But, notwithstanding the public manner in which our blessed Saviour now asserted his claim to the character of the Messiah no man attempted to seize him; Providence not suffering them to put their malicious designs in execution, because his hour, or the time of his suffering was not yet come.

The debate being ended, Jesus again repeated what he had before told them; namely, that he should shortly depart from them; and that they should then seek him, but not be able to find him. "I go my way, and ye shall seek me, and shall die in your sins: whither I go, ye can not come." John viii: 21. As if he had said, After my ascension into heaven, when the Roman armies shall spread horror and desolation in every corner of the land, ye shall then earnestly wish for the coming of the Messiah, in expectation of being delivered by his powerful arm from your cruel enemy: but ye shall then find your mistake; ye shall die in your sins, and be forever excluded from the mansions of happiness.

The Jews by no means comprehended the departure of which our Lord told them. They even fancied he would destroy himself, because they thought the only retreat where they could not find him was the gloomy habitation of the grave. To which the blessed Jesus replied, Your vile insinuation discovers at once the wickedness of your hearts, and the baseness of your original. Ye are from the earth, and therefore subject to all the evil passions that infect human nature, the source of temptation to every sin. Ye therefore must believe that I am the bread of life, the heavenly manna, the light of the world, the true Messiah, if ye are desirous of being cleansed from those pollutions which flow from your earthly origin; but if you still continue in your unbelief, you shall die in your sins.

The Jews now, in order to vindicate themselves, demanded what sort of a person he pretended to be? To which Jesus answered, "Even the same that I said unto you from the beginning," that is, at the beginning of this discourse, "the light of the world;" adding, "I have many things to say, and to judge of you: but he that sent me is true; and I speak to the world those things which I have heard of him." John viii: 26.

This discourse, however plain it may appear, was not understood by the perverse Jews; they did not perceive that he spake to them of the Father. But Jesus told them, that when they crucified him they would be convinced, by the miracles accompanying that awful hour—the resurrection from the dead, the effusion of the Holy Spirit on the disciples, and the destruction of the Jewish nation—who he was, and the Father that sent him. "When ye have lifted up the Son of Man, then shall ye know that I am he, and that I do nothing of myself; but as my Father hath taught me, I speak these things." John viii: 28.

He added, that though he should be crucified as a malefactor, that punishment would not be inflicted on him as a consequence of being deserted by his Father; because he would never leave him in any period of his sufferings, or even at the hour of his death, as he always acted agreeably to his will.

These words induced many of the people to believe him to be the Messiah. Perhaps by lifting him up, they did not understand his crucifixion, but his ascen sion to the throne of David; and hence supposed that he now entertained sentiments worthy of the Messiah, and were therefore very ready to acknowledge him as such, and believe the doctrine he had delivered concerning his mission. But Jesus told them, that if they persevered in the belief and practice of his word, they should in reality become his disciples, have a title to that honorable appellation, be fully instructed in every doctrine of the gospel, and not only freed from the slavery of sin and its consequences, but from the ceremonial laws delivered by Moses. "If ye continue my word, then are ye my disciples indeed; and ye shall know the truth, and the truth shall make you free." John viii: 31, 32.

The Jews, on hearing him mention that they should be made free, answered, "We be Abraham's seed, and were never in bondage to any man." This assertion, if taken literally, was absolutely false, the whole nation, at that very time, being in bondage to the Romans; nor were their ancestors any strangers to slavery, having severely felt the hand of tyranny in Egypt, Assyria, and Babylon. The expression, therefore, according to some writers, must be taken in a metaphorical sense, to signify spiritual bondage: it was a freedom by truth, a freedom in respect of religion, which they now asserted. They meant that they were the descendants of illustrious ancestors, and, during the worst of times, had preserved sentiments in religion and government worthy the posterity of Abraham; nor had the hottest persecution of the Assyrian kings been able to compel them to embrace the religion of the heathen. In respect of truth, "We were never in bondage to any man: how sayest thou, Ye shall be made free?"

In answer to this question, Jesus told them, that those who gave themselves up to the practice of sin, and the gratification of their sinful appetites, were absolute slaves; and how far they might deserve that appellation, it was incumbent on them to consider. "Verily, verily, I say unto you, whosoever committeth sin is the servant of sin." And, as a slave can not be assured of the continuance of his master's favor, or be certain of abiding continually in the family, so my Father can, when he pleases, discard such habitual sinners, and deprive you of the external economy of religion, of which you so highly boast, as you have, through sin, rendered yourselves bondmen to his justice. If ye are desirous of becoming the children of God, and of remaining forever in his family, you must submit to the authority of his Son, and embrace his doctrine, which will induce him to adopt you as co-heirs with himself. It is he only that can make you free indeed, and place you in the city of the heavenly Jerusalem, without the least danger of being removed. I well know that you are, in a natural sense, the seed of Abraham, but, in a moral one, the offspring of Satan; for many of you are desirous of destroying me, because I enjoy a greater degree of sanctity than you are willing to acquire. "I know that ye are Abraham's seed: but ye seek to kill me, because my word hath no place in you. I speak that which I have seen with my Father: and ye do that which you have seen with your father. They answered and said unto him, Abraham is our father." John viii: 37–39.

Notwithstanding their claim to immediate descent from that father of the faithful, Jesus told them, that if they were the spiritual progeny of Abraham, they would resemble that great and good man in his righteousness; and therefore, instead of endeavoring to take away the life of a person who came with a revelation from God, they would believe on him, in imitation of Abraham, who was justly styled the father of the faithful, and the friend of God. "If ye were Abraham's children, ye would do the works of Abraham. But now ye seek to kill me, a man that hath told you the truth, which I have heard of God; this did not Abraham." John viii: 39, 40.

The Jews, incensed at our Lord, rushed on him, and attempted to stone him; but Jesus, by miraculously concealing himself, passed unhurt through the crowd, and retired out of the temple. With what patience did our blessed Redeemer bear, and with what "meekness of wisdom" did he answer the most virulent and opprobrious language. And shall we too keenly resent the reflections which are thrown upon us? May but our conscience witness for us, and we need not fear all that are against us!

CHAPTER XIX.

Our Lord continues to work miracles, in Confirmation of his Mission and Doctrine — Calls forth and sends out seventy Disciples — Preaches to the People of Judea, by way of Parable.

THE great Preacher of Israel, having defeated the cruel designs of the obstinate Jews, in passing on his way, saw a man who had been blind from his birth. The sight of so affecting an object could not fail to excite the compassion of the benevolent Saviour of mankind. Nor could the affronts and indignities he had just received from the Jews hinder him from "working the works of him that sent him," and dispensing blessings on that rebellious and ungrateful nation. Accordingly, he beheld this poor blind man, not with a transient view, but fixed on him the eyes of pity, and resented him with the riches of his adorable love.

The disciples, observing the affectionate regard of heir Master to this object of compassion, and probaly imagining that he was going to extend his usual mercy to this unfortunate object, asked their Master whether his blindness was occasioned by his own sin, or the sin of his parents? They had often heard their Master say, that afflictions were commonly the punishment of particular sins, and had learned, from the law of Moses, that sin was the fruitful source of evil; and that the Lord punished the iniquities of the fathers upon the children. Their Master kindly answered, that neither his own nor the sins of the parents were the immediate cause of this peculiar affliction; but that he was born blind, "that the works of God should be made manifest in him:" particularly his sovereignty in bringing him blind into the world, his power in conferring the faculty of sight upon him, and his goodness in bearing witness to the doctrine by which men are to be saved.

We may learn, by this pertinent reply of the Saviour of the world, that a curious inquiry into the cause of afflictions in other men may be safely avoided; and that we ought to suppose every calamity subservient to the glory of Omnipotence; never imputing to their personal sins whatever miseries we behold in others, lest, like the disciples in the present case, we assign to sin what owes its origin to the glory of our Maker.

Having assigned the cause of this person's blindness, namely, "that the works of God should be made manifest in him," Jesus added, "I must work the works of him that sent me while it is day; the night cometh when no man can work," (John ix: 4;) intimating to his disciples, and all the sons of men, his unwearied labor in the work of his Almighty Father. In this he was employed day and night, during the time of his sojourning in the flesh. To this alone he directed all his thoughts and all his intentions. This he esteemed even as his meat and drink; and for this he suffered the neglect of his ordinary food, that he might finish the blessed, the benevolent work of human salvation. A work, to accomplish which he left the courts of heaven, and, during the execution of it, went about doing good.

It was now the Sabbath-day, and the blessed Jesus was going to perform a miracle, in which there was to be a small degree of servile work; and therefore he told his disciples, that they need not be surprised to see him work miracles of that kind on the Sabbath-day. For though they should imagine that he might defer them till the day of rest was over, his time on earth was so short, that it was necessary for him to embrace every opportunity that offered of working miracles. Perhaps he chose to perform this work on the Sabbath, because he knew the Pharisees would, for that reason, inquire into it with the utmost attention, and consequently render it more generally known. But, however this be, our blessed Saviour, who was now going to confer sight on one that was born blind, took occasion from thence to speak of himself as one appointed to give light also to the minds of men involved in darkness: "As long as I am in the world, I am the light of the world." John ix: 5.

Having declared the salutary design of his coming into the world, "he spat on the ground, and made clay of the spittle, and he anointed the eyes of the blind man with the clay, and said unto him, Go, wash in the pool of Siloam, (which is, by interpretation, Sent.) He went his way, therefore, and washed, and came seeing." John ix: 6, 7.

This miraculous operation could not fail of producing a general curiosity and surprise; it induced those who had seen this blind man in his dark and deplorable condition, to be very particular in their inquiries into the means of so singular a miracle. It was doubtless, the subject of general conversation, and, it is natural to think, should also have proved the means of a general conversion; but, as it too frequently happens, a perverse curiosity prevented its salutary effects npon their souls. Unbelief, and hardness of heart, led some of them even to doubt of the plainest fact—a fact the most evident and indisputable, and plainly the work of the Divinity—and others, to persecute at once both the object and the author of it! "The neighbors, therefore, and they which before had seen him that he was blind, said, Is not this he that sat and begged? Some said, This is he: others said, He is like him: but he said, I am he." John ix: 8, 9. The man, transported with gratitude and joy, and perceiving his neighbors to doubt the identity of his person proclaimed himself to be the very same whom they lately saw begging in total darkness. I am he thus wonderfully blest with sight, by the peculiar mercy of the Almighty! I am he, who was blind from my birth, whom ye have all seen, and many relieved in my miserable distress! I am he who was, even from my mother's womb, involved in total darkness, but now enjoy the enlivening light of day!

So ingenuous an acknowledgment of the fact excited their curiosity to know how this admirable effect was produced. "How were thine eyes opened?" To this question he readily replied, "A man that is called Jesus, made clay, and anointed mine eyes, and said unto me, Go to the pool of Siloam, and wash: and I went and washed, and I received sight." John ix: 11. They then asked him where the person was who had performed so stupendous a work? To which the man answered, "I know not:" for Jesus had retired while the man went to wash his eyes in the pool of Siloam, probably to avoid the applauses which would naturally have been given him, and which we see, through the whole gospel, he generally studied to avoid.

The neighbors, either stimulated by envy, or excited by a desire of having the truth of this extraordinary event searched to the bottom, brought the man before the council, as the proper judges of this affair. Accordingly, he was no sooner placed before the assembly, than the Pharisees began to question him, "how he had recovered his sight?" Not daunted by this awful assembly, though terrible to a man of his mean circumstances, he boldly answered, "He put clay on mine eyes, and I washed, and do see." John ix: 15.

On hearing this account of the miracle, the Pharisees declared, that the author of it must be an impostor, because he had, by performing of it, violated the Sabbath-day. But others, more candid in their way of thinking, gave it as their opinion, that no deceiver could possibly work a miracle of that kind, because it was too great and beneficial for an evil being to have either the inclination or power to perform.

The court being thus divided in their opinions with regard to the character of Jesus, they asked the man himself what he thought of the person who had conferred on him the blessing of sight? To which he boldly and plainly answered, "He is a prophet." But the Jews, wanting to prove the whole a cheat, started another objection, namely, that this person was not born blind, though all his neighbors had really testified to the truth of it. Accordingly, they called his parents, and asked them, Whether he was their son? if he had been born blind? and by what means he had obtained his sight? To which they answered, that he was truly their son, and had been born blind; but, with regard to the manner in which he received his sight, and the person who had conferred it on him, they could give no information: their son was of age, and he should answer for himself. "These words spake his parents, because they feared the Jews; for the Jews had agreed already, that if any man did confess that he was Christ, he should be put out of the synagogue." John ix: 22.

The road from Galilee to Jerusalem lay through Samaria, and the inhabitants were those which entertained the most inveterate hatred against all who worshipped in Jerusalem. Jesus, being no stranger to this disposition of the Samaritans, thought proper to send messengers before him, that they might, against his arrival, find reception for him in one of the villages. The prejudiced Samaritans, finding the intention of his journey was to worship in the temple at Jerusalem, refused to receive either him or his disciples into their houses.

The messengers, being thus disappointed, returned to Jesus, and gave him an account of all that had passed; at which James and John were so exceedingly incensed, that they proposed to their Master to call fire from heaven, in order to destroy such inhospitable wretches; alleging, in excuse for such violent proceedings, the example of the prophet Elijah: "Lord, wilt thou that we command fire to come down from heaven, and consume them, even as Elias did?" Luke ix: 54.

Our Lord, desirous of displaying an example of humility on every occasion, sharply rebuked them for entertaining so unbecoming a resentment for this offence. "Ye know not," said he, "what manner of spirit ye are of." Ye are ignorant of the sinfulness of the disposition ye have now expressed; nor do ye consider the difference of times, persons, and dispensations. The severity exercised by Elijah on the men who came from Ahab to apprehend him, was a just reproof of an idolatrous king and people; very proper for the times, and very agreeable to the characters, both of the prophet who gave it, and of the offenders to whom it was given, and, at the same time, not unsuitable to the Mosaic dispensation. But the gospel breathes a very different spirit: and the intention of the Messiah's coming into the world, was not to destroy, but to save the lives of the children of men.

Ye wise of this world, who reject saving knowledge, behold here an instance of patience, under a real and unprovoked injury, which you can not parallel among all your boasted heroes of antiquity! An instance of patience, which expressed infinite sweetness of disposition, and should be imitated by all the human race, especially by those who call themselves the disciples of Christ.

As our blessed Saviour's ministry, was from this time till its final period, to be confined to Judea and the countries beyond Jordan, it was necessary that some harbingers should be sent into every town and village he was to visit, to prepare his way. Accordingly, he called his seventy disciples unto him, and, after instructing them in the duties of their mission, and the particulars they were to observe on their journey, he sent them into different parts of the country, to those particular places whither he himself intended to follow them, and preach the doctrines of the gospel to the inhabitants. Our Lord, according to his own declaration, dispatched these disciples on the same important message as he had done the twelve before.

The harvest was plenteous in Judea and Perea, as well as in Galilee, and the laborers also few; and being never more to preach in Chorazin, Bethsaida, and Capernaum, the cities wherein he had usually resided, he reflected on the reception he himself had met with from the inhabitants of those cities. He foresaw the terrible consequences that would flow from their rejecting his doctrine, and the many kind offers he had made them. He was grieved for their obstinacy: and, in the overflowing tenderness of his soul, he lamented the hardness of their hearts. "Woe," said he, "unto thee, Chorazin! woe unto thee, Bethsaida! for if the mighty works had been done in Tyre and Sidon, which have been done in you, they had a great while ago repented, sitting in sackcloth and ashes. But it shall be more tolerable for Tyre and Sidon at the judgment, than for you. And thou, Capernaum, which art exalted to heaven, shalt be thrust down to hell." Luke x: 13–15. To which our Saviour added, as some consolation to his disciples, "He that heareth you, heareth me, and he that despiseth you, despiseth me; and he that despiseth me, despiseth him that sent me." Luke x: 16.

Such a token of heavenly regard could not fail of comforting the seventy, and alleviating their minds, when thinking of the ill usage they expected to meet with during the course of their mission. They well knew that the preaching of Christ himself had been often despised, and often unsuccessful, with respect to to many of his hearers; and, therefore, they had no very great reason to expect that they should find a more welcome reception than their Master.

The seventy disciples, having received their instructions, and the power of working miracles, from the Messiah, departed to execute their important commission in the cities and villages of Judea and Perea. And, after visiting the several places, publishing the glad tidings of salvation, and working many miracles in confirmation of their mission, they returned to their Master with great joy, saying, "Lord, even the devils are subject unto us through thy name!"

From this appeal, it seems that they knew not the extent of their delegated power, and were pleasingly surprised to find the apostate spirits trembling at their command. To which their great Master replied, "I beheld Satan as lightning fall from heaven." You will be no longer astonished, that the devils are subject to the power I have given you, when I tell you that their prince is not able to stand before me; and, accordingly, when I first put on the veil of human nature, to destroy him and his works, I saw him, with the swiftness of the lightning's flash, fall from heaven: adding, in order to increase their joy, and prove that he had really cast Satan down from the seat of heaven, that he would increase their power. "Behold," says he, "I give unto you power to tread on serpents and scorpions, and over all the power of the enemy: and nothing shall by any means hurt you." Luke x: 19.

Lest they should exult beyond measure in the honor thus conferred on them, which was merely temporary, our Lord adds, "Notwithstanding, in this rejoice not, that the spirits are subject unto you; but rather rejoice, because your names are written in heaven." Luke x: 20.

Nor could the blessed Jesus reflect on the unsearchable wisdom and goodness of the divine dispensations to mankind, without feeling extraordinary joy; so that his beneficent heart overflowed with strains of gratitude: "I thank thee, O Father, Lord of heaven and earth, that thou hast hid these things from the wise and prudent, and hast revealed them unto babes: even so, Father, for so it seemed good in thy sight." Luke x: 21.

When the disciples had executed their commission, Jesus left Samaria, and retired into Judea, and in the way was met by a certain lawyer, or scribe, who, being desirous of knowing whether the doctrines preached by Jesus were the same with those before delivered by Moses, asked him, What he should do to inherit eternal life? It is really amazing that any mortal should ask a question like this with a view to tempt, not to be instructed. This was, however, the case; but the blessed Jesus, though no stranger to the most secret thoughts of the heart, did not reply, as he had before done to the Pharisees, "Why temptest thou me, thou hypocrite?" He turned the scribe's weapons against himself; what, says he, is written in the law, of which thou professest thyself a teacher? "How readest thou?" That law will teach thee what thou must do to be saved; and happy will it be for thee, if thou compliest with its precepts. The scribe answered, it is there written, "Thou shalt love the Lord thy God with all thy heart, and with all thy soul, and with all thy strength, and with all thy mind; and thy neighbor as thyself." Luke x: 27.

Our Lord then shows the strength and spirituality of the law: "Thou hast answered right: this do, and thou shalt live." Perform these commands, and thou hast fulfilled the duties of an Israelite; for on these two commandments hang all the law and the prophets.

Where is the man that can fulfill the law? The lawyer, who, in all probability, expected no such answer, being conscious of his defects, and consequently of the impossibility of obtaining eternal life on those conditions, was willing, as the sacred historian informs us, "to justify himself;" was willing to stifle the rising suggestions of his own conscience, and, at the same time, to make a show of his own devotion; and, in order to do this, he said to Jesus, "And who is my neighbor?" a question very likely to be asked by a bigoted Jew, whose narrow notions led him to despise all who were not of his own fold — all who were not the natural descendants of his father Abraham.

To remove their obstinate attachment to their own principles, open their hearts to a more generous and noble way of thinking, and show them the only foundation of true love, and the extensive relation they and all mankind stand in to each other, our Saviour delivered the following most beautiful and instructive parable:

A certain person, in his journey from Jerusalem to Jericho, had the misfortune to fall into the hands of robbers, who, not content with taking his money, stripped him of his raiment, beat him in a deplorable manner, and left him for dead. While he continued in this miserable condition, utterly incapable of assisting himself, a certain priest happened to travel the same road, "and when he saw him, he passed by on the other side. And likewise a Levite, when he was at the place, came and looked on him, and passed by on the other side." So little compassion had these ministers of religion for a brother in the most deplorable circumstances of distress, that they continued their journey, without offering to assist so miserable an object, notwithstanding their sacred characters obliged them to perform, on every occasion, the tender offices of charity and compassion. It was a brother, a descendant of Abraham, in distress, and therefore these hypocrites could offer no reasons to palliate their inhumanity. Their stony hearts could behold the affecting object of an unfortunate Israelite, lying on the road naked and cruelly wounded, without being the least affected with his distress.

Though these teachers of religion were hypocrites, and wholly destitute of grace and charity, compassion glowed in the heart of a Samaritan, who, coming to the spot where this helpless object lay, ran to him; and though he found him to be a person of a different nation, and one who professed a religion opposite to his own, yet the hatred which had been instilled into his mind from his earliest years, and every objection arising from the animosity subsisting between the Jews and Samaritans, were immediately silenced by the tender sensations of pity, awakened by the sight of such complicated distress; his bowels yearned toward the miserable object; though a Jew, he flew to him, and assisted him in the most tender manner.

It was the custom in these eastern countries for travelers to carry their provision with them; so that this compassionate Samaritan was enabled, though in the desert, to give the wounded man a little wine to recruit his spirits. He also bound up his wounds, pouring into them wine and oil, placed him on his own beast, and walked himself on foot to support him. In this manner he conducted him to an inn, took care of him during the night, and, in the morning, when business called him to pursue his journey, recommended him to the care of the host, left what money he could spare, and desired that nothing might be denied him; for whatever was expended he would repay at his return.

Having finished the parable, Jesus turned himself to the lawyer, and asked him, "Which now of these three, thinkest thou, was neighbor to him that fell among thieves?" The lawyer, struck with the truth and evidence of the case, replied, without the least hesitation, "He that showed mercy unto him." Upon which Jesus replied, "Go, and do thou likewise." Perform all the good offices in thy power, extend thy kindness to every one who stands in need of thy assistance, whether he be an Israelite, an heathen, or a Samaritan. Consider every man as thy neighbor in respect to works of charity, and make no inquiry with regard to his country or religion, but with regard to his circumstances.

CHAPTER XX.

The humble Jesus resides with Martha and Mary, two obscure Women of Bethany — Improves a Circumstance which occurred at the Feast of Dedication — Prescribes a mode of Prayer to his Disciples and future Followers — Revisits some of the Pharisaical Tribe.

THE feast of dedication approaching, Jesus turned his course toward Jerusalem, and in the evening came to the house of Martha and Mary, the sisters of Lazarus, at Bethany. Martha was desirous of expressing her regard for the divine guest, by providing for him and his disciples the best entertainment in her power. But her sister, who was of a more contemplative disposition, sat at the feet of Jesus, listening with the utmost attention to his doctrine; for the great Redeemer of mankind never omitted any opportunity of declaring the gracious offers of the Almighty, and his unspeakable love for the children of men. Martha, being greatly fatigued with the burden of the service, complained to Jesus of the little care Mary took to assist her. "Lord, dost thou not care that my sister hath left me to serve alone? Bid her therefore that she help me." Luke x: 40.

But Martha's officiousness incurred our Lord's re proof, who commended Mary for her attentive application to his doctrine: "Martha, Martha, thou art careful and troubled about many things: but one thing is needful: and Mary hath chosen that good part which shall not be taken away from her." Luke x: 41.

When Jesus repaired to Jerusalem, to celebrate the feast of dedication, he was informed, that the beggar he had restored to sight, had been, by the council, cast out of the synagogue. This information excited the pity of the Son of God; and he resolved to make him full amends for the injury he had suffered. It was not long before he met the suffering person, and said to him, "Dost thou believe on the Son of God? He answered and said, Who is he, Lord, that I might believe on him? And Jesus said unto him, Thou hast both seen him, and it is he that talketh with thee. And he said, Lord, I believe. And he worshiped him." John ix: 35.

We have hinted that the beggar was thoroughly convinced the person who opened his eyes was a messenger from heaven. It is, therefore, no wonder, that as soon as he knew Jesus was the person who had performed so great a work, he readily believed him to be the Son of God.

Our Saviour having thus given the poor man ample proof of his Messiahship, directed his discourse to the people, and said unto them, "For judgment I am come into this world; that they which see not might see, and that they which see might be made blind." John ix: 39. The meaning of our Saviour, though he alluded to the blind man, was spiritual. He did not intend to represent the design of his coming, but the effect it would have on the minds of men; as it would demonstrate what character and disposition every person possessed. The humble, the docile, and the honest, though they were immersed in the night of darkness, with regard to religion and the knowledge of the Scriptures, should be enlightened by his coming, as the blind man had enjoyed the invaluable gift of sight from his hands; but those who were wise, learned, and enlightened, in their own opinion, should appear in their true character, absolutely ignorant, foolish, and blind.

The Pharisees, who happened to be present when he spake these words to the people, imagined that he intended to throw a reflection on their sect, which the common people, from their skill in the law, held in great veneration. Accordingly, they asked him, with disdain, "Are we blind also?" Dost thou place us, who are teachers, and have taken such pains to acquire the knowledge of the Scriptures, on a level with the vulgar? To which Jesus answered, "If ye were blind, ye should have no sin: but now ye say, We see; therefore your sin remaineth." If ye had not enjoyed the faculties and opportunities of discerning the proofs of my mission, you might have been considered as blind; but as ye are superior to the vulgar in point of learning, and, at the same time, your hearts averse from acknowledging the truth, your enlightened understanding will only aggravate your guilt.

Having condemned the obstinacy and prejudice of the sect, in rejecting the most evident tokens of the divinity of his mission, he continued the reproof, by describing the character of a true and false teacher. It was our Lord's custom, always to allude to objects before him; and being now in the outer courts of the temple, near the sheep, which were there exposed to sale, for sacrifice, he compared the teachers among the Jews to shepherds, and the people to sheep—a metaphor often used by the old prophets. He considered two kinds of bad shepherds, or teachers: the one, who instead of entering in by the door to lead the flocks to the richest pastures, entered some other way, with an intention only to kill, to steal, and to destroy; the other, who, though they entered by the door to feed their flocks, with the dispositions of hirelings, yet when the wolf appeared, they deserted the sheep, having no love for any but themselves. By the former he plainly alluded to the Pharisees, who had cast the man born blind out of the synagogue, for no other reason than because he would not act contrary to the dictates of his conscience, and agree with them in declaring Jesus to be an imposter. But though they had cast him out of their church, Christ received him into his, which is the true church, the spiritual inclosure, where the sheep go in and out, and find pasture.

To illustrate the allusion, it should be observed, that the sheep which were brought to be sold, were inclosed in little folds, within the outer court of the temple; so that the shepherd himself could not enter, till the porter had opened the door. And, from this circumstance, the following parabolical discourse may be easily understood. "Verily, verily, I say unto you, He that entereth not by the door into the sheepfold, but climbeth up some other way, the same is a thief and a robber." John x: 1. Believe me, that whosoever, in any age of the church, assumed the office of a teacher, without a commission from me, was a thief and a robber; and, in the present age, he is no better who assumes that office without my commission, and particularly without believing on me. "But he that entereth in by the door is the shepherd of the sheep. To him the porter openeth; and the sheep hear his voice: and he calleth his own sheep by name, and leadeth them out. And when he putteth forth his own sheep, he goeth before them, and the sheep follow him for they know his voice." John x: 2–4.

The doctrine here inculcated is, that good men are obedient to the instructions of true and faithful teachers, who, in every case, show them their duty with the greatest plainness, not concealing it because it may be disagreeable in their inclinations.

The feast of the dedication being now over, Jesus departed from Jerusalem, and retired into the parts of Perea beyond Jordan. Here his ministry was attended with great success; for the inhabitants of the country, remembering what had been told them by John the Baptist concerning Jesus, and being sensible that the doctrine and miracles of our blessed Saviour were fully equal to what the Baptist had foretold, firmly believed him to be the Messiah.

According to this supposition, which seems th most agreeable to reason, the inhabitants of thes countries enjoyed the doctrines and miracles of the Son of God for a very considerable time. But, however this may be, the evangelist tells us, that while he was executing his ministry beyond Jordan, he happened to pray publicly, with such fervency, that one of his disciples, who was exceedingly affected both with the matter and manner of his address, begged he would teach them to pray. "And it came to pass, that as he was praying in a certain place, when he ceased, one of his disciples said unto him, Lord, teach us to pray, as John also taught his disciples. And he said unto them, When ye pray, say, Our Father which art in heaven, Hallowed be thy name: Thy kingdom come: Thy will be done, as in heaven, so in earth. Give us day by day our daily bread: and forgive us our sins; for we also forgive every one that is indebted to us: And lead us not into temptation; but deliver us from evil." Luke xi: 1-4.

Soon after, our blessed Saviour cast out a devil, when some, who were present, ascribed the miracle to Beelzebub. "And he was casting out a devil, and it was dumb. And it came to pass when the devil was gone out, the dumb spake; and the people wondered. But some of them said, He casteth out devils through Beelzebub the prince of the devils." Luke xi: 14, 15. However strange this argument may seem, and however weak and absurd it must appear to impartial judges, yet it had a considerable effect on illiterate persons, especially on those whose prejudices and interests it favored. The Pharisees pretended, that as Jesus had all along been at great pains to oppose the traditions which most of the teachers of that age considered as the essentials of religion, and the principal branches of piety, they concluded that he must be a very wicked person.

They also supposed that a false prophet had the power of working signs and wonders; and thence concluded, that our Saviour performed all his miracles by the assistance of evil spirits, with an intention to turn the people from the worship of the true God.

Another pretended reason for ascribing his miracles to evil spirits was that the demons themselves, when they departed out of the persons possessed, honored him with the title of Messiah. Their arguments, though evidently founded on falsehood, contributed largely to the infidelity of the Jews; and, however we may be surprised that such weak reasons should have any effect, considering what multitudes were witnesses of the many miracles the blessed Jesus performed on the sick of all sorts, on the blind, the deaf, the dumb, the maimed, the lame, on paralytics, lunatics, demoniacs, and other miserable objects; nay, on the dead, whom he raised again to life; on the winds and the seas; in a word, on every part of nature; yet experience hath abundantly convinced us, that notwithstanding all these evidences, their own superstitious opinions fixed that headstrong people in their infidelity.

CHAPTER XXI.

EXPLANATION OF THE ORIGIN AND OPINIONS OF THE DIFFERENT SECTS AMONG THE JEWS — OUR LORD TEACHES THE MULTITUDE BY PLAIN DISCOURSE, AND ALSO BY PARABLES.

HAVING undertaken to write the history of the life of our blessed Lord and Saviour Jesus Christ, we can not omit a distinct account of the different sects of the Jews, a people with whom he was most intimately concerned, both as a necessary elucidation of many circumstances, as well as an important verification of many things foretold concerning the Messiah.

Josephus reckons four principal sects among the Jews: namely, the Pharisees, the Sadducees, (called also Herodians,) the Essenes, and the Galileans. The evangelists, however, mention only two, the Pharisees and Sadducees.

The rise of the Pharisees is unknown. They claim, indeed, the celebrated Hillel for their founder—as he is by some supposed to have lived during the pontificate of Jonathan, about a hundred and fifty years before the birth of Christ; but others, with more reason, suppose that he was cotemporary with the famous Someas, who lived about the time of Herod, long before whom the sect of the Pharisees was in high repute. It is, therefore probable that they claim Hillel rather as an ornament, than as the author of the sect.

One of the most famous tenets of the Pharisees, was that of an oral tradition handed down from Moses, and to which they attributed the same divine authority as to the sacred books. This being strenuously opposed by the Sadducees and Samaritans, rendered these equally detested by them. But none more incurred their hatred than the blessed Jesus, who embraced every occasion of reproving them for the unjustifiable preference they gave this pretended tradition to the written word of God, and for condemning those as apostates, worthy of death, who did not pay the same, or even a greater regard, to the former than to the latter.

Another tenet they embraced, in opposition to the Sadducees, was that of the existence of angels, the immortality of the soul, the resurrection of the dead, and future rewards. But, with regard to the last, they excluded all who were notoriously wicked from having any share in the happiness of eternity; supposing, that as soon as death had put a period to their lives, their souls were conveyed into everlasting punishment.

A third tenet was, that all things were subject to fate; or, as some expressed it, to the heavens. It is not easy to conceive what they meant by this: Josephus, indeed, will have it, that they designed to reconcile the fatality or predestination of the Essenes with the free-will of the Sadducees.

If so, this is not the only absurdity, or even contradiction, which they held; but a certain learned prelate seems to have proved that they attribute all to fate, or to that chain of causes to which the Creator has subjected all things from the beginning; among which the influence of the heavenly bodies were considered the principal. This seems to be hinted at by St. James, in the beginning of his epistle to the new converts, where he explodes that Pharisaical leaven by the most beautiful exposition of the immutability of God, the giver of all good, to the mutability of the planets; which, according to that notion, must necessarily vary their aspects from a malign to a benevolent one, and the contrary, even by their natural motions and change of position. This tenet of the Pharisees was, therefore, a source of dislike to the doctrines delivered by the blessed Jesus, as these affirm that men are the authors of their own unbelief, disobedience, and obstinacy; and consequently answerable for that, and all the train of evils these vices draw after them.

But the most distinguished character of the Pharisees, and that which rendered them more obnoxious to the just censures of our blessed Saviour was, their supererogatory attachment to the ceremonial law, their frequent washings, fastings, and prayings, their giving alms publicly, seeking for proselytes, scrupulous tithings, affected gravity of dress, gesture, and mortified looks: their building the tombs of the prophets, to tell the world that they were more righteous than their ancestors, who murdered them, though they were themselves plotting the death of one greater than all the prophets; their over-scrupulous observance of the Sabbath, to the exclusion of the works of the greatest charity, and many others of the like nature; while they were wholly negligent of the moral and eternal law of mercy and justice, of charity and humility, and the like indispensable virtues. The very best of them contented themselves with abstaining from the actual commission of any enormous act, while they indulged themselves in the most wicked thoughts and desires Nay, some, more hardened in their vices, made no scruple, not only of coveting, but destroying, poor widows' houses, of committing the vilest oppressions, injustice, and cruelties, and of encouraging these enormities in their followers, under the specious cloak of religion and sanctity. Well, therefore, might the great Redeemer of mankind compare them to whited sepulchres, beautiful indeed without, but within full of rottenness and corruption.

The last erroneous opinion we shall mention of the Pharisees, common, indeed, to all the other sects, but more exactly conformable to their haughty, rapacious, and cruel temper, was, their expectation of a powerful, conquering Messiah, who was to bring the whole world under the Jewish yoke; so that there was scarce an inhabitant of Jerusalem, however mean, that did not expect to be made a governor of some opulent province under that wonderful prince. How unlikely was it, then, that the preaching of the meek, and humble Jesus, whose doctrine breathed nothing but humility, peace, sincerity, and contempt of the world, and universal love and beneficence, should ever be relished by that proud, that covetous, that hypocritical sect, or even by the rest of the people, while these, their teachers, so strenuously opposed it?

The sect of the Sadducees is said to have been founded by Saddoc, a disciple of Antigonus, of Socho. Their chief tenet was, that our serving God ought to be free, either from slavish fear of punishment, or from selfish hope of reward; that it should be disinterested, and flow only from the pure love and fear of the Supreme Being. They added, that God was the only immaterial being; in consequence of which they denied the existence of angels, or any spiritual substances, except the Almighty himself. It is, therefore, no wonder that the Sadducees took every opportunity of opposing and ridiculing the doctrine of the resurrection.

Another of their tenets, equally opposite to the Pharisees and to the doctrine of Christ, was, that man was constituted absolute master of all his actions, and stood in no need of any assistance to choose or act; for this reason, they were always very severe in their sentences, when they sat as judges. They rejected all the pretended oral traditions of the Pharisees, admitting only the texts of the sacred books, and preferred those of Moses to all the rest of the inspired writings. They are charged with some other erroneous tenets, by Josephus and the Talmudists; but those already mentioned are abundantly sufficient for the purpose. The notions of a future life, universal judgment, eternal rewards and punishments, to men whom a contrary doctrine had long soothed into luxury, and an overgrown fondness for temporal happiness, which they considered as the only reward for their obedience, must of necessity appear strange and frightful; and, as such, could not fail of meeting with the strongest opposition from them; especially, if we add, what Josephus observes, that they were, in general, men of the greatest quality and opulence, and, consequently, too apt to prefer the pleasures and grandeur of this life to those of another.

The sect of Galilean, or Gaulonites, so called from Judas, the Galilean or Gaulonite, appeared soon after the banishment of Archelaus, when his territories were made a Roman province, and the government given to Coponius. For the Jews, considering this as an open attempt to reduce them to slavery, Judas took advantage of their discontent; and, to ripen them for an insurrection, Augustus furnished them with a plausible pretence by issuing, about this time, an edict for surveying the whole province of Syria, and laying on it a proportional tax. Judas, therefore, who was a man of uncommon ambition, took occasion from this incident to display all his eloquence, in order to convince the Jews that such a submission was nothing less than base idolatry, and placing men on a level with the God of Jacob, who was the only Lord and Sovereign that could challenge their obedience and subjection. The party which he drew after him became so considerable, that they threw every thing into confusion, laid the foundation for those frightful consequences that ensued, and which did not end but with the destruction of Jerusalem.

The Essenes, though not mentioned by the evangelist, made a very considerable sect among the Jews, and are highly celebrated by Josephus, Philo, Pliny, and several Christian writers, both ancient and modern. It is impossible to trace their origin, or even the etymology of their name. This, however, is certain, that they were settled in Judea in the time Jonathan, the brother and successor of Judas Maccabeus, about a hundred and fifty years before Christ.

The Essenes distinguished themselves, by their rules and manner of life,—laborious and contemplative The former divided their time between prayer and labor; such as the exercise of some handicraft, or the cultivation of some particular spot of ground, where they planted and sowed such roots, corn, &c., as served for their food; and the latter, between prayer, contemplation, and study. In this last they confined themselves to the sacred books and morality, without troubling themselves with any branch of philosophy. But the contemplative and laborious had their synagogues, their stated hours for prayer, for reading and expounding the sacred books. The latter was always performed by the elders, who were seated at the upper end of the synagogue, according to their seniority; while the younger, who were permitted to read the lessons, were placed at the lower. Their expositions were generally of the allegorical kind, in which they seem to have excelled all their Jewish brethren. But they paid the greatest regard to the five books of Moses, and considered that lawgiver as the head of all the inspired penmen; they even condemned to immediate death whoever spoke disrespectfully either of him or his writings. Upon this account they studied, read, and expounded him, more than all the rest, and seem to have drawn their religion chiefly from the Pentateuch. The doctrines and expositions of the elders were received with implicit faith, and in their practice they conformed with an entire submission to all their sect.

With respect to their faith, they believed in the existence of angels, the immortality of the soul, and a future state of rewards and punishments, like the Pharisees; but seem to have had no notion of the resurrection. They considered the souls of men as composed of a most subtle ether, which, immediately after their separation from the cage or prison, as they called it, were adjudged to a place of endless happiness or misery: that the good took their flight over the ocean, to some warm or delightful regions prepared for them; while the wicked were conveyed to some cold, intemperate climates where they were left to groan under an inexpressible weight of misery. They were likewise entirely opposed to the Sadducean doctrine of free-will, attributing all to an eternal fatality, or chain of causes. They were averse to all kinds of oaths, affirming that a man's life ought to be such that he may be credited without them. The contemplative sort placed the excellency of their meditative life in raising their minds above the earth, and placing their thoughts on heaven; when they had attained this degree of excellency, they acquired the character of prophets.

In their practice, they excelled all the other sects in austerity. If we may credit Philo, it was a fundamental maxim with them, upon their entrance into the contemplative life, to renounce the world, and to divide among their friends and relations their properties and estates. They never ate till after sunset, and the best of their food was coarse bread, a little salt, and a few stomach herbs. Their clothing was made of coarse wool, plain, but white; they condemned all sorts of unctions and perfumes, as luxurious and effeminate. Their beds were hard, and their sleep short. Their heads, or superiors, were generally chosen according to seniority, unless there started up among the brotherhood some more conspicuous for learning, piety, or prophetic spirit. Some of them, indeed, were so contemplative that they never stirred out of their cell, or even looked out of their window, during the whole week, spending their time in reading the sacred books, and writing comments upon them. On the Sabbath-day they repaired to their synagogues early in the morning, and continued there the whole day in prayer, singing psalms, or expounding the sacred books.

Having endeavored to explain the origin and tenets of the several sects among the Jews, we now return to the history of our blessed Saviour, whom we left preaching in the country beyond Jordan, where he was surrounded by an innumerable multitude of people.

In the audience of this vast assembly, he gave his disciples, in general, a charge to beware of the leaven of the Pharisees, namely, hypocrisy; because all their actions would be brought to light, either in this world, or in that which is to come; and therefore exhorted them to be very careful never to do anything which could not bear the light, but to let the whole of their behaviour be honest, just, and good. "Beware ye of the leaven of the Pharisees, which is hypocrisy. For there is nothing covered that shall not be revealed; neither hid, that shall not be known. Therefore whatsoever ye have spoken in darkness shall be heard in the light; and that which ye have spoken in the ear, in closets, shall be proclaimed upon the house-tops." Luke xii: 1–3.

This argument against hypocrisy he improved as a reason for their acquiring another quality, which would much better serve all the ends they could propose; namely, an undaunted resolution in the performance of their duty, founded on a firm confidence in God, who would bring to light the most secret word and thought, publicly condemn the wicked, and justify his faithful servants and children.

CHAPTER XXII.

THE BLESSED JESUS ACCEPTS THE PHARISEE'S INVITATION — DELIVERS DIVERS PARABLES, REPRESENTING THE REQUISITES FOR ADMITTANCE INTO THE KINGDOM OF GOD — THE CARE OF THE REDEEMER FOR EVERY ONE OF HIS PEOPLE — THE RECEPTION OF A PENITENT SINNER AND THE PUNISHMENT OF MISUSING THE BENEFITS OF THE GOSPEL.

OUR Saviour was invited by one of the Pharisees to his house. Though he knew that this invitation arose not from a generous motive, yet, as he never shunned any opportunity of doing good, even to his most implacable enemies, he accepted it. At his entering the Pharisee's house, they placed before him, a man that had a dropsy, doubtless with an intention to accuse him for healing on the Sabbath-day; being persuaded that he would work a miracle in favor of so melancholy an object. Jesus, who knew the secret thoughts of their hearts, asked the lawyers and Pharisees whether it was "lawful to heal on the Sabbath-day?" But they refusing to give any answer to the question, Jesus laid his hand on the diseased person, and immediately his complexion returned, his body was reduced to its ordinary dimensions, and his former health and strength renewed in an instant. So surprising a miracle might surely have convinced these

CHRIST BLESSES LITTLE CHILDREN.

Pharisees, that the author must have been endued with power from on high; but, instead of being persuaded that he was a person sent from God, and labored only for the benefit of the children of men, they were contriving how they might turn this miracle to his disadvantage. Our Lord, however, soon disconcerted their projects, by proving that, according to their own avowed practice, he had done nothing but what was truly lawful. "Which of you," said he, "shall have an ass or an ox fallen into a pit, and will not straightway pull him out on the Sabbath-day?" If a calamity happens to one of your beasts, you make no scruple of assisting it on the Sabbath, though the action may be attended with considerable labor; and surely I may relieve a descendant of Abraham, when nothing more is requisite than touching him with my hand. This argument was conclusive, and so plain, that the grossest stupidity must feel its force, and the most virulent malice could not contradict it.

As the entertainment approached, our blessed Lord had an opportunity of observing the pride of the Pharisees, and remarking what an anxiety each of them expressed to obtain the most honorable place at the table. Nor did he let their ridiculous behaviour pass without a proper animadversion; in which he observed, that pride generally exposed a person to many affronts, and that humility is the surest method of gaining respect. "When thou art bidden," said he, "of any man to a wedding, sit not down in the highest room; lest a more honorable man than thou be bidden of him; and he that bade thee and him, come and say to thee, Give this man place; and thou begin with shame to take the lowest room. But when thou art bidden, go and sit down in the lowest room; that when he that bade thee cometh, he may say unto thee, Friend, go up higher; then shalt thou have worship in the presence of them that sit at meat with thee. For whosoever exalteth himself shall be abased; and he that humbleth himself shall be exalted." Luke xiv: 8, &c.

Having thus addressed the guests in general, he turned to the master of the house, and said unto him, "When thou makest a dinner or a supper, call not thy friends, nor thy brethren, neither thy kinsmen, nor thy rich neighbors; lest they also bid thee again, and a recompense be made thee. But when thou makest a feast, call the poor, the maimed, the lame, and the blind." Luke xiv: 12, 13. Be very careful not to limit thy hospitality to the rich, but let the poor also partake of thy bounty. "And thou shalt be blessed; for they can not recompense thee: for thou shalt be recompensed at the resurrection of the just." Luke xiv: 14.

One of the Pharisees, enraptured with the delightful prospect of the happiness good men enjoyed in the heavenly Canaan, cried out, "Blessed is he that shall eat bread in the kingdom of God!" Blessed is he, who, being admitted into the happy regions of Paradise, shall enjoy the conversation of the inhabitants of those heavenly countries; as those spiritual repasts must regale and invigorate his mind beyond expression. In answer to which our blessed Saviour delivered the parable of the marriage-supper, representing, by the invitation of the guests, the doctrine of the gospel, and the success those beneficent invitations to the great feast of heaven should meet with among the Jews; foretelling, that though it was attended with every inviting circumstance, they would disdainfully reject it, and prefer the pleasures of a temporal existence to those of an eternal state; while the Gentiles, with the greatest cheerfulness, would embrace the beneficent offer, and thereby be prepared to sit down with Abraham, Isaac, and Jacob, in the happy mansions of the kingdom of heaven. But, as this parable was afterward spoken by our blessed Saviour in the temple, we shall defer our observations on it, till we come to the history where it was again delivered.

When Jesus departed from the Pharisee's house, great multitudes of people thronged him to hear his doctrine; but mistook the true intention of it, expecting he was going to establish the Messiah's throne in Jerusalem, and render all the nations of the world tributary to his power. The benevolent Jesus therefore took this opportunity to undeceive them, and to declare, in the plainest terms, that his kingdom was not of this world; and, consequently, that those who expected, by following him, to obtain temporal advantages, would find themselves wretchedly mistaken; as, on the contrary, his disciples must expect to be persecuted from city to city, and hated of all men for his name's sake; though it was requisite for those who would be his true followers, to prefer his service to the richest grandeur and pleasure of the world, and to show, by their conduct, that they had much less respect and value for the dearest objects of their affection than for him. "If any man come to me, and hate not his father, and mother, and wife, and children, and brethren, and sisters, yea, and his own life also, he can not be my disciple. And whosoever does not bear his cross, and come after me, can not be my disciple." Luke xiv: 26.

And in order to induce them to weigh this doctrine attentively in their minds, he elucidated it with two opposite cases—that of an unthinking builder, and of a rash warrior. The former was obliged to leave the structure unfinished, because he had foolishly begun the building before he had computed the cost; and the latter, reduced to the dilemma of being ingloriously defeated, or meanly suing for peace previous to the battle, having rashly declared war before he had considered the strength of his own and his enemy's army. "So likewise, whosoever he be of you," added the blessed Jesus, "that forsaketh not all that he hath, he can not be my disciple." Luke xiv: 33.

The publicans and sinners, roused by the alarming doctrine of our Lord, listened to it attentively. This opportunity was readily embraced by the great Redeemer of mankind, who not only condescended to preach to them the happy tidings of eternal life, but even accompanied them to their own houses; that, if possible, the seeds of the gospel might take root in their hearts. But this condescension of the meek and humble Jesus was considered, by the haughty Pharisees, as an action too mean for the character of a prophet. They murmured, and were highly displeased at a condescension, which ought to have given the greatest joy. But Jesus soon showed them their mistake, by repeating to them the parables of the lost sheep and piece of money; intimating thereby, the great care all prophets and pastors ought to take of those committed to their care, and the obligation they lay under of searching diligently for every wandering sinner, whose conversion is a grateful offering to the Almighty. "There is joy in the presence of the angels of God over one sinner that repenteth." Luke xv: 10.

To illustrate this doctrine still further, and show to the greatest sinner the willingness of God to receive him into his grace and favor, if convinced of his unworthy and lost condition in himself, and imploring forgiveness through the merits of Jesus Christ, and the renewal of his heart by the efficacious influences of his spirit, he delivered the expressive parable of the prodigal son.—Luke xv:

There are three expositions given of this instructive representation, each of which seems to have some place in the original design; for it should be observed, and carefully remembered, that the parables and doctrines of our Saviour are by no means to be confined absolutely to one single point of view, since, they frequently have relation to different objects, and consequently prove the riches and depth of the manifold wisdom of God.

In this parable, for instance, the great and principal doctrine, intended to be particularly inculcated, is, that sinners, upon their repentance and faith, are gladly received into favor; or that there is joy in heaven over one sinner that repenteth. There are, however, two other expositions of this parable; the first is that of the greatest part of the ancients, who expounded it of Adam. He was made in the image of God, and endowed with many other excellent gifts, which he might have used happily, had he been content to stay in his Father's house; but, like this younger brother, who foolishly desired his portion of goods to himself, that he might be his own master, and under no confinement or restriction he was unwilling to remain under the obedience of the divine precept, he was desirous of having a free use of things in Paradise, and by the devil's instigation effected a wretched independency, which caused him to break the divine command, and eat of the forbidden tree, to obtain the knowledge of good and evil. Thus he lost for himself, and his posterity, the substance put at first into his possession; but his heavenly Father, on his and his posterity's return, hath provided such grace and compassion for them, that they may be reinstated in their former place and favor. And the same grace not being granted to the higher order of intellectual beings, the fallen spirits, is the cause of their murmuring against God and men, represented by the answer of the elder brother in this parable.

Others, secondly, with a much greater show of probability, expound this parable of the two people, the Jews and Gentiles, who have both one Father, even God; and while they both continued in their Father's house, the true church, they wanted for nothing; there was plenty of food for the soul, there was substance enough for them both. But the latter, represented by the younger brother, possessed of his share of knowledge, went into a strange country, left God, and spent his substance, the evidence and knowledge of the Almighty, fell into idolatry, and wasted all he had in riotous living—all his knowledge of God in the loose and absurd ceremonies of idolatry. Then, behold a mighty famine arose in that land; the worship of the true God was banished the country. In this dreadful dearth and hunger, he joined himself to the devil, and worked all "uncleanness with greediness." But finding nothing to satisfy his spiritual hunger, this prodigal long estranged from his Father, reflecting on his spiritual famine, and his own severe wants, humbly confessed his faults, returned to his offended Father, was readmitted into favor, and blessed with the privileges of the gospel. But the elder brother, the Jewish church, daily employed in the field of legal ceremonies, and who had long groaned under the yoke of the law, seeing the Gentiles received into the covenant of the Gospel, obtain the remission of sins, and the hope of everlasting life, murmured against the benevolent acts of the Almighty. God, however, out of his great compassion, pleaded pathetically the cause with the elder brother, offered him all things, upon supposition of his continuing in his obedience, and declared that he had delivered the nation from the heavy yoke of the ceremonial law.

Thus the parable has a very clear and elegant exposition; the murmuring of the elder brother is explained to us without the least difficulty; and as the offence of receiving the Gentiles to pardon and peace, through Jesus Christ, was so great a stumbling block to the Jews, it is natural to imagine that our Saviour intended to obviate and remove it by this excellent parable.

It is, however, evident, both from the context and the occasion of delivering it, that the third interpretation is the first in design and importance. The publicans and sinners drew near to hear Jesus. This gave occasion to a murmuring among the Pharisees; and upon their murmuring, our Saviour delivered this and two other parables, to show, that if they would resemble God, and the celestial host, they should, instead of murmuring, rejoice at seeing sinners willing to embrace the doctrines of the gospel, because there is joy, in the presence of God and his angels, "over one sinner that repenteth, more than over ninety and nine just persons that need no repentance."

The obstinacy and malicious temper of the Pharisees, who opposed every good doctrine, made a deep impression on the mind of the blessed Jesus: he did not, therefore, content himself barely with justifying his receiving sinners, in order to their being justified and saved through him, but, in the presence of the scribes and Pharisees, turned himself to his disciples, and delivered the parable of the artful steward, as an instance of the improvements made by the children of this world, in embracing every opportunity and advantage for improving their interests. "There was," said he, "a certain rich man which had a steward; and the same was accused unto him that he had wasted his goods. And he called him, and said unto him, How is it that I hear this of thee? Give an account of thy stewardship; for thou mayest be no longer steward." Luke xvi: 1, 2.

This reprimand of his lord, and the inward conviction of his own conscience, that the accusation was just, induced him to reflect on his own ill management of his lord's affairs, and in what manner he should support himself when he should be discharged from his service. "What shall I do?" said he, "for my lord taketh away from me the stewardship? I can not dig; to beg I am ashamed." Luke xvi: 3.

In this manner he deliberated with himself, and at last resolved on the following expedient, in order to make himself friends who would succor him in his distress: "I am resolved what to do, that, when I am put out of the stewardship, they may receive me into their houses. So he called every one of his lord's debtors unto him, and said unto the first, How much owest thou unto my lord? And he said, An hundred measures of oil. And he said unto him, Take thy bill, and sit down quickly, and write fifty. Then said he to another, And how much owest thou? And he said, An hundred measures of wheat. And he said unto him, Take thy bill, and write fourscore." Luke xvi: 4, &c.

To illustrate this parable, we beg leave to observe that the riches and trade of the Jews, originally, consisted principally in the products of the earth; they were, if we may be allowed the expression, a nation of farmers and shepherds; so that their wealth, chiefly, arose from the produce of their flocks and herds, and the fruits of the earth, their corn, their wine, and their oil.

Thus, the steward, to secure the friendship of his lord's tenants, bound them to him under a lasting obligation; and his master, when he heard of the proceedings of the steward, commended him, not because he acted honestly, but because he had acted wisely: he commended the art and address he had shown, in producing a future subsistence; he commended the prudence and ingenuity he had used with regard to his own interest, and to deliver him from future poverty and distress. "For the children of this world," added the blessed Jesus, "are in their generation wiser than the children of light." They are more prudent and careful, more anxious and circumspect, to secure their possessions in this world, than the children of light are to secure in the next an eternal inheritance. "And I say unto you, Make to yourselves friends of the mammon of unrighteousness; that, when ye fail, they may receive you into everlasting habitations." Luke xvi: 9.

This advice of our Saviour is worthy our most serious attention; the best use we can make of our riches being to employ them in promoting the salvation of others. For, if we use our abilities and interests in turning sinners from the evil of their ways; if we spend our wealth in this excellent service, from pure motives, and to the glory of God, we shall have the good-will of all the heavenly beings, who will greatly rejoice at the conversion of sinners, and, with open arms, receive us into the mansions of felicity.

CHAPTER XXIII.

Our Lord is applied to in behalf of poor Lazarus — Cures ten Persons of the Leprosy in Samaria, and restores Lazarus to life.

SOON after our blessed Saviour had finished these discourses, one of his friends named Lazarus, fell sick at Bethany, a village about two miles from the countries beyond Jordan, where Jesus was now preaching the gospel. The sisters of Lazarus, finding his sickness was of a dangerous kind, thought proper to send an account of it to Jesus; being firmly persuaded, that he who had cured so many strangers, would readily come and give health to one whom he loved in so tender a manner. "Lord," said they, "behold he whom thou lovest is sick:" they did not add, Come down and heal him, make haste and save him from the grave; it was sufficient for them to relate their necessities to their Lord, who was both able and willing to help them from their distress.

"When Jesus heard that, he said, This sickness is not unto death." This declaration of the benevolent Jesus being carried to the sisters of Lazarus, must have strangely surprised them, and exercised both theirs' and his disciples' faith; since it is probable, that before the messenger arrived at Bethany, Lazarus had expired. Soon after, Jesus positively assured his disciples that "Lazarus was dead."

The evangelist, in the beginning of this account, tells us, that Jesus loved Martha, and her sister, and Lazarus, and also, that after he had received the message, he abode two days in the same place where he was. His design in this might be to intimate, that his lingering so long after the message came, did not proceed from a want of concern for his friends, but happened according to the counsels of his own wisdom. For the length of time which Lazarus lay in the grave put his death beyond all possibility of doubt, removed every suspicion of fraud, and consequently afforded Jesus a fit opportunity of displaying the love he bore to Lazarus, as well as his undoubted resurrection from the dead. His sisters, indeed, were, by this means, kept awhile in painful anxiety on account of their brother's life, and at last pierced by the sorrows of seeing him die; yet they must surely think themselves abundantly recompensed by the evidence, according to the gospel, from this astonishing miracle, as well as by the inexpressible surprise or joy they felt, when they again received their brother from the dead.

Jesus having declared his resolution of returning into Judea, Thomas, conceiving nothing less than destruction from such a journey, yet unwilling to forsake his Master, said, "Let us also go, that we may die with him." Let us not forsake our Master in this dangerous journey, but accompany him into Judea, that if the Jews, whose inveteracy we are well acquainted with, should take away his life, we may also expire with him.

The journey to Judea being thus resolved on, Jesus departed with his disciples, and, in his way to Bethany passed through Samaria and Galilee. "And as he entered into a certain village, there met him ten men that were lepers, which stood afar off: and they lifted up their voices, and said, Jesus, Master, have mercy on us. And when he saw them, he said unto them, Go, show yourselves unto the priests. And it came to pass, that as they went they were cleansed." Luke xvii: 12.

Among these miserable objects, one of them was a native of the country, who perceiving that his cure was complete, came back, praising God for the great mercy he had received. He had before kept at a distance from our Saviour, but being now sensible that he was entirely clean, he approached his benefactor, that all might have an opportunity of beholding the miracle, and fell on his face at his feet, thanking him, in the most humble manner, for his condescension in healing him of so terrible a disease. Jesus, in order to intimate that those who were enlightened with the knowledge of the truth, ought, at least, to have shown as great sense of piety and gratitude as this Samaritan, asked, "Were there not ten cleansed? but where are the nine? There are not found that returned to give glory to God, save this stranger." Luke xvii: 17, 18.

Jesus and his disciples now continued their journey toward Bethany, where he was informed, by some of the inhabitants of that village, that Lazarus was not only dead, as he had foretold, but had now lain in the grave four days. The afflicted sisters were overwhelmed with sorrow; so that many of the Jews from Jerusalem came to comfort them concerning their brother.

It seems the news of our Lord's coming had reached Bethany before he arrived at the village; for Martha, the sister of Lazarus, being informed of his approach, went out and met him; but Mary, who was of a more melancholy and contemplative disposition, sat still in the house. No sooner was she come into the presence of Jesus, than, in an excess of grief, she poured forth her complaint: Lord, said she, if thou hadst complied with the message we sent thee, I well know that thy interest with Heaven had prevailed: my brother had been cured of his disease, and preserved from the chambers of the grave.

Martha, doubtless, entertained a high opinion of our Saviour's power: she believed that death did not dare to approach his presence; and, consequently, if Jesus had arrived at Bethany before her brother's dissolution, he had not fallen a victim to the king of terrors. But she imagined it was not in his power to heal the sick at a distance; though, at the same time, she seemed to have some dark and imperfect hopes that our blessed Saviour would still do something for her. "But I know," said she, "that even now, whatsoever thou wilt ask of God, God will give it thee." She thought that Jesus could obtain whatsoever he desired by prayer; and therefore did not found hopes on his power, but on the power of God, through his intercession. She doubtless knew that the great Redeemer of mankind had raised the daughter of Jairus, and the widow's son at Nain, from the dead; but seems to have considered her brother's resurrection as much more difficult, probably because he had been longer dead.

But Jesus, who was willing to encourage this imperfect faith of Martha, answered, "Thy brother shall rise again." As these words were delivered in an indefinite sense, with regard to time, Martha understood them only as an argument of consolation, drawn from the general resurrection, and accordingly answered, "I know that he shall rise again at the resurrection at the last day." She was firmly persuaded of that important article of the Christian faith, the "resurrection of the dead;" at which important hour she believed her brother would rise from the dust. And here she seems to have terminated all her hopes, not thinking that the Son of God would call her brother from the sleep of death. Jesus, therefore, to instruct her in the great truth, replied, "I am the resurrection and the life." I am the author of the resurrection, the fountain and giver of that life they shall then receive; and therefore can, with the same ease, raise the dead now, as at the last day. "He that believeth in me, though he were dead, yet shall he live; and whosoever liveth and believeth in me shall never die. Believest thou this?" To which Martha answered, "Yea, Lord; I believe that thou art the Christ, the Son of God, which should come into the world." I believe that thou art the true Messiah, so long promised by the prophets, and therefore believe that thou art capable of performing every instance of power that thou art pleased to claim.

Martha now left Jesus, and called her sister, according to his order. Mary no sooner heard that Jesus was come, than she immediately left her Jewish comforters, who increased the weight of her grief, and flew to her Saviour. The Jews, who suspected she was going to weep over the grave of her brother, followed her to that great Prophet who was going to remove all her sorrows. Thus the Jews, who came from

Jerusalem to comfort the two mournful sisters, were brought to the grave of Lazarus, and made witnesses of his resurrection.

As soon as Mary approached the great Redeemer of mankind, she fell prostrate at his feet, and, in a flood of tears, poured out her complaint: "Lord, if thou hadst been here my brother had not died." No wonder the compassionate Jesus was moved at so affecting a scene: on this side stood Martha, pouring forth a flood of tears; at his feet lay the affectionate Mary, weeping and lamenting her dear departed brother; while the Jews, who came to comfort the afflicted sisters, unable to confine their grief, joined the common mourning, and mixed their friendly tears, in witness of their love for the departed Lazarus, and in testimony to the justice of the sisters' grief, for the loss of so amiable, so deserving a brother. Jesus could not behold the affliction of these two sisters, and their friends, without having a share in it himself; his heart was melted at the mournful scene; "he groaned in spirit, and was troubled."

To remove the doubts and fears of these pious women, he asked them where they had buried Lazarus? not that he was ignorant where the body of the deceased was laid; he who knew that he was dead, when so far distant from him, and could raise him up by a single word, must have known where his remains were deposited: to which they answered, "Lord, come and see." The Son of God, to prove that he was not only so, but a most compassionate man, and to show us that the tender affections of the human heart, when kept in due bonds, and that friendly sorrow, when not immoderate, and directed to proper ends, are consistent with the highest sanctity of the soul, joined in the general mourning. He wept even to the time he was going to give the most ample proof of his divinity.

By his weeping, the Jews were convinced that he loved Lazarus exceedingly; but some of them interpreted this circumstance to his disadvantage; or, according to their mean way of judging, they fancied he had suffered him to fall by the stroke of death, for no other reason in the world, but for want of power and affection to rescue him. And thinking the miracle said to have been wrought on the blind man, at the feast of the tabernacles, at least as difficult as the curing an acute distemper, they rather called the former in question, because the latter had been neglected. "Could not this man," said they, "which opened the eyes of the blind, have caused that even this man should not have died?"

Our Lord, regardless of their question, but grieving for the hardness of their hearts and blindness of their infidelity, groaned within himself, as he walked toward the sepulchre of the dead. At his coming to the grave, he said, "Take ye away the stone." To which Martha answered, "Lord, by this time he stinketh: for he hath been dead four days." She meant to intimate, that her brother's resurrection was not now to be expected; but Jesus gave her a solemn reproof, to teach her that there was nothing impossible with God, and that the power of the Almighty is not to be circumscribed within the narrow bounds of human reason. "Said I not unto thee, that if thou wouldst believe, thou shouldst see the glory of God?" i. e., Have but faith, and I will display before thee the power of Omnipotence.

The objections of Martha being thus obviated, she, with the rest, awaited the great event in silence; and, in pursuance with the command of the Son of God, took away the stone from the place where the dead was laid. Jesus had, on many occasions, publicly appealed to his own miracles, as the proofs of his mission, though he did not generally make a formal address to his Father before he worked those miracles. But being now to raise Lazarus from the dead, he prayed for his resurrection, to convince the spectators that it could not be effected without an immediate interposition of the Divine power. "Father," said he, "I thank thee that thou hast heard me. And I know that thou hearest me always: but because of the people which stand by, I said it, that they may believe that thou hast sent me." John xi: 41, 42. I entertain no doubt of thy empowering me to do this miracle, and therefore did not pray for my own sake: I well know that thou hearest me always. I prayed for the sake of the people, to convince them that thou lovest me, hast sent me, and art continually with me.

After returning thanks to his Father for this opportunity of displaying his glory, "he cried with a loud voice, Lazarus, come forth!" This loud and efficacious call of the Son of God awakened the dead; the breathless clay was instantly reanimated; and he who had lain four days in the tomb obeyed immediately the powerful sound. "And he that was dead came forth bound hand and foot with grave-clothes; and his face was bound about with a napkin. Jesus saith unto them, Loose him, and let him go." John xi: 44. It would have been the least part of the miracle, had Jesus, by his powerful word, unloosed the napkin wherewith Lazarus was bound; but he brought him out in the same manner as he was lying, and ordered the spectators to loose him, that they might be the better convinced of the miracle; for, in taking off the grave-clothes, they had the fullest evidence both of his death and resurrection. For, on the one hand, the manner in which he was swathed must soon have killed him, if he had been alive when buried; which consequently demonstrated, beyond all exception, that Lazarus had been dead several days before Jesus called him again to life; besides, in stripping him, the linen probably offered, both to their eye and smell, abundant proofs of his putrefaction; and by that means convinced them that he had not been in a swoon, but was really dead. On the other hand, by his lively countenance appearing, when the napkin was removed, his fresh color, and his active vigor, those who came near, and handled him, must be convinced that he was in perfect health, and had an opportunity of proving the truth of the miracle by the closest examination. There is something exceedingly beautiful in our Lord's behavior on this occasion: he did not utter one upbraiding word, either to the doubting sisters or the malicious Jews, nor did he let fall one word of triumph or exultation; "Loose him, and let him go," were the only words we have recorded. He was on this, as on all other occasions, consistent with himself, a pattern of perfect humility and modesty.

Such was the astonishing work wrought by the Son of God at Bethany; and, in the resurrection of Lazarus, thus corrupted, and thus raised by the powerful call of Jesus, we have a striking emblem and a glorious earnest of the resurrection of our bodies from the grave at the last day, when the same powerful mandate which spoke Lazarus again into being, shall collect the scattered particles of our bodies, and raise them to immortality.

Such an extraordinary power, displayed before the face of a multitude, and near to Jerusalem, even overcame the prejudices of some of the most obstinate among them. Many believed that Jesus could be no other than the great Messiah so long promised; though others, who still expected a temporal prince, and therefore unwilling to acknowledge him for their Saviour, were filled with indignation, particularly the chief priests and elders. But this miracle, as well as all the rest he had wrought in confirmation of his mission, was too evident to be denied; and, therefore, they pretended that his whole intention was to establish a new sect, which would endanger both their church and nation. "Then gathered the chief priests and the Pharisees a council, and said, What do we? for this man doeth many miracles. If we let him thus alone, all men will believe on him; and the Roman shall come, and take away both our place and nation." John xi: 47, 48.

The common people, astonished at his miracles, will, if we do not take care to prevent it, certainly set him up for the Messiah; and the Romans, under pretence of a rebellion, will deprive us both of our liberty and religion. Accordingly, they came to a resolution to put him to death. This resolution was not, however, unanimous; for Nicodemus, Joseph of Arimathea, and other disciples of our Saviour, then members of the council, urged the injustice of what they proposed to do, from the consideration of his miracles and innocence.

But Caiaphas, the high priest, from a principle of human policy, told them, that the nature of government often required certain acts of injustice, in order to secure the safety of the state. "Ye know nothing at all, nor consider that it is expedient for us that one man should die for the people, and that the whole nation perish not." John xi: 49, 50.

The council having thus determined to put Jesus to death, deliberated, for the future, only upon the best methods of effecting it; and, in all probability, agreed to issue a proclamation, promising a reward to any person who would deliver him into their hands. For this reason, our blessed Saviour did not now go up to Jerusalem, though he was within two miles of it; but went to Ephraim, a city on the borders of the wilderness, where he abode with his disciples, being unwilling to go far into the country, because the passover, at which he was to suffer, was now at hand.

While in retirement, the blessed Jesus foretold the ruin of the Jewish state; after which, he continued to preach his divine mission over the adjacent countries, healing the sick as he went along, and rebuking sin. At length he returned to Jerusalem, into which he made a public entry, accompanied by a multitude of many thousands. This drew upon him the malice of he Pharisees; but this had no effect upon his conduct; he continued to preach daily in the temple and lsewhere, to the multitude who thronged to hear him.

CHAPTER XXIV.

Our Saviour commends even the smallest Act, proceeding from a truly benevolent Motive —Predicts the demolition of the magnificent Temple of Jerusalem, and delivers several instructive Parables.

JESUS, some time after, repaired with his disciples, into the court of the temple, called the treasury, from several chests being fixed to the pillars of the portico surrounding the court, for receiving the offerings of those who came to worship in the temple. While he continued in this court, he "beheld how the people cast money into the treasury: and many that were rich cast in much. And there came a certain poor widow, and she threw in two mites, which make a farthing. And he called unto him his disciples, and saith unto them, Verily I say unto you, that this poor widow hath cast more in than all they which have cast into the treasury. For all they did cast in of their abundance; but she of her want did cast in all that she had, even all her living." Mark xii: 41, &c.

Though the offering given by this poor widow was in itself very small, yet, in proportion to the goods of life she enjoyed, it was remarkably large; for it was all she had, even all her living. In order, therefore, to encourage charity, and show that it is the disposition of the mind, not the magnificence of the offering, that attaches the regard of the Almighty, the Son of God applauded this poor widow, as having given more in proportion than any of the rich. Their offerings, though great in respect to hers, were but a small part of their estates; whereas her offering was her whole stock. And from this passage of the gospel we should learn, that the poor, who in appearance are denied the means of doing charitable offices, are encouraged to do all they can. For how small soever the gift may be, the Almighty, who beholds the heart, values it, not according to what it is in itself, but according to the disposition with which it is given.

On the other hand, we should learn from hence, that it is not enough for the rich that they exceed the poor in gifts of charity; they should bestow in proportion to their income; and they would do well to remember, that a little given, where a little only is left, appears a much nobler offering in the sight of the Almighty, and discovers a more benevolent and humane temper of mind, than sums much larger bestowed out of a plentiful abundance.

The disciples now remembered that their Master, at the conclusion of his pathetic lamentation over Jerusalem, had declared that the temple should not any more be favored with his presence, till they should say, "Blessed is he that cometh in the name of the Lord." A declaration of this kind could not fail of greatly surprising his disciples; and, therefore, as he was departing from that sacred structure, they desired him to observe the beauty of the building; insinuating, that they thought it strange he should intimate an intention of leaving it desolate; that so glorious a fabric, celebrated in every corner of the earth, was not to be deserted rashly; and that they should think themselves supremely happy, when he, as the Messiah, and descendant of David, should take possession of it, and erect his throne in the midst of Jerusalem. And, as they went out of the temple, one of his disciples said unto him, "Master, see what manner of stones and what buildings are here!"

The eastern wall of the temple, which fronted the Mount of Olives, whither the disciples, with their Master, were then retiring, was built from the bottom of the valley to a prodigious height, with stones of an incredible bulk, firmly compacted together, and therefore made a very grand appearance at a distance. The eastern wall is supposed to have been the only remains of Solomon's temple, and had escaped when the Chaldeans burnt it. But this building, however strong, or costly it appeared, our Saviour told them should be totally destroyed. "Seest thou," said he, "these great buildings? there shall not be left one stone upon another, that shall not be thrown down." Mark xiii: 2. That noble edifice, raised with much labor, and at a vast expense, shall be razed to the very foundation. The disciples, therefore, when they heard their Master affirm, that not so much as one of these enormous stones, which had withstood the fury of Nebuchadnezzar's army, and survived the destructive hand of time, was to be left one upon another, they perceived that the whole temple was to be demolished, but did not suspect that the sacrifices were to be taken away, and a new mode of religion introduced, which rendered the temple unnecessary. They, therefore, flattered themselves, that the fabric then standing, however glorious it might appear, was too small for the numerous worshipers who would frequent it, when all the nations of the world were subject to the Messiah's kingdom, and was, therefore, to be pulled down, in order to be erected on a more magnificent plan, suitable to the idea they had conceived of his future empire. Filled with these pleasing imaginations, they received the news with pleasure, meditating, as they walked to the mountain, on the glorious things which were shortly to come to pass. When they arrived on the Mount of Olives, and their Master had taken his seat on some eminence, from whence they had a prospect of the temple, and part of the city, his disciples drew near, to know when the demolition of the old structure was to happen, and what were to be the signs of his coming, and of the end of the world. "And as he sat upon the Mount of Olives, the disciples came unto him privately, saying, Tell us, when shall these things be? and what shall be the sign of thy coming, and of the end of the world?" Matt. xxiv: 3.

The disciples, by this request, seemed desirous of knowing what signs should precede the erection of that extensive empire, over which they supposed the Messiah was to reign; for they still expected he would govern a secular kingdom. They, therefore, connected the demolition of the temple with their Master's coming, though they had not the least notion that he was to destroy the nation, and change the form of religious worship. They, therefore, meant by the "end of the world," or, as the words should have been translated, the end of the ages, the period of the political government, then executed by the heathen procurators;

and considered their Master's coming to destroy the constitution then subsisting, as a very desirable event. They also thought the demolition of the temple proper, as they expected a larger and more superb building, proportioned to the number of the Messiah's subjects, would be erected in its stead.

That this is the real sense of the disciples' question, will sufficiently appear, if we consider that the disciples were delighted with the prospect; whereas, if they had meant, by the end of the world, the final period of all things, the destruction of the temple would have exhibited to them, in their present temper of mind, a melancholy prospect, which they could not have beheld without a deep concern. Our blessed Saviour, therefore, was careful to convince them of their mistake, by telling them, that he was not come to rule a secular empire, as they supposed, but to punish the Jews for their perfidy and rebellion, by destroying both their temple and nation. "Take heed," said he, "that no man deceive you. For many shall come in my name, saying, I am Christ; and shall deceive many."

This caution was far from being unnecessary, because, though his disciples were to see their Master ascend into heaven, they might take occasion, from the prophecy, to think that he would appear again on earth, and, therefore, be in danger of seduction by the false Christs that should arise. "And when ye shall hear of wars, and rumors of wars: see that ye be not troubled: for all these things must come to pass, but the end is not yet." Before this nation and temple are destroyed, terrible wars will happen in the land; "For nation shall rise against nation, and kingdom against kingdom: and there shall be famines, and pestilences, and earthquakes, in divers places." Matt. xxiv: 7. These are the preludes of the important event, forerunners of the evils which shall befall this nation and people. At the same time you shall meet with hot persecutions ; walk therefore circumspectly, and arm yourselves, both with patience and fortitude, that you may be able to perform your duty, through the whole course of these persecutions; for ye shall be brought before the great men of the earth for my sake. "But when they shall lead you, and deliver you up, take no thought before hand what ye shall speak, neither do ye premeditate; but whatsoever shall be given you in that hour, that speak ye: for it is not ye that speak, but the Holy Ghost." Mark xiii: 11.

During this time of trouble and confusion, he told them, the perfidy of mankind should be so great toward one another, that "brother shall betray the brother to death, and the father the son; and children shall rise up against their parents, and shall cause them to be put to death." The unbelieving Jews, and apostate Christians, shall commit the most enormous and inhuman crimes. It is, therefore, no wonder that the perfidy and wickedness of such pretended Christians should discourage many disciples, and greatly hinder the propagation of the gospel. But he who lives by faith, during these persecutions, and is not led away by false Christians, shall escape that terrible destruction, which, like a deluge, will overflow the land. And when Jerusalem shall be surrounded with armies, pagan armies, bearing on their standards the images of their gods, the "abomination of desolation" mentioned by the prophet Daniel, then let him who readeth the predictions of that prophet understand, that the end of the city and sanctuary, together with the ceasing of sacrifices and oblations there predicted, is come, and consequently the final period of the Jewish polity. "Then let them which are in Judea flee to the mountains; and let them which are in the midst of it depart out." Luke xxi: 21. "Let him which is on the house-top, not come down to take anything out of his house: neither let him which is in the field return back to take his clothes." Matt. xxiv: 17, 18. Then shall be fulfilled the awful predictions of the prophet Daniel, and the dreadful judgments denounced against the impenitent and unbelieving. In those days of vengeance, the women who are with child, and those who have infants hanging at their breasts, shall be particularly unhappy, because they cannot flee from the impending destruction. "But pray ye that your flight be not in the winter," when the badness of the roads, and the rigor of the season, will render speedy traveling very troublesome, if not impossible; "neither on the Sabbath-day," when you shall think it unlawful. "For then shall be great tribulation, such as was not since the beginning of the world to this time, no, nor ever shall be." This is confirmed by what Josephus tells us, that no less than eleven hundred thousand perished in the siege.

The heavenly prophet added, that except the days of tribulation should be shortened, none of the inhabitants of Jerusalem and Judea, of whom he was speaking, should escape destruction: in confirmation of which Josephus tells us, that the quarrels which raged during the siege were so fierce and obstinate, that both within the walls of Jerusalem, and without in the neighboring country, the whole land was one continued scene of horror and desolation; and had the siege continued much longer, the whole nation of the Jews had been totally destroyed, according to our Lord's prediction. "But," added our blessed Saviour, "for the elect's sake, whom he hath chosen, he hath shortened the days." By the elect, are meant such of the Jews as had embraced the doctrines of the gospel, and particularly those who were brought in with the believing Gentiles.

As it is natural, in time of trouble, to look with eager expectation for a deliverer, our blessed Saviour cautioned his disciples not to listen to any pretences of that kind, as many false Christs would arise, and deceive great numbers of the people. A prediction that was fully accomplished, during the terrible siege of Jerusalem by the Romans; so Josephus tells us, that many arose, pretending to be the Messiah, boasting that they would deliver the nation from all its enemies. And the multitude, always too prone to listen to deceivers who promise temporal advantages, giving credit to those deceivers, became more obstinate in their opposition to the Romans, and thereby rendered their destruction more severe and inevitable. And what still increased the infatuation of the people, was their performing wonderful things during the war; and accordingly, Josephus calls them magicians and sorcerers. Hence we see the propriety of the caution given by the Son of God, who foretold that "they should show great signs and wonders, insomuch that, If it were possible, they would deceive the very elect. But take heed; behold, I have foretold you all things." And, as the partizans of the false Christ might pretend, that the Messiah was concealed awhile for fear of the Romans, and the weaker sort of Christians, without this warning, have imagined that Christ was actually returned to deliver the nation in its extremity, and to punish their enemies, who now so cruelly oppressed them, and that he would show himself as soon as it was proper, the blessed Jesus thought proper to caution them against this particular; "Wherefore if they shall say unto you, Behold, he is in the desert; go not forth: behold, he is in the secret chambers; believe it not. For as the lightning cometh out of the east, and shineth even unto the west, so shall also the coming of the Son of Man be." Matt. xxiv: 26, &c. The coming of the Son of Man shall be like lightning, swift and destructive. But he will not come personally; his servants only shall come, the Roman armies, who by his command, shall destroy this nation, as eagles devour their prey.

Having thus given them a particular account of the various circumstances which should precede the destruction of Jerusalem, he next described that catastrophe itself, in all the pomp of language and imagery made use of by the ancient prophets when they foretold the destruction of cities and kingdoms. "But in those days, after that tribulation, the sun shall be darkened, and the moon shall not give her light; and the stars of heaven shall fall, and the powers that are in heaven shall be shaken." Mark xiii: 24. "And upon the earth distress of nations, with perplexity; the sea and the waves roaring; men's hearts failing them for fear, and for looking after those things which are coming on the earth." Luke xxi: 25, 26.

Whoever shall compare the prediction of our Saviour

with the history Josephus wrote of the war, can not fail of being struck with the wisdom of Christ, and acknowledge that his prediction was truly divine: for as the Jewish nation was at this time in the most flourishing state, the event here foretold appeared altogether improbable. Besides, the circumstances of the destruction are very numerous and surprisingly great: and the whole delivered without any ambiguity. It is, therefore, a prophecy of such a kind as could never have been uttered by any impostor, and consequently the person who delivered it was acquainted with the secret counsels of heaven, and was truly divine.

Having thus generally described the future state of retribution, our Lord passed to the consideration of the general judgment, when those rewards and punishments should be distributed to their utmost extent. This could not fail of animating his disciples to a vigorous discharge of their duty: and by the striking representation of the last judgment he has here given, must greatly tend to rouse the consciences of men from their lethargy, and consider, before it be too late, "the things which belong to their peace."

Then shall the kingdom of heaven, the gospel kingdom, in the last dispensation of it, when the kingdom of grace is going to be swallowed up in the kingdom of glory, "be likened unto ten virgins, which took their lamps, and went forth to meet the bridegroom. And five of them were wise, and five were foolish." They that were foolish took their lamps, but put no oil in their vessels; knowing that it was uncertain when the bridegroom would arrive, and that they might in all probability wait long for his coming. Nor were they mistaken: for the bridegroom did not come as soon as they expected. "While the bridegroom tarried, they all slumbered and slept. And at midnight there was a great cry made, Behold, the bridegroom cometh; go ye out to meet him. Then all those virgins rose, and trimmed their lamps. And the foolish said unto the wise, Give us of your oil; for our lamps are gone out. But the wise answered, saying, Not so; lest there be not enough for us and you: but go ye rather to them that sell, and buy for yourselves. And while they went to buy, the bridegroom came; and they that were ready went in with him to the marriage: and door was shut. Afterward came also the other virgins, saying, Lord, Lord, open to us. But he answered and said, Verily I say unto you, I know you not. Watch therefore, for ye know neither the day nor the hour wherein the Son of Man cometh." Matt. xxv: 6, &c.

In order to understand this parable, we must remember that it alludes to the custom of the eastern people. It was usual with them for the bridegroom to bring his bride home in the evening, sooner or later, as circumstances might happen; and, that they might be received properly at his house, his female acquaintances, especially those of the younger sort, were invited to come and wait with lamps, till some of his retinue, dispatched before the rest, informed them that he was near at hand; upon which they trimmed their lamps, went forth to welcome him, and conduct him, with his bride, into the house; for which they were honored as guests at the marriage feast, and shared in the usual festivities. To ten such virgins our blessed Saviour compares those to whom the gospel is preached; because this was the general number appointed to wait on the bridegroom: and to these all Christian professors may be likened, who, taking their lamp of Christian profession, go forth to meet the bridegroom; that is, consider themselves candidates for the kingdom of heaven, and desire to be admitted, with Christ, the celestial bridegroom, into the happy mansions of immortality.

We must remember, that there always was, and always will be, a mixture of good and bad in the church, till the great day of separation arrives. The weakness of the foolish is represented by their taking no oil in their vessels, with their lamps; that is, the foolish professors content themselves with the bare lamp of profession, and never think of furnishing it with the oil of divine grace, the fruit of which is a life of holiness. Whereas, the wise, well knowing that a lamp, without the supply of oil, would be speedily extinguished—that faith, without love or holiness, will be of no consequence—take care to secure a supply for themselves of the divine grace, and to display in their lives the works of love and charity. While those virgins, though differently supplied, waiting the coming of the bridegroom, all slumbered and slept; that is, as some think, all Christians, both good and bad, the sincere and the hypocrite, lie down together in the sleep of death, and while the bridegroom delays his coming, slumber in the chambers of the dust. But others suppose, that this argues the want of vigilance and care, even in the wise as well as foolish; that few, if any, are so attentive as they ought to be to the coming of the Lord.

The Jews have a tradition, that Christ's coming to judgment will be at midnight: which agrees with that particular in the parable, "At midnight there was a cry made, Go ye out to meet him." But, however this be, whether he will come at midnight, or in the morning, it will be awfully sudden and alarming. The great cry will be heard to the end of the earth; the trumpet shall sound, and the mighty archangel's voice pierce even the bowels of the earth and the depths of the ocean: "Behold the bridegroom cometh: go ye out to meet him." The graves, both earthly and watery, must surrender their clayey tenants, and all will then begin to think how they may prepare themselves to find admittance to the marriage-supper of the Lamb: "Then all those virgins arose, and trimmed their lamps." But the foolish soon perceived their folly; their lamps were gone out, totally extinguished, and they had no oil to support the flame. In like manner the hypocrite's hope shall perish. But the wise were in much happier condition: they had oil in their vessels, sufficient for themselves, but none to spare; for, when the foolish virgins would have procured some from them, they denied their request, fearing there would not be enough for both.

There are here beautifully represented nominal and sincere Christians. The former, having only the bare lamp of a profession, and who have not been solicitous to gain the oil of divine grace, by a constant use of the means assigned, will fare like the foolish virgins; while the latter, whose hearts are filled with divine oil, will, like the wise virgins, enter into the joy of the Lord. But the foolish, going to purchase oil, missed the bridegroom, and, behold, "the door was shut." They at last, however, reached the gate, and, with great importunity, cried, "Lord, Lord, open unto us." But he answered, and said, "Verily I say unto you, I know you not." As you denied me on earth, I deny you now; depart from me, I know you not. How justly, therefore, did our blessed Saviour bid us all watch, that we may be found ready whenever he cometh, or commands, by the king of terrors, our attendance before his judgment seat. Let us not refuse this kind invitation of being constantly prepared to meet the heavenly Bridegroom; let us get our lamps filled with oil, that we may be ready to follow our great Master into the happy mansions of the heavenly Canaan.

But, as this duty was of the utmost importance, our blessed Saviour, to show us more clearly the nature and use of Christian watchfulness, to which he exhorts us at the conclusion of the parable of the ten virgins, added another, wherein he represented the different characters of a faithful and slothful servant, and the difference of their future acceptation. This parable, like the former, is intended to stir us up to a zealous preparation for the coming of our Lord, by diligence in the discharge of our duty, and by a careful improvement of our souls in holiness; and, at the same time, to expose the vain pretences of hypocrites, and to demonstrate that their fair speeches and outward forms, without the power of godliness, will be of no service whatever in the last day of account.

The Son of Man, said he, may, with respect to his final coming to judge the world, be likened unto "a man traveling into a far country, who called his own servants, and delivered unto them his goods. And unto one he gave five talents, to another two, and to another one; to every one according to his several ability: and straightway took his journey." Immediately on his master's departure, he who had received the five talents lost no time, but traded with the same, and his increase was equal to his industry and application; he made them other five talents. He that received two talents did the same, and had equal success. But he that received one, very unlike the conduct of his fellow servants, went and digged in the earth, and hid his lord's money, idle, useless, unemployed, and unimproved. After a long time, and at an hour when they did not expect it, the lord of those servants returned, called them before him, and ordered them to give an account of their several trusts. Upon which, he that had received five talents, as a proof of his fidelity, produced other five talents, saying "Lord, thou deliveredst unto me five talents; behold, I have gained besides them five talents more." Matt. xxv: 20. His lord, highly applauding his industry and fidelity said to him, "Well done, thou good and faithful servant. thou hast been faithful over a few things, I will make thee ruler over many things: enter thou into the joy of thy lord." Matt. xxv: 21. In like manner also, he that had received two talents, declared he had gained two other; upon which he was honored with the same applause, and admitted into the same joy with his fellow servant; their master having regard to the industry and fidelity of his servants, not to the number of the talents only, but the greatness of their increase. After this, he that had received the one talent came, and, with a shameful falsehood, to excuse his vile indolence, said, "Lord, I knew thee that thou art a hard man, reaping where thou hast not sown, and gathering where thou hast not strewed: and I was afraid, and went and hid thy talent in the earth; lo, there thou hast that is thine." Matt. xxv: 24, 25. The perversion of even the smallest portion of grace greatly excited the resentment of his lord, who answered, "Thou wicked and slothful servant, thou knewest that I reap where I sowed not, and gather where I have not strewed: thou oughtest therefore to have put my money to the exchangers, and then at my coming I should have received mine own with usury. Take, therefore, the talent from him, and give it unto him that hath ten talents. For unto every one that hath shall be given, and he shall have abundance: but from him that hath not shall be taken away even that which he hath. And cast ye the unprofitable servant into outer darkness: there shall be weeping and gnashing of teeth." Matt. xxv: 26, &c.

Such is the parable of the talents, as delivered by our blessed Saviour; a parable containing the measures of our duty to God, and the motives which enforce it, all delivered in the plainest and simplest manner. But its views are so extensive and affecting, that while it instructs the meanest capacity, it engages reverence and attention from the greatest, and strikes an impression on the most approved understanding. We are to consider God as our Lord and Master, the author and giver of every good gift, and ourselves as his servants or stewards, who, in various instances and measures, have received from his goodness such blessings and abilities as may fit us for the several stations and offices of life to which his providence may appoint us. But then we are to observe, that these are committed to us as a trust or loan, for whose due management we are accountable to the donor. If we faithfully acquit ourselves of this probationary charge, we shall receive far greater instances of God's regard and favor; but if we are remiss and negligent, we must expect to feel his resentment and displeasure. A time will come, and how near it may be, none of us can tell, when our great Master will demand a particular account of every talent he hath committed to our care. This time may, indeed, be at a distance; for it is uncertain when the king of terrors will receive the awful warrant to terminate our existence here below: yet it will certainly come, and our eternal happiness or misery depends upon it; so that we should all have it continually in our thoughts, and engraven, as with the point of a diamond, on the tables of our hearts.

We learn, from this instructive parable, that infinite Wisdom hath intrusted men with different talents, and adjusted them to the various purposes of human life. But though the gifts of men are unequal, none can with justice complain; since whatever is bestowed, be it more or less, is a favor entirely unmerited. Each then should be thankful, and satisfied with his portion; and, instead of envying the more liberal endowments of others, apply himself to the improvement of his own. And it should be observed, that the difficulty of the task is in proportion to the number of talents committed to each. He who had received five, was to gain other five; and he who had received two was to account for other two. Surely, then, we have no reason to complain, if our Master has laid on us a lighter burden, a more easy and less service, than he has on others; especially, as our interest in the favor of the Almighty does not depend on the number of our talents, but on our diligence and application in the management of them: so that the moral design of this parable is, to engage our utmost attention to improve such talents as our heavenly Father has thought proper to bestow upon us.

CHAPTER XXV.

Our blessed Lord is anointed by a poor but pious Woman — The perfidious Judas consents to betray his Master — The humble Jesus washes the Feet of his Disciples, and foretells that Disciple who was to betray him into the hands of his inveterate Enemies.

THE blessed Jesus used frequently to retire in the evening from the city to the Mount of Olives, and there spend the night, either in some village or the gardens, either to avoid falling into the hands of his enemies, or for the sake of a little retirement. They did not, indeed, presume to attack him, while he was surrounded by his followers, in the day-time; but, in all probability, had he lodged within the city, they would have apprehended him during the darkness and silence of the night.

When our blessed Saviour had finished these parables, he added a short account of his own death, in order to fortify his disciples against a greater trial than they had yet met with; namely, the sufferings of their Master. "And it came to pass, when Jesus had finished all these sayings, he said unto his disciples, Ye know that after two days is the feast of the passover, and the Son of Man is betrayed to be crucified. Then assembled together the chief priests, and the scribes, and the elders of the people, into the palace of the high priest, who was called Caiaphas, and consulted that they might take Jesus by subtilty, and kill him. But they said, Not on the feast day, lest there be an uproar among the people." Matt. xxvi: 1, &c.

When the evening approached, our blessed Saviour, with his disciples, repaired to Bethany, and entered the house of Simon the leper—probably one who experienced the healing efficacy of his power. But while he sat at meat, a woman, who had also, doubtless, been an object of his mercy, came and poured a box of precious ointment upon his head. This action displeased his disciples, who knew that their Master was not delighted with luxuries of any kind: and therefore they rebuked the woman, imagining that it would have been more acceptable to the Son of God, if the ointment had been sold, and the money distributed among the sons and daughters of poverty and affliction. To reprove the disciples, Jesus told them, that it had pleased the divine Providence to order that there should always be persons in necessitous circumstances, that the righteous might never want occasions for exercising their charity; but that those who did not testify their love to him, would never more have the opportunity of doing it, as the time of his ministry was near its period, when the king of terrors should enjoy a short triumph over his body; and therefore this woman had seasonably anointed him for his burial. And to make them sensible of their folly, in blaming the woman for this expression of love to him he assured them, that she should be highly esteemed for this action in every part of the world, and her memory live to the latest period of time.

Judas Iscariot, (one of the twelve, having been more forward than the rest in condemning the woman, thought the rebuke was particularly directed to him,) stung with the guilt of his own conscience, arose from the table, and went immediately into the city, to the high priest's palace, where he found the whole council assembled. His passion would not suffer him to reflect on the horrid deed he was going to commit: he immediately promised, for the reward of thirty pieces of silver, to betray into their hands his Lord and Master. Having thus engaged with the rulers of Israel, to put into their hands a person who had often invited them, in the most pathetic manner, to embrace the gracious terms of the gospel offered by the Almighty, he sought an opportunity to betray him in the absence of the multitude

Our Lord, who well knew that the time of his suffering drew nigh, desired, therefore, to celebrate the passover with his disciples. He was now going to finish the mighty work for which he came into the world; and therefore would not neglect to fulfill the smallest particular of the law of Moses. He therefore sent two of his disciples into the city to prepare a lamb, and make it ready for eating the passover; telling them that they should meet a man, bearing a pitcher of water, who .would conduct them to his house, and show them a large upper room, furnished, where they were to make ready for him. He was willing, in this last transaction, to convince his disciples, that he knew every thing that should befall him; that his sufferings were all foretold by the Almighty;

and that they were all, on his own account, submitted unto voluntarily.

When night approached, Jesus left Bethany, and every thing being ready for him at the time he entered into the city, he sat down at the appointed hour. But knowing that his sufferings were now near, he told his disciples, in the most affectionate manner, that he had greatly longed to eat the passover with them before he suffered, in order to show them the strongest proofs of his love. These proofs were to give them a pattern of humility and love, by washing their feet; instructing them in the nature of his death, and a propitiatory sacrifice; instituting the sacrament, in commemoration of his sufferings; comforting them by the tender discourses recorded John xiv, xv, xvi, in which he gave them a variety of excellent directions, together with many gracious promises; and recommending them to the kind protection of his heavenly Father. "With desire I have desired to eat this passover with you before I suffer. For I say unto you, I will not any more eat thereof, until it be fulfilled in the kingdom of God."

Having thus spoken, he rose from the table, laid aside his garments, like a servant, and with all the officiousness of a humble minister, washed the feet of his disciples without distinction, though one of them, Judas Iscariot, was a monster of impiety; that they might at once behold a conjunction of love and humility, of self-denial and indifference represented by a person glorious beyond expression, their great Lord and Master. He washed their feet, (according to a custom which prevailed in those hot countries, both before and after meat,) in order to show them an example of the utmost humility and condescension. The omnipotent Son of the Father lays every thing aside, that he may serve his followers; heaven stoops to earth, one abyss calls upon another, and the miseries of man, which were almost infinite, are exceeded by a mercy equal to the immensity of the Almighty. He deferred this ceremony, which was a customary civility paid to honorable strangers at the beginning of their feast, that it might be preparatory to the second, which he intended should be a feast to the whole world, when all the followers of the blessed Jesus should have an opportunity, in a spiritual manner, of feeding on his flesh, and drinking his blood. When our blessed Saviour came to Peter, he modestly declined it; but his Master told him, if he refused to submit implicitly to all his orders, he could have no part with him. On which Peter cried out, "Lord, not my feet only, but also my hands and my head." But Jesus told him, that the person washed had no reason to wash any part of the body except the feet, which he might have dirtied by walking from the bath: adding, "Ye are all clean, as to the outward laver, but not as to the inward and spiritual laver: I well know that one of you will betray me."

When our gracious Lord had finished this menial service, he asked his disciples, if they knew the meaning of what he had done, as the action was purely emblematical? You truly, added he, style me Master and Lord; for I am the Son of God and the Saviour of the world. But if I, your Master and your Lord, have condescended to wash your feet, you surely ought to perform, with the utmost pleasure, the humblest offices of love one to another. I have set you a pattern of humility, and I recommend it to you.

And certainly nothing can more effectually show us the necessity of this heavenly temper of mind, than its being recommended to us by so great an example; a recommendation which, in the present circumstances, was particularly seasonable; for the disciples having heard their great Master declare that the kingdom of heaven was at hand, their minds were filled with ambitious thoughts. And therefore our blessed Saviour added, Ye need not be ashamed to follow my example in this particular; for no servant can think it beneath him to condescend to perform those actions his Lord has done before him. And therefore, if he knows his duty, he will be happy if he practices it. He, moreover, added, that though he had called them all to the apostleship, and knew the secret dispositions of every heart before he chose them, they need not be surprised that one among them should prove a traitor, as thereby the Scripture would be fulfilled: "He that eateth bread with me, hath lifted up his heel against me."

As our blessed Saviour was now to be but a short time with his disciples, he thought proper to take his farewell of them, which he did in a most affectionate manner. These melancholy tidings greatly troubled them. They were unwilling to part with so kind a friend, so dear a master, so wise a guide, and so profitable a teacher; especially, as they thought they should be left in a forlorn condition, a poor and helpless prey to the rage and hatred of a blind and malicious generation. They seemed willing to die with their Lord, if that might be accepted. Why can not I follow thee? I will lay down my life for thee! was the language of one, and even all of them; but they could not support the thought of a disconsolate separation. Their great and compassionate Master, seeing them thus dejected, endeavored to cheer their drooping spirits: "Let not your hearts be troubled." Listen attentively to what I am going to deliver for your consolation: "I am going to prepare a place for you; I will come again, and receive you to myself, that where I am there ye may be also." A reviving word of promise. They were one day to meet again their dear, their affectionate Master, in a place where they should live together to eternity.

But death makes so vast a distance between friends, and the disciples then knew so little of a future state, that they seemed to doubt whether they should, after their parting, meet their great Redeemer. They neither knew the place where he was going, nor the way that led to his kingdom: "Lord," said they, "as we know not whither thou goest, how can we know the way?" In answer to this question, he told them, that he was "the way, the truth, and the life;" as if he had said, Through the propitiatory sacrifice I am about to offer, the sacred truths I have delivered, and the divine assistance which I shall hereafter dispense, you are to obtain that happiness which I go to prepare for you. But, lest these arguments should not be sufficient to quiet their minds, he had still another, which could not fail of success: "If ye love me," says he, "ye will rejoice, because I said, I go to the Father:" intimating, that he would consider it as a proof of their love to him, if they ceased to mourn. They doubtless thought, that by grieving for his death, they expressed their love to their Master, and it might seem strange that our Saviour should put so contrary an interpretation on their friendly sorrow, or require so unnatural a thing of them, as to rejoice at his departure. What, (they might think,) shall we rejoice at so amiable a friend's removal from us? or can we be glad that he retires and leaves us in this vale of misery? No, it is impossible; the human heart, on so melancholy an occasion, can have no disposition to rejoice.

Our blessed Saviour, therefore, adds this reason, to solve the seeming paradox: because he was going to his Father; that is, he was going to ascend to the right hand of infinite Power, from whence he would send them all the assistance they could desire. It must not, however, be supposed, that he meant by these words, that his disciples should not be concerned at his death, or that they could not love him unless they expressed a visible joy on this occasion. That would, indeed, have been a hard interpretation of their grief: he knew their grief flowed from love; and that if their love had not been strong, their sorrow had been much less. Indeed, their Master was fully convinced that love was the occasion of their sorrow; and, therefore, he used these arguments to mitigate it, and direct it in a proper course. Nor did our Lord intend to intimate that all sorrow for so worthy a friend was unlawful, or an unbecoming expression of their love: doubtless he was not displeased to see his disciples so tenderly affected at his removal from them. He who shed tears at the grave of Lazarus, blended with sighs and groans, can not be thought to forbid them wholly at his own. He therefore did not chide his disciples with angry reproaches, as though they had been entirely in the wrong, but gently reasoned with them by kind persuasions: "Let not your hearts be troubled;" as rather pitying than condemning their sorrow.

Soon after Jesus had spoken these things, his heart was greatly troubled to think that one of his disciples should prove his enemy; he complained of it at the table, declaring that one of them should betray him. This moving declaration greatly affected the disciples; and they began every one of them to say to their Master, "Lord, is it I?" But Jesus giving them no decisive answer, John, the beloved disciple, whose sweet disposition, with other amiable qualities, is perpetuated in the peculiar love his great Master bore him, and was now reclining on his bosom, asked him, who among the disciples could be guilty of so detestable a crime? Jesus told him, that the person to whom he should give the sop, when he had dipped it, was he who should betray him. Accordingly, as soon he had dipped the sop in the dish, he gave it to Judas Iscariot, saying to him, at the same time, "That thou doest, do quickly." Judas received the sop, without knowing anything of what his Master had told the beloved disciple: nor did any of the disciples, except St. John, entertain the least suspicion that Judas was the person who would betray their Master.

The innocent disciples were, indeed, so deeply affected with his declaration that one of them should betray him, that they did not remark the words of Jesus to his apostate disciple; but continued to ask him who was the person, that should be guilty of so base a crime? Willing, at last, to satisfy their importunity, the blessed Jesus declared, that the person who dipped his hand with him in the dish should betray him. This, to the eleven, was a joyful declaration, but confounding, in the highest degree, to Judas. Impudent as he was, it struck him speechless, pointing him out plainly, and displaying the foulness of his heart. While Judas continued mute with confusion, the blessed Jesus declared that his death should be brought according to the decrees of Heaven, though that would not, in the least mitigate the crime of the person who betrayed him: adding, "it had been good for that man if he had not been born." Judas, having now recovered himself a little, asserted his innocence, by a question which implied a denial of the charge. But his Master soon silenced him, by positively affirming that he was really the person.

As various conjectures have been formed concerning the motives which induced the perfidious Judas cruelly to deliver up his innocent Master into the hands of his enemies, it may not be improper to cite those which appear to be most probable, though the decision must be entirely left to the reader.

Some are of opinion, that he was induced to commit this villainy by the resentment of the rebuke given him by his Master, for blaming the woman who came with the precious ointment, and anointed the head of Jesus, as he sat at meat in the house of Simon the leper. But, though this had, doubtless, its weight with the traitor, yet it could not, I think, be his only motive; because the rebuke was given in general to all the disciples, who had certainly been forward with him in censuring the woman. Nor can we imagine, even if he had been rebuked alone, that so mild a reproof could provoke any person, however wicked, to the horrid act of murdering his friend; much less Judas, whose covetous disposition must have disposed him to bear every thing from his Master, from whom he expected the highest preferment, if he should openly declare himself the Messiah, and take the reins of government into his own hands.

Others think, that Judas betrayed his Master through covetousness. But, if we understand by covetousness, the reward given by the priests, this opinion is equally defective; for the sum was too small for the most sordid wretch to think equivalent to the life of a friend, especially when he expected from him the highest posts and advantages.

Others attribute the perfidy of Judas to his doubting whether his Master was the Messiah; and that he betrayed him in a fit of despair. But, of all the solutions, this is the worst founded. For, if Judas believed his Master to be an imposter, he must have observed something in his behaviour which led him to form such an opinion of him; and, in that case, he would doubtless have mentioned it to the chief priests and elders, when he made the contract with them; which it is plain he did not, as they would have reminded him of it, when he came back and expressed his remorse for what he had done.

In fine, the supposition that Judas believed his Master to be an imposter, is directly confuted by the solemn declaration he made to the priests, when he declared the deepest conviction of the innocence of our great Redeemer: "I have sinned," says he, "in betraying innocent blood."

It must be remembered, that the remorse he felt for his crime, when he saw his Master condemned, was too bitter to be endured; so that he fled even to the king of terrors for relief.

L

CHAPTER XXVI.

JESUS INSTITUTES THE SACRAMENT, IN COMMEMORATION OF HIS DEATH AND SUFFERINGS — SETTLES A DISPUTE WHICH AROSE AMONG HIS DISCIPLES — PREDICTS PETER'S COWARDICE IN DENYING HIS MASTER — FORTIFIES HIS DISCIPLES AGAINST THE APPROACHING SHOCK — FORETELLS PETER'S COWARDICE AGAIN — PREACHES TO, AND PRAYS WITH HIS DISCIPLES FOR THE LAST TIME — PASSIONATE ADDRESS OF OUR LORD TO HIS FATHER IN THE GARDEN.

THE great Redeemer, ever mindful of the grand design of his mission, even the salvation of lost and perishing sinners, was not in the least affected by the treachery of his apostate disciple: for, knowing that he must become a sacrifice for sin, &c., he instituted the sacrament of his supper, to perpetuate the memory of it through all ages. Accordingly, as they were eating the paschal supper, "Jesus took bread, and blessed it, and brake it, and gave it to the disciples, and said, Take, eat; this is my body." Matt. xxvi : 26. Observe this rite no longer in remembrance of your deliverance from Egypt, but in remembrance of me, who, by dying for you, will bring you out of the spiritual bondage, a bondage far worse than the Egyptian under which your fathers groaned, and will establish you in the glorious liberty of the children of God. Do it in remembrance of me, who, by laying

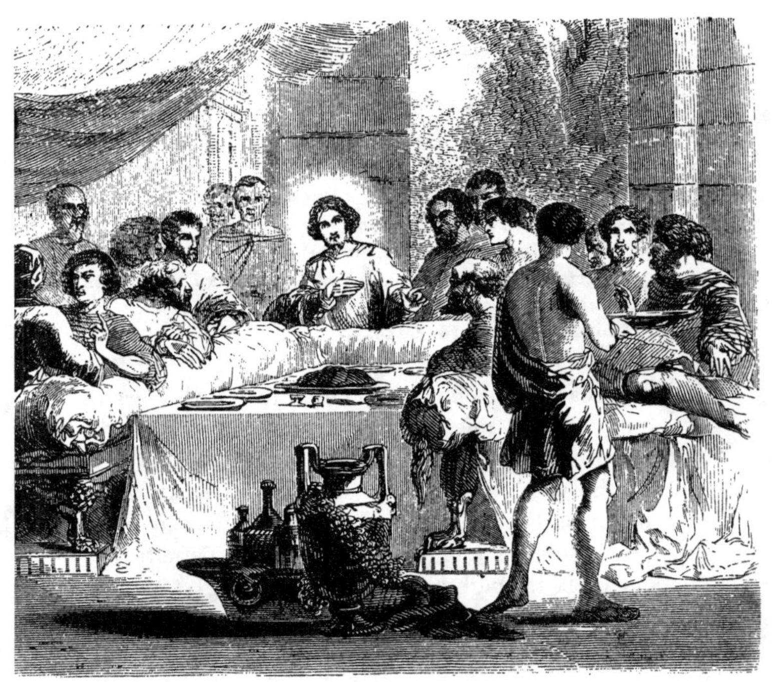

THE SACRAMENT.

down my life, will ransom you from sin, from death, from hell, and will set open the gates of heaven to you, that you may enter immortality in triumph.

Having given the bread to his disciples, he also took the cup, and gave it to them, saying, "Drink ye all of it; for this is my blood of the new testament, which is shed for many for the remission of sins." Matt. xxvi: 27, 28.

All of you, and all of my disciples, in all ages, must drink of this cup, because it represents my blood shed for the remission of the sins of mankind: my blood by which the new covenant between God and man is ratified. It is, therefore, my blood of the new covenant; so that this institution exhibits to your joyful meditation, the grand basis of the hopes of the children of men, and perpetuates the memory of it to the end of the world. He added, "I will not drink henceforth of the fruit of the vine, until that day when I drink it new with you in my Father's kingdom." Matt. xxvi: 29.

The manifestation of the Son of God is the most illustrious, the most momentous event, that is possible to engage the meditations of men. To his life and death, his resurrection and ascension into glory, we are indebted for our hopes and assurances of pardon, for our peace and happiness. To procure our salvation, he made the most amazing condescension from the dignity he enjoyed with his Father, by putting on the veil of flesh; he poured divine instruction from his lips, and shone forth with an all-perfect and all-lovely example. For our benefit, he submitted to a course of the most cruel treatment from his bitter enemies, to the agonies of the cross, and to the stroke of the king of terrors. For our happiness, he arose again with power and luster, ascended into the mansions of eternal happiness, manages our affairs with the Father, and holds the reins of government. With the greatest wisdom and goodness, therefore, the beneficent Jesus instituted a rite, that should recall his love to our memories, and awake each pious passion in our breast; a rite which, by the breaking of bread, and the pouring out of wine, should represent to us, in a striking manner, that most signal proof of the affection both of him and his heavenly Father, when his tender frame was exposed to wounds and bruises, when streams of the most precious blood issued from his sacred veins.

Our blessed Saviour, after delivering the sacramental cup, and telling them that his blood was shed for them, mentioned the treachery of Judas a second time: "Behold, he is at hand that doth betray me." Matt. xxvi: 46. This second declaration was made, very properly, after the institution of the sacrament, which exhibits the highest instance of our great Redeemer's love to mankind, his dying to obtain the remission of their sins; for it abundantly proves, that the person who could be deliberately guilty of such an injury to so kind a friend, must have been a monster, the oulness of whose ingratitude cannot be described by the force of language.

It is thought that some of the disciples, particularly struck with horror at the thought of Judas' treachery, rebuked him, by asking him, with surprise, how he could betray his Master? This accusation Judas, no doubt, repelled, by impudently denying the fact; but consciousness of guilt giving edge to the reproaches of his brethren, and to every circumstance of the affair, he immediately left the company, exceedingly displeased at thinking himself insulted and affronted.

The important, the awful scene, now approached, when the great work was to be finished. The traitor, Judas, was gone to the chief priests and elders, for a band of soldiers to apprehend him; but this did not discompose the Redeemer of mankind: he took occasion to meditate on the glory that would accrue both to himself and his Almighty Father, from those sufferings, and spake of it to his disciples. "Now," said he, "is the Son of Man glorified, and God is glorified in him." He told them that, having already done honor to his Father, by the past actions of his life, and being about to honor him still farther by his sufferings and death, which would display his perfections, particularly his infinite love to the human race, in the most astonishing and amiable light, he was, in his turn, to receive honor from his Father: intimating, that his human nature was to be exalted to the right hand of Omnipotence, and that his mission from God was to be supported by irrefragable attestations. But his disciples imagining that he spake of the glory of a temporal kingdom, their ambition was again revived, and they began to dispute, with as much keenness as ever, which of them should be greatest in that kingdom. This contention Jesus suppressed by the arguments he had formerly used for the same purpose. Among the Gentiles said he, they are reckoned the greatest who have the greatest power, and have exercised it in the most absolute manner; but your greatness shall be very different from theirs: it shall not consist in being unlimited with regard to tyrannical power, even though it should be joined with an affectation of titles, which denote qualities truly honorable; but whosoever desires to be great, or chief, among you, let him be so by his humility, and the service he renders to the rest, in imitation of me, your Master, whose greatness consists in this, that I am become the servant of you all: adding, as they had continued with him in his temptation, he would bestow upon them such a kingdom as his Father had appointed for him. At the same time, to check their ambition, and lead them to form a just notion of his kingdom, he told them, that he was soon to leave them, and that whither he was going, they could not at that time follow him; for which reason, instead of contending with one another which of them should be greatest, they would do well to be united among themselves in the happy bond of love. For by loving one another sincerely and fervently, they would prove themselves his disciples, to the conviction of mankind, who could not be ignorant that love was a distinguishing part of his character.

Having thus spoken, they finished the passover with singing a hymn, and went out to the Mount of Olives. On their arrival at the place which was to be the scene of his sufferings, he desired them to fortify themselves by prayer, and forewarned them of the terrible effects his sufferings would have upon them; they would make them all stumble that very night, agreeably to the prophecy of Zechariah: "I will smite the shepherd, and the sheep of flock shall be scattered abroad." To strengthen their faith, therefore, he not only mentioned his own resurrection, but told them they should see him in Galilee, after he was risen from the dead.

On our blessed Saviour's mentioning the offence that his disciples would take at his suffering, Peter recollected what had been said to him in particular, before they left the house. Grieved, therefore, afresh, to find his Master entertain such thoughts of him, and being now armed with a sword, the vehemence of his temper urged him to boast a second time of his courageous and close attachment to his Master. "Though all men," said he, "should be offended because of thee, yet will I never be offended." But Jesus, knowing that human confidence and security were weak and frail, thought proper to forewarn him again of his danger, and told him, that the cock should not crow before he had denied him.

Peter, however, still continued to repeat his confidence; I will die with thee, but never deny thee. The disciples all joined with Peter in professing their fixed resolution of suffering death, rather than that they would deny their Master; but the event fully confirmed the prediction of our Saviour. From hence we may learn, how ignorant men are of their own hearts, and that the strongest resolutions in their own strength avail them nothing.

The compassionate Redeemer of mankind, not willing to lose one single moment of the short time of his ministry that yet remained, continued to instruct his disciples in the great truths he came into the world to explain; and, from the vines which were growing round him on the Mount of Olives, he began his excellent discourse with the parable of the vine, to the following import:

Hitherto, said the blessed Jesus, the Jewish church and nation have been the peculiar care of Providence; as a choice and goodly vine, likely to bring forth much fruit is the special care of the husbandman. But, from henceforth, my church, my disciples, and the professors of my religion, of what country or nation soever they be, shall become the people of God, and the peculiar care of Divine Providence. I will be to them the root and stock of a vine, of which they are the branches, and my Father the husbandman and vine-dresser.

As, in the management of a choice vine, the skillful vine-dresser cuts off all barren and superfluous branches, that they may not burden nor exhaust the tree, and prunes and dresses the fruitful branches, that they may grow continually, and so bear more fruit; thus, in the government of my church, all useless, wicked, and incorrigible members, my Father, sooner or later, by his judgments, cuts off and destroys; but those who are sincerely pious and good, he, by the various and merciful dispensations of his providence toward them, tries, purifies, and amends, that they may daily improve, and be more and more abundant in all good works.

Now ye, my apostles, are such members as these, being purified in heart and mind, and prepared for every good work, by your lively faith in me, and sincere resolutions to obey my commands. Continue steadfastly in this state, and then you may be sure of deriving all spiritual blessings from me, as the branches receive sap and nourishment from the vine. But as a branch, without continuing in the vine, can not bear any fruit, but presently dries up and perishes, so ye, unless ye continue steadfast in your communion with me, (by a lively faith and sincere obedience, so as to receive grace and spiritual blessings,) can never bring forth any good fruit of true holiness and righteousness but will fall into vanity, superstition, and wickedness, and, at last, utterly perish. I am, as it were, I say, the root and stock of the vine, whereof ye are the branches. He that continues to adhere to me, by a constant faith in me, shall bring forth much fruit unto everlasting life; even as a branch which continues to grow in a vine, and receives sap and nourishment from it. But he that does not continue his relation to me in this manner, becomes a false and useless professor, and shall be cast out from me, and perish forever; even as a fruitless branch is cut off from the vine, and left to wither and dry, and is at last burned in the fire. If you continue in me, by believing my words, and holding fast what ye believe, and obeying and practicing it accordingly, no power or malice, either of man or of devils, shall be able to hurt you or oppose your doctrines. For, though I be absent from you in body, I yet will hear your prayers, and my Father himself also will hear you; and whatsoever ye shall ask, for the glory of the Almighty, and the propagation of my true religion in the world, shall certainly be granted you. But, above all things, carefully remember to demonstrate your continuance in me, by abounding in all good works of holiness, righteousness, and charity. This is the honor which my Father desires and expects from you; even as it is the glory and desire of the vine-dresser, that his vine should bring forth much fruit. And this is the honor that I myself expect from you, that ye shall prove yourselves to be really and indeed my disciples, by imitating my example, and obeying my commands. This ye are bound to do, not only in duty, but in gratitude also; for, as my Father hath loved me, so have I also loved you; and ye, in like manner, ought to love me again, that you may continue to be loved by me. But the way to express your love toward me, and to continue to be loved by me, is to keep my commandments; even as I, by keeping my Father's commandments, have expressed my love toward him, and continue to be loved by him.

These things have I spoken to you before my departure, that the comfort ye have taken in my presence may be continued in my absence, and even increase until the coming of the Holy Spirit, as it will be upon this condition, which I have so often repeated to you, that you keep my commandments. And the principle of these commandments is, that ye love one another: not after the common fashion of the world, but in such a manner as I have loved you; nor can you be ignorant what sort of love that is, when I tell you that I am now going to lay down my life for you. This is the highest instance in which it is possible for a man to express his love toward his greatest friends and benefactors; but this I am now going to do for you and for all mankind. I might, indeed, justly call you servants, considering the infinite distance between me and you, and the obligation ye have to obey my commandments, but I have not treated you as servants, (who are not admitted into their master's counsels,) but as friends, revealing to you the whole will of my Father with all freedom and plainness.

I have, I say, behaved myself to you as to the nearest friends. Not that you first obliged me, or did any acts of kindness for me; but I have freely, and of my own good pleasure, chosen you to be my apostles, and the preachers of my gospel, that you may go and declare the will of God to the world, and bring forth much and lasting fruit, in the conversion of men to the knowledge of the truth, and to the profession and practice of true religion. In the performance of this work, whatsoever ye shall ask of my Father, in my name, in order to enable you to perform it effectually and with full success, shall certainly be granted you.

Now all these things which I have spoken unto you concerning the greatness of my love toward you, in choosing you to be my apostles, in revealing unto you the whole will of my Father, and in laying down my life for you, I have urged and inculcated upon you for this reason chiefly, as I at first told you, that ye may learn, after my example, to "love one another." The world, indeed, you must expect, will hate and persecute you, on my account. But this you ought not to be surprised or terrified at, knowing that it is no worse treatment than I myself have met with before you. Be not, therefore, surprised when ye meet with opposition; nor think to find better treatment in the world than I myself have done. Remember what I have already told you, that the disciple is not above his master; nor is he that is sent greater than he that sent him. If men had generally and readily embraced my doctrine, you might, indeed, have had some reason to expect that they would willingly have received yours also. But since I myself have suffered great indignities and persecutions from wicked and perverse, from obstinate and incorrigible men, only for opposing their vices, it is highly reasonable that you should expect to undergo the like treatment, upon the like account. In all which sufferings you will, moreover, have this further comfortable consideration to support you, that the justice of your own cause, and the injustice of your persecutors, will, by that means, most evidently appear; seeing ye are persecuted only for professing and preaching, in my name, the doctrine of true religion; and they persecute you only because they know not God, and out of mere malice will not bear to be instructed in his commands. Indeed, had not I appeared to the world with all possible demonstrations of authority and truth, teaching them a most holy and undeniable doctrine, sufficient to reform their manners and amend their lives, and moreover demonstrated my divine commission by such proofs as ought to satisfy and convince the most doubting and suspicious minds, they might have had some plea and excuse of ignorance for their unbelief. But now, since all reasonable evidence has been offered them, and proper methods used for their conversion and salvation, and yet they willfully and obstinately reject these means of grace, it is plain they have no excuse for their sin; but they oppose and persecute you only because they will not forsake their worldly lusts, and out of mere malice will not bear to be instructed in the commands of the Almighty. So that they who oppose and persecute you, as they have before persecuted me, show plainly that they are haters of God, and of his most holy commandments; which is, as I have already told you, a plain evidence of the justice of your own cause, and of the injustice of your persecutors. If I had not, I say, done such works among them as no man ever did, they might, indeed, have had some appearance of excuse for their sin. But now, having seen abundant proofs of my authority, and undeniable evidence of the truth of my doctrine, and yet willfully and obstinately persisting to oppose it, because inconsistent with their lusts, it is plain that their dishonoring me is a dishonor done to my Father himself, and a direct contempt of his commands; so that they are utterly inexcusable. But it is no wonder, when men have given themselves wholly up to be governed by worldly affections, passions, and vices, they should act contrary to all the reason and evidence in the world: for this is but the natural consequences of obstinate and habitual wickedness; and hereby is only fulfilled in me what holy David long since prophetically complained of, that they hated him without a cause.

But notwithstanding all the opposition that wicked and incorrigible men will make against my doctrine, there will not be wanting powerful promoters of it, who shall effectually overcome all opposition. For the Comforter, whom I said, I will send you from heaven, even that "Spirit of truth," which cometh forth and is sent from the Father, shall, when he cometh, with wonderful efficacy, bear testimony to the truth of my doctrine, and cause it to be spread through the world with incredible success. Nay, and ye yourselves also, though now so weak, fearful, and doubting, shall then very powerfully bear testimony to the truth of all the things whereof ye, having been all along present with me, have been eye-witnesses from the beginning.

Thus have I warned you beforehand, of the opposition and persecution ye must expect to meet with in the world, that when it cometh ye may not be surprised and terrified, so as to be discouraged thereby from persisting in the performance of your duty.

Having finished his discourse, "Jesus lifted up his eyes to heaven, and prayed," with great fervency, to his Father. (The prayer itself is recorded in the seventeenth chapter of John.)

His prayer being ended, Jesus and his disciples came down from the Mount of Olives, into a field below, called Gethsemane, through which the brook Cedron ran, and, in it, on the other side of the brook, was a garden, called the Garden of Gethsemane. Here he desired his disciples to sit down till he should retire to pray, taking with him Peter, James, and John, those three select disciples, whom he had before chosen to be witnesses of his transfiguration, and now to be eye-witnesses of his passion, leaving the other disciples at the garden door, to watch the approach of Judas and his band.

The sufferings he was on the point of undergoing, were so great, that the very prospect of them excited this doleful exclamation; "My soul is exceeding sorrowful, even unto death; tarry ye here, and watch." On this great occasion, he sustained those grievous sorrows in his soul, by which, as well as by dying on the cross, he became a sin-offering, and accomplished the redemption of mankind.

He now withdrew from them about a stone's cast, and his human nature being overburdened beyond measure, he found it necessary to retire and pray, that if it was possible, or consistent with the salvation of the world, he might be delivered from the sufferings which were then lying on him. It was not the fear of dying on the cross which made him speak or pray in such a manner. To suppose this, would infinitely degrade his character. Make his sufferings as terrible as possible, clothe them with all the aggravating circumstances of distress, yet the blessed Jesus, whose human nature was strengthened by being connected with the divine, could not but shrink at the prospect of such sufferings as he had to endure. He addresses his divine Father, with a sigh of fervent wishes, that the cup might, if possible, be removed from him. In the Greek, it is, "O that thou wouldst remove this cup from me!" And having first knelt and prayed, he fell prostrate on his face, accompanying his address with due expressions of resignation, adding, immediately, "Not as I will, but as thou wilt."

At length he obtained relief, being heard on account of his perfect and entire submission to the will of his heavenly Father. "And when he arose up from prayer, and was come to his disciples, he found them sleeping for sorrow." This circumstance shows how much his disciples were affected with their Master's sufferings. The sensations of grief which they felt, on seeing his unspeakable distress, so overpowered them, that they sank into a sleep.

Our blessed Saviour, for the last time, came to his disciples, and seeing them still asleep, he said, "Sleep on now, and take your rest; behold, the hour is at hand, and the Son of Man is betrayed into the hands of sinners. Rise, let us be going: behold, he is at hand that doth betray me." Matt. xxvi: 45, 46. The event will soon be over, which causes your sorrow: I am betrayed, and ready to be delivered unto death.

CHAPTER XXVII.

The blessed Redeemer is taken by a band of Soldiers, at the information of the traitor Judas — Heals a Wound given the High Priest's Servant by Simon Peter — Fulfillment of our Lord's Prediction concerning Peter — The Saviour of the World is arraigned at the Bar of the Sanhedrim, and tried by the Jewish Council.

JUDAS, who had often resorted to the garden of Gethsemane, with the disciples of our Lord, knowing the spot and the usual time of his Master's repairing thither, informed the chief priests and elders that the time for apprehending Jesus was now come. They therefore sent a band of soldiers with him, and servants carrying lanterns and torches to show them the way; because, though it was always full moon at the passover, the sky might be dark with clouds, and the place whither they were going was shaded with trees. At the same time, a deputation of their number accompanied the band, to see that every one did his duty.

Judas having thus received a band of men and officers from the chief priests and Pharisees, they went thither with lanterns, and torches, and weapons; for they were exceedingly anxious to secure and get him into their hands; and the soldiers having, perhaps, never seen Jesus before, found it necessary that Judas should distinguish him, and point him out to them by some particular sign. The treacherous Judas went before the band, at a small distance, to prepare them for the readier execution of their office, by kissing his Master, which was the token agreed upon, that they might not mistake him, and seize a wrong person. "And he that was called Judas, one of the twelve, went before them, and drew near unto Jesus to kiss him." Stung with remorse at the horrid engagement into which he had entered, and not being now able to retract from the execution of it, he determined to make use of art in his vile proceedings, and weakly imagined he could deceive him whom he was about to betray, on a supposition that when he should give the kiss, it might be considered by his Master as a singular mark of his affection. When, therefore, they approached near the spot, Judas (who was at the head of the band,) suddenly ran forward, and coming up to Jesus, said, "Hail Master! and kissed him. And Jesus said unto him, Friend, wherefore art thou come? Betrayest thou the Son of Man with a kiss?" Before, however, Judas could make any reply, the band (who had fixed their eyes on the person he had kissed) arrived immediately, and surrounded Jesus.

The artifice and wicked designs of the base and perfidious Judas are here manifestly displayed. In order to conceal his villainy from his Master and his disciples, he walked hastily, and, without waiting for the band, went up directly and saluted him, wishing, perhaps, to have that considered as a token of apprising him of his danger. But Jesus did not fail to convince him that he knew the meaning and intent of his salutation; saying, "Betrayest thou the Son of Man with a kiss?" Judas certainly concealed his treachery so well that Peter did not suspect him, or it is probable he would have struck at him rather than at Malchus, the high priest's servant.

The appointed time of our Lord's sufferings being now come, he did not, as formerly, avoid his enemies; but, on the contrary, on their telling him they sought Jesus of Nazareth, he replied, "I am he;" thereby intimating to them, that he was willing to put himself into their hands. At the same time, to show them that they could not apprehend him without his own consent, he, in an extraordinary manner, exerted his divine power; he made the whole band fall back, and threw them to the ground. "Jesus, therefore, knowing all things that should come upon him, went forth and said unto them, Whom seek ye? They answered him, Jesus of Nazareth. Jesus said unto them, I am he; and Judas also, who betrayed him, stood with them. As soon, then, as he had said unto them, I am he, they went backward, and fell to the ground." But the soldiers and the Jews, imagining, perhaps, that they had been thrown down by some demon or evil spirit, with whom the Jews said he was in confederacy, advanced toward him a second time. "Then he asked again, Whom seek ye? And they said, Jesus of Nazareth. Jesus answered, I told you that I am he;" expressing again his willingness to fall into their hands. "If, therefore, ye seek me, let these go their way." If your business be with me alone, suffer my disciples to pass: for the party had surrounded them also. He seems to have made this request to the soldiers, that the saying might be fulfilled which he spake, "Of them which thou gavest me, have I lost none." For, as he always proportioned the trials of his people to their strength, so here he took care that the disciples should escape the storm, which none but himself could sustain.

At length one of the soldiers, more daring than the rest, rudely caught Jesus and bound him; upon which Peter drew his sword and smote off the ear of the high priest's servant, who, probably, was showing greater forwardness than the rest in this business: "Then Simon Peter, having a sword, drew it, and smote the high priest's servant, and cut off his right ear: the servant's name was Malchus." The enraged disciple was on the point of singly attacking the whole band, when Jesus ordered him to sheath his sword, telling him that his unseasonable and imprudent defence might prove the occasion of his destruction. "Then said Jesus unto him, Put up thy sword into his place: for all they that take the sword shall perish with the sword." Matt. xxvi: 52. He told him likewise, that it implied both a distrust of God who can always employ a variety of means for the safety of his people, and also his ignorance in the Scriptures. Thinkest thou," said he, "that I can not now pray to my Father, and he shall presently give me more than twelve legions of angels? But how then shall the Scriptures be fulfilled, that thus it must be?" Matt. xxvi: 53, 54.

The word legion, was a Roman military term, being a name which they gave to a body of five or six thousand men; wherefore, in regard that the band which surrounded them was a Roman cohort, our Lord might make use of this term, by way of contrast, to show what an inconsiderable thing the cohort was, in comparison of the force he could summon to his assistance — more than twelve legions, not of soldiers, but of angels. He was yet tenderly inclined to prevent any bad consequences which might have followed from Peter's rashness, by healing the servant, and adding, in his rebuke to him, a declaration of his willingness to suffer; "The cup which my Father hath given me, shall I not drink it?"

The circumstance of his healing the ear of Malchus by touching it, evidently implies that no wound or distemper was incurable in the hand of Jesus; neither was any injury so great, that he could not forgive. It seems somewhat surprising, that this evident miracle did not make an impression upon the chief priests, especially as our Lord put them in mind, at the same time, of the other miracles; for, having first said, "Suffer ye thus far; and he touched his ear and healed him," he added, "Be ye come out as against a thier, with swords and staves? When I was daily with you in the temple, ye stretched forth no hands against me: but this is your hour, and the power of darkness." Luke xxii: 51, &c. The priests had kept at a distance, for some time, but drew near when they understood that Jesus was in their power; for they were proof against all conviction, being obstinately bent on putting him to death. And the disciples, when they saw their Master in the hands of his enemies, forsook him, and fled, according to his prediction; notwithstanding they might have followed him without any danger, as the priests had no design against them. "Then all the disciples forsook him, and fled. Then the band, and the captain and officers, took Jesus, and bound him."

But it was not the cord which held him; his infinite love was, by far, the strongest bond. He could have broken those weak ties, and exerted his divinity in a more wonderful manner: he could have stricken them all dead, with as much ease as he had before thrown them on the ground; but he patiently submitted to this, as to every other indignity which they chose to offer him, so meek was he under the greatest injuries. Having thus secured him, they led him away. "And there followed him a certain young man, having a linen cloth cast about his naked body; and the young men laid hold on him; and he left the linen cloth, and fled from them naked." This, perhaps, was the proprietor of the garden, who, being awakened by the noise, came out with the linen cloth in which he had been lying, cast round his naked body; and, having a respect for Jesus, followed him, forgetting the dress he was in.

They first led Jesus to Annas, father-in-law of Caiaphas, who was the high priest that year. Annas having himself discharged the office of high priest, was consequently a person of distinguished character, which, together with his relation to the high priest, made him worthy of the respect they now paid him. But he refused, singly, to meddle in the affair; they therefore carried Jesus to Caiaphas himself, at whose palace the chief priests, elders, and scribes were assembled, having staid there all night, to see the issue of their stratagem. This Caiaphas was he that advised the council to put Jesus to death, even admitting he was innocent, for the safety of the whole Jewish nation. He seems to have enjoyed the sacerdotal dignity during the whole course of Pilate's government in Judea; for he was advanced by Valerius Gracchus, Pilate's prede cessor, and was divested of it by Vitellius, governor of Syria, after he had deposed Pilate from his procuratorship.

The apprehending of their dear Master could not but strike his disciples with horror and amazement: though he had forewarned them of that event, such was their consternation, that they fled different ways; some of them, however, recovering out of the panic that had seized them, followed the band at a distance, to see what the issue would be. Of this number was Peter, and another disciple, whom John has mentioned without giving his name, and who therefore is supposed to have been John himself. This disciple, being acquainted at the high priest's, got admittance for himself first, and soon after for Peter, who had come with him. "And Simon Peter followed Jesus, and so did another disciple. That disciple was known unto the high priest, and went in with Jesus into the palace of the high priest. But Peter stood at the door without. Then went out that other disciple, which was known unto the high priest, and spake unto them that kept the door, and brought in Peter. And when they had kindled a fire in the midst of the hall, and were set down together, Peter sat down amongst them." The maid-servant, who kept the door, concluding Peter to be a disciple also, followed after him to the fire, and looking earnestly at him, charged him with the supposed crime. "Then said the damsel that kept the door unto Peter, Art not thou, also, one of this man's disciples?" This blunt attack threw Peter into such confusion, that he flatly denied his having any connection with Jesus; replying, "I am not," and adding,

"I know not, neither understand I what thou sayest." As if he had said, I do not understand any reason for your asking me such a question.

Thus the very apostle who had before acknowledged his Master to be the Messiah, the Son of the living God, and had so confidently boasted of his fortitude and firm attachment to him in the greatest dangers, proved himself an arrant deserter of his cause upon trial. His shameful fears were altogether inexcusable, as the enemy who attacked him was one of the weaker sex, and the terror of the charge was in a great measure taken off by the insinuation made in it, that John was likewise known to be Christ's disciple; for, as he was known at the high priest's, he was consequently known in that character. "Art thou not also one of this man's disciples?" Art thou not one of them, as well as he who is sitting with you? Nothing can account for this conduct of Peter, but the confusion and panic which had seized him on this occasion. As his inward perturbation must have appeared in his countenance and gesture, he did not choose to stay long with the servants at the fire. He went out, therefore, into the porch, where he was a little concealed. "And he went into the porch; after he had been some time there, another maid saw him, and began to say to them that stood by, This is one of them; and he again denied, with an oath, I know not the man;" adding perjury to falsehood.

After Peter had been thus attacked without doors, he thought proper to return and mix with the crowd at the fire. "And Simon Peter stood and warmed himself." From this circumstance, it is clear, that the ensuing was the third denial; and that Peter left the porch, where the second denial happened, and was come again into the hall. "Here one of the servants of the high priest (being his kinsman, whose ear Peter cut off,) saith, Did not I see thee in the garden with him? Peter then denied again, and immediately the cock crew." The words of Malchus' kinsman bringing to Peter's remembrance what he had done to that man, threw him into such a panic, that when those who stood by repeated the charge, he impudently denied it: "He even began to curse and to swear, saying, I know not this man of whom you speak." For, when they heard Peter deny the charge, they supported it by an argument drawn from the accent with which he pronounced his answer. Surely thou art one of them; for thou art a Galilean, and thy speech agreeth thereto; so that, being pressed on all sides, to give his lie the better color, he profaned the name of God, by imprecating the bitterest curses on himself, if he was telling a falsehood. Perhaps he hoped, by these acts of impiety, to convince them effectually that he was not the disciple of the holy Jesus.

Thus the apostle denied his Master three distinct times, with oaths and asseverations, totally forgetting the vehement protestations he had made a few hours before, that he would never deny him. He was, probably, permitted to fall in this manner, to teach us two lessons: first that the strongest resolutions, formed in our own strength, can not withstand the torrent of temptation; secondly, that the true disciples of Christ, though they fall, may be brought to a conviction of their sin; for he no sooner denied his Master the third time, than the cock crew, and first awakened in him a consciousness of his sin. "And the Lord turned and looked upon Peter; and Peter remembered the words of the Lord, how he had said unto him, Before the cock crow, thou shalt deny me thrice. And Peter went out and wept bitterly."

When the band of soldiers arrived at the high priest's with Jesus, they found there all the chief priests, and scribes, and the elders, assembled: "And as soon as it was day, the elders of the people, and the chief priests and the scribes came together, and led him into their council. And the high priest asked Jesus of his disciples, and his doctrine." He inquired of him what his disciples were? for what end he had gathered them? whether it was to make himself a king? and what the doctrine was which he taught them? In these questions there was a great deal of art; for, as the crime laid to our Saviour's charge, was, that he had set up for the Messiah, and deluded the people, they expected that he would claim that dignity in their presence, and so would, on his own confession, have condemned him without any farther progress. This was unfair, as it was artful and ensnaring. To oblige a prisoner, on his trial, to confess what might take away his life, was a very iniquitous method of proceeding; and Jesus expressed his opinion thereof with very good reason, and complained of it, bidding them prove what they had laid to his charge, with witnesses. "Jesus answered him, I spake openly to the world; I ever taught in the synagogue, and in the temple, whither the Jews always resort; and in secret have I said nothing. Why asked thou me? ask them which heard me, what I have said unto them: behold, they know what I said." It was greatly to the honor of our blessed Redeemer, that all his actions were done in public, under the eyes even of his enemies; because, had he been carrying on any imposture, the lovers of goodness and truth had thus abundant opportunities of detecting him with propriety; he, therefore, in his defence, appealed to that part of his character, but his answer was construed to be disrespectful; "for, when he had thus spoken, one of the officers, which stood by, struck Jesus with the palm of his hand, saying, Answerest thou the high priest so?" To which he meekly replied, with the greatest serenity, "If I have spoken evil, bear witness of the evil; but if well, why smitest thou me?" Show me, prove before this court, wherein my crime consists, or record it on the evidence on the face of my trial; which if you can not, how can you answer for this inhuman treatment to a defenceless prisoner, standing on his trial before the world, and in open court? Thus Jesus became an example of his own precepts, "Whosoever shall smite thee on thy right cheek, turn to him the other also," (Matt. v: 39,) bearing the greatest injuries with a patience that could not be provoked.

When the council found that Jesus declined answering the questions whereby they expected to have drawn from him an acknowledgment of his being the Messiah, they proceeded to examine many witnesses to prove his having assumed that character; as they considered such a pretension as blasphemy in his mouth, who being only a man, according to their opinion, could not, without the highest affront of the divine Majesty, pretend to the title of the Son of God, as it belonged to the Messiah.

But, in this examination, they acted like interested and enraged persecutors, rather than as impartial judges, forming their questions in the most artful man ner, in order, if possible, to draw expressions from him, which they might pervert into suspicions of guilt, as some foundation for condemning Jesus, who had so long and faithfully labored for their salvation.

Their witnesses, however, disappointed them, some of them disagreeing in their story, and others mentioning things of no manner of importance. At last, two persons agreed in their depositions; namely, in hearing him say, that he was able to destroy the temple of God, and to raise it in three days. But this testimony was absolutely false; for our great Redeemer never said he could destroy and build the temple of Jerusalem in three days, as they affirmed. It is true, that after banishing the traders from the temple, when the Jews desired to know by what authority he undertook to make such reformation, he referred them to the miracle of his resurrection; bidding them "destroy this temple," pointing probably to his body, "and in three days he would raise it up." The witnesses, therefore, either through malice or ignorance, perverted his answer into an affirmation that he was able to destroy and build the magnificent temple of Jerusalem in three days; and the judges considered this assertion as blasphemy, because it could only be done by the divine power.

Our Saviour made no reply to the evidences that were produced against him, which greatly incensed the high priest; who, supposing that he intended, by his silence, to put an affront on the council, rose from his seat, and, with great perturbation, demanded the reason of so remarkable a conduct. "Answerest thou nothing? said he: What is it which these witness against thee?" And some of the council added, "Art thou the Christ?" To which our blessed Saviour answered, If I should tell you plainly, you would not believe me; and if I should demonstrate it to you by the most evident and undeniable arguments, ye would neither be convinced or let me go. The high priest, finding all his attempts to trepan our Saviour in vain, said to him, I adjure you solemnly, by the dreadful and tremendous name of God, in whose presence you stand, that you tell me plainly and truly, whether you are the Messiah, the Son of God.

The consequence attending the confession of the truth, did not intimidate the blessed Jesus; for, being adjured by the chief magistrate, he immediately acknowledged the charge: adding, Ye shall shortly see a convincing evidence of this truth, in that wonderful and unparalleled destruction which I will send upon the Jewish nation; in the quick and powerful progress which the gospel shall make upon the earth; and finally, in my glorious appearance in the clouds of heaven, at the last day, the sign you have so often demanded in confirmation of my mission.

Upon our blessed Saviour's making this answer, a number of them cried out at once, "Art thou the Son of God?" To which our great Redeemer replied, "Ye say that I am;" a manner of speaking among the Jews, which expressed a plain and strong affirmation of the thing expressed. When the high priest heard this second assertion, he rent his clothes, with great indignation, and said unto the council, Why need we trouble ourselves to seek for more witnesses, Ye yourselves, nay, this whole assembly, are witnesses that he hath spoken manifest and notorious blasphemy? What think ye? To which they all replied, that for assuming to himself the character of the Messiah, he deserved to be put to death.

Then began the servants and common people to fall upon him, as a man already condemned: spitting upon him, buffeting him, and offering all manner of rudeness and indignities. They blindfolded him; and some of the council, in order to ridicule him for having professed to be the great Prophet, bid him exercise his prophetical gift, in declaring who had smitten him.

Such was the treatment of the Son of God, the Saviour of sinners, which, though derogatory to his character, he bore with patience and resignation, leaving his people an example to follow his steps, and to submit to the will of God in all things, nor murmur at any of the dispensations of his providence.

CHAPTER XXVIII.

Our blessed Saviour is carried before the Roman Governor — The traitor Judas becomes his own Executioner — Pilate publicly acquits Jesus, and refers his case to the decision of Herod.

THE blessed Jesus being thus condemned by the unanimous voice of the grand assembly, it was resolved to carry him before the governor, that he likewise might pass sentence on him. The Roman governors of Judea generally resided at Cesarea; but at the great feast they came up to Jerusalem, to prevent or suppress tumults, and to administer justice, it being a custom for the Roman governors of provinces to visit the principal towns under their jurisdiction, on this latter account. Pilate being accordingly come to Jerusalem, some time before the feast, had been informed of the great ferment among the rulers, and the true character of the person on whose account it was raised, for he entertained a just notion of it: "He knew that for envy they had delivered him." He knew the cause of their envy, was impressed with a favorable opinion of Jesus, and wished, if possible, to deliver him from his vile persecutors.

Early in the morning, the Jewish council brought Jesus to the hall of judgment, or governor's palace.

They themselves, however, went not into the hall, but stood without, lest they should be defiled, and rendered incapable of eating the passover.

Now Judas Iscariot, who had delivered his Master into the hands of the council, finding his project turn out very different from what he expected, was filled with the deepest remorse for what he had done. He saw all his golden dreams of temporal honors and advantages sunk at once to nothing; he saw his kind, his indulgent Master, condemned, and forsaken by all his followers. He saw all this, and determined to make all the satisfaction in his power for the crime he had committed. Accordingly, he came and confessed openly his sin, before the chief priests and rulers, offered them the money they had given him to commit it, and earnestly wished he could recall the fatal transaction of the preceding night. It seems he thought this was the most public testimony he could possibly give of his Master's innocence and his own repentance. I have, said he, committed a most horrid crime, by betraying an innocent man to death. But this moving speech of Judas had no effect on the callous hearts of the Jewish rulers. They affirmed that, however he might think the prisoner innocent, and for that reason had sinned in bringing the sentence of death upon his head, they were not to blame; because they knew him a blasphemer, who deserved to die. "What is that to us?" said they, "see thou to that." Nay, they even refused to take the money they had given him, as a reward for performing the base act of betraying his Master.

The deepest remorse now seized upon the wretched Judas, and his soul was agitated by the horrors of despair. The innocence and benevolence of his Master-the many favors he himself had received from him, and the kind offices he had done for the sons and daughters of affliction, crowded at once into his mind, and rendered his torments intolerable. Racked with these agonizing passions, and unable to support the misery, he threw down the wages of his iniquity in the temple, and confessing, at the same time, his own sin, and the innocence of his master, went away in despair, and hanged himself.

Thus perished Judas Iscariot, the traitor, a miserable example of the fatal influence of covetousness, and a standing monument of divine vengeance, to deter future generations from acting in opposition to the dictates of conscience, through a love for the things of this world; for which this wretched mortal betrayed his Master, his Friend, his Saviour, and accumulated such a load of guilt on himself, as sunk his soul into the lowest pit of perdition.

The pieces of silver cast down by Judas were gathered up, and delivered to the priests, who, thinking it unlawful to put them into the treasury, because they were the wages of a traitor, agreed to lay them out in purchasing the potter's field, and to make it a common burial-place for strangers.

We have already observed that the chief priests and elders refused to go themselves into the judgment hall, lest they should contract some pollutions in the house of a heathen, which would have rendered them unfit for eating the passover. The same reason also hindered them from entering the governor's palace, on other festivals, when that magistrate attended in order to administer justice; a kind of structure was therefore erected, adjoining to the palace, which served instead of a tribunal, or judgment-seat. This structure, called, in the Hebrew, *Gabbatha*, was finely paved with small pieces of marble, of different colors, being always exposed to the weather. One side of this structure joined to the palace, and a door was made in the wall, through which the governor passed to the tribunal. By this contrivance, the people might stand round the tribunal in the open air, hear and see the governor when he spake to them from the pavement, and observe the whole administration of justice, without danger of being defiled, either by him or any of his retinue.

Before this tribunal the great Redeemer of mankind was brought, and the priests and elders having taken their places around the pavement, the governor ascended the judgment-seat, and asked them what accusation they had to bring against the prisoner? Though nothing was more natural than for the governor to ask this question, yet the Jews thought themselves highly affronted by it, and haughtily answered, If he had not been a very great and extraordinary malefactor, we should not have given you this trouble at all, much less at so unseasonable an hour.

Pilate then examined Jesus: and, finding he had not been guilty either of rebellion or sedition, but that he was accused of particulars relating to the religion and customs of the Jews, grew angry, and said, What are these things to me? Take him yourselves, and judge him according to your own law: plainly insinuating that, in his opinion, the crime they laid to the prisoner's charge was not of a capital nature; and that such punishments as they were permitted by

Cæsar to inflict, were adequate to any misdemeanor that Jesus was charged with. But this proposal of the Roman governor was absolutely refused by the Jewish priests and elders, because it condemned the whole proceeding; and therefore they answered, We have no power to put any one to death, as this man certainly deserves, who has attempted not only to make innovations in our religion, but also to set up himself for a king.

The eagerness of the Jews to get Jesus condemned by the Roman governor, who often sentenced malefactors to be crucified, tended to fulfill the saying of our great Redeemer, who, during the course of his ministry, had often mentioned what kind of death he was, by the counsel of his Father, appointed to die.

Pilate, finding it impossible to prevent a tumult unless he proceeded to try Jesus, ascended again the judgment-seat, and commanded his accusers to produce their accusations against him. Accordingly, they accused him of seditious practices, affirming that he had used every method in his power to dissuade the people from paying taxes to Cæsar, pretending that he himself was the Messiah, the great King of the Jews, so long expected. But they brought no proof of these assertions. They only insinuated they had already convicted him of this assertion, which was absolutely false. Pilate, however, asked him, Is it true what these men lay to your charge, that you have indeed attempted to set up yourself as King of the Jews? To which Jesus replied, Have you ever, during your stay in this province, heard any thing of me that gave you reason to suspect me guilty of secret practices and seditious designs against the government;

or do you found your question only on the present clamor and tumult that is raised against me? If this be the case, be very careful lest you be imposed on merely by the ambiguity of a word; for, to be "King of the Jews," is not to erect a temporal throne in opposition to that of Cæsar, but a thing of very different nature; the kingdom of the Messiah is a heavenly kingdom. To which Pilate replied, Am I a Jew? Can I tell what your expectations are, and in what sense you understand these words? The rulers and chiefs of your own people, who are the most proper judges of these particulars, have brought you before me, as a riotous and seditious person: if this be not the truth, let me know what is, and the crime thou hast been guilty of. Jesus answered, I have, indeed, a kingdom, and this kingdom I have professed to establish. But then it is not of this world, nor have my endeavors to establish it any tendency to cause disturbances in the government. For, had that been the case, my servants would not have suffered me to have fallen into the hands of the Jews. But I tell you plainly, my kingdom is wholly spiritual. I reign in the hearts of my people, and subdue their wills and affections into a conformity to the will of God. You acknowledge, then, in general, answered Pilate, that you have professed to be a king? To which the blessed Jesus replied, In the sense I have told you, I have declared, and do now declare, myself to be a king. For this very end I was born, and for this purpose I came into the world, that I should bear witness to the truth; and whosoever sincerely loves and is always ready to embrace the truth, will hear my testimony, and be convinced of it. Pilate answered, "What is truth?" and immediately went out to the Jews, and said unto them, I have again examined this man, but can not find him guilty of any fault, which, according to the Roman law, is worthy of death.

The generous declaration made by the governor, of the innocence of our blessed Saviour, had no effect on the superstitious and bigoted Jews. They even persisted in their accusations with more vehemence than before, affirming that he attémpted to raise a sedition in Galilee: "He stirreth up," said they, "the people, beginning from Galilee to this place."

Jesus, however, made no answer at all to this heavy charge. Nay, he continued silent, notwithstanding the governor himself expressly required him to speak in his own defence. A conduct so extraordinary, in such circumstances, astonished Pilate exceedingly; for he had great reason to be persuaded of the innocence of our dear Redeemer. The truth is, he was altogether ignorant of the divine counsel by which the whole affair was directed.

There were many reasons which induced the blessed Jesus not to make a public defence. He came into the world purely to redeem lost and undone sinners, by offering up himself a sacrifice for them; but had he pleaded with his usual force, the people had, in all probability, been induced to ask his release, and consequently his death had been prevented. Besides, the gross falsehood of the accusation, known to all the inhabitants of Galilee, rendered any reply absolutely needless.

In the mean time, the chief priests continued to accuse him with great noise and tumult. And the meek and humble Jesus still continuing mute, Pilate spake again to him, saying, Wilt thou continue to make no defence? Dost thou not hear how vehemently these men accuse thee? But Pilate, recollecting what the chief priests had said with regard to a sedition in Galilee, asked, If Jesus came out of that country? and on being informed he did, he immediately ordered him to be carried to Herod, who was also then at Jerusalem. The governor supposed that Herod, in whose dominion the sedition was said to have been raised, must be a much better judge of the affair than himself; besides, his being a Jew rendered him more versed in the religion of his own country, and gave him greater influence over the chief priests and elders; he therefore considered him as the most proper person to prevail on the Jewish council to desist from their cruel persecution. But if, contrary to all human probability, he should, at their solicitation, condemn Jesus, Pilate hoped to escape the guilt and infamy of putting an innocent person to death. He might also propose, by this action, to regain Herod's friendship, which he had formerly lost, by encroaching, in all probability, on his privileges. But however that be, or whatever motive induced Pilate to send our great Redeemer to Herod, the latter greatly rejoiced at this opportunity of seeing Jesus, hoping to have the pleasure of beholding him perform some great miracle. In this he was, however, disappointed; for, as Herod had apostatized from the doctrine of John the Baptist, to which he was once probably a convert, and had even put his teacher to death, the blessed Jesus, however liberal of his miracles to the sons and daughters of affliction, would not work them to gratify the curiosity of a tyrant, nor even answer one of the many questions he proposed to him.

Herod finding his expectations thus cut off, ordered the blessed Saviour to be clothed with an old robe, resembling in color those worn by kings, and permitted his attendants to insult him. From Herod's dressing him in this manner, it evidently appears, that the chief priests and elders had accused him of nothing, but his having assumed the character of the Messiah; for the affront put upon him was plainly in derision of that profession..

The other head of accusation, namely, his having attempted to raise a sedition in Galilee, on account of tribute paid to Cæsar, they did not dare to mention, as Herod could not fail of knowing it to be a gross and malicious falsehood. And, no crime worthy of death being laid to his charge, Herod sent him again to Pilate. It seems, that though he was displeased with the great Redeemer of mankind for refusing to work a miracle before him, yet he did not think proper to comply with the wishes of his enemies.

PILATE DELIVERS UP JESUS.

CHAPTER XXIX.

THE ROMAN GOVERNOR, FOR WANT OF EVIDENCE, PROPOSES TO ACQUIT AND RELEASE JESUS THREE SEVERAL TIMES; BUT, AT THE PRESSING INSTIGATION OF THE JEWS, HE CONDEMNS AND DELIVERS HIM UP.

THE Roman governor, in order to acquire popular applause, used generally, at the feast of the passover, to release a prisoner nominated by the people. At this feast there was one in prison, named Barabbas, who, at the head of a number of rebels, had made an insurrection in the city, and committed murder during the confusion.

The multitude, being now assembled before the governor's palace, began to call aloud on him to perform the annual office of mercy, customary at that festival.

Pilate, glad of this opportunity, told them, that he was very willing to grant the favor they desired: and asked them, whether they would have Barabbas or Jesus released unto them? But, without waiting for an answer, he offered to release Jesus, knowing that the chief priests had delivered him through envy; especially as Herod had not found him guilty of the crimes laid to his charge.

While these particulars were transacting, Pilate received a message from his wife, then with him at Jerusalem, and who had that morning been greatly affected by a dream, which gave her much uneasiness. The dream had so great an effect on this Roman lady, that she could not rest till she had sent an account of it to her husband, who was then sitting with the tribunal on the pavement, and begged him to have no hand in the death of the righteous person he was then judging. The people had not yet determined whether they would have Jesus or Barabbas released to them; therefore, when Pilate received the message from his wife, he called the chief priests and rulers together, and, in the hearing of the multitude, made a speech to them, in which he gave them an account of the examination which Jesus had undergone, both at his own, and Herod's tribunal, declaring that in both courts it had turned out honorably to his character: for which reason he proposed to them, that he should be the object of the people's favor. Pilate did the priests the honor of desiring to know their inclination in particular, perhaps with a design to soften their stony hearts, and, if possible, to move them for once to pity an injured but innocent man. But he was persuaded, that if pity was absolutely banished from their callous breasts, his proposals would have been acceptable to the people, whom he expected would embrace the first opportunity of declaring in his favor; yet, in this he was disappointed. They cried out, all at once, "Away with this man, and release unto us Barabbas."

Pilate himself was astonished at this determination of the multitude, and repeated his question; for he could hardly believe what he had himself heard. But, on their again declaring that they desired Barabbas might be released, he asked them what he should do with Jesus, which is called Christ. As if he had said, You demanded that Barabbas should be released; but what shall I then do with Jesus? You can not surely desire me to crucify him, whom so many of you have acknowledged as your Messiah? "But they cried, saying, Crucify him, crucify him. Then Pilate said unto them, Why, what evil hath he done? And they cried out the more exceedingly, Crucify him." They were so resolutely determined to have him destroyed, that notwithstanding the governor urged them again and again to desire his release, declared his innocence, and offered several times to dismiss him, they would not hear it, uttering their rage, sometimes in hollow, distant, inarticulate murmurs, and sometimes in furious outcries—to such a pitch were their passions raised by the craft and artful insinuations of the priests. Pilate, finding it therefore in vain to struggle with their prejudices, called for water, and washed his hands before the multitude, crying out, at the same time, that the prisoner had no fault, and that he himself was innocent of his blood.

By this action and declaration, Pilate seems to have intended to make an impression on the Jewish populace, by complying with the institution of Moses, which orders, in case of an unknown murder, the elders of the nearest city to wash their hands publicly, and say, "Our hands have not shed this blood." Deut. xxi: 7. And, in allusion to this law, the Psalmist says, "I will wash my hands in innocence." According, therefore, to the Jewish rite, Pilate made the most solemn and public demonstration of the innocence of our Redeemer, and of his resolution of having no hand in his death. But, notwithstanding the solemnity of this declaration, the Jews continued inflexible, and cried out, with one voice, "His blood be on us, and on our children." Dreadful imprecation! it shocks humanity! An im precation which brought on them the dreadful vengeance of Omnipotence, and is still a heavy burden on that people! The governor, finding it impossible to alter their choice, released unto them Barabbas. And, as it was the general practice of the Romans to scourge those criminals they condemned to be crucified, Pilate ordered the blessed Jesus to be scourged, before he delivered him to the soldiers to be put to death.

The soldiers having scourged Jesus, and received orders to crucify him, carried him into the pretorium, or common hall, where they added the shame of disgrace to the bitterness of his punishment; for, sore as he was by reason of the stripes they had given him, they dressed him in a purple robe, in derision of his being King of the Jews. Having dressed him in this robe of mock majesty, they put a reed in his hand instead of a scepter, and, after plaiting a wreath of thorns, they put it on his head for a crown, forcing it down in so rude a manner, that his temples were torn, and his face besmeared with his most precious blood. To the Son of God, in this condition, the rude soldiers bowed the knee, pretending to do it out of respect; but, at the same time, gave him severe blows on the head, which drove the points of the wreath afresh into his temples, and then spit on him, to express their highest contempt. The governor, whose office obliged him to be present at this shocking scene of inhumanity, was ready to burst with grief. The sight of an innocent and eminently holy person, treated with such shocking barbarity, raised in his breast the most painful sensations of pity. And though he had given sentence that it should be as the Jews desired, and had delivered our dear Redeemer to the soldiers to be crucified, he was in hopes that if he showed him to the people in that condition, they must relent, and earnestly petition for him to be released. Filled with this thought, he resolved to carry him out, and exhibit to their view a spectacle capable of softening the most envenomed, obdurate, and enraged enemy: and went out himself, and said unto them, Though I have sentenced this man to die, and have scourged him as one that is to be crucified, yet I once more bring him before you, that I may again testify how fully I am persuaded of his innocence, and that ye may yet have an opportunity of saving his life. As soon as the governor had finished his speech, Jesus appeared on the pavement, his hair, his face, his shoulders all clotted with blood, and the purple robe daubed with spittle of the soldiers. And that the sight of Jesus in this distress might make the greater impression on the people, Pilate, while coming forward, cried out, "Behold the man!" As if he had said, will nothing make you relent? Have ye lost all the feelings of humanity, and bowels of compassion? Can you bear to see the innocent, a son of Abraham, thus injured? But all this was to no purpose; the priests, whose rage and malice had extinguished not only the sentiments of justice and feelings of pity natural to the human heart, but also that love which countrymen bear for each other, no sooner saw Jesus, than they began to fear the fickle populace might relent; and, therefore, laying decency aside, they led the way to the multitude, crying out, with all their might, Crucify him! crucify him!

Pilate, vexed to see the Jewish rulers thus obstinately bent on the destruction of one from whom they had nothing to fear that was dangerous, either with regard to their church or state, passionately told them, that if they would have him crucified, they must do it themselves; because he would not suffer his people to murder a man who was guilty of no crime. But this they also refused, thinking it dishonorable to receive permission to punish a person who had been more than once publicly declared innocent by his judge. Besides, they considered with themselves, that the governor might afterward have called it sedition, as the permission had been extorted from him. Accordingly, they told him, that even though none of the things alleged against the prisoner were true, he had committed such a crime in presence of the council itself, as by the law deserved the most ignominious death. He had spoken blasphemy, calling himself the Son of God, a title which no mortal could assume, without the highest degree of guilt: "We have a law, and by our law he ought to die, because he made himself the Son of God."

When Pilate heard that Jesus called himself the Son of God, his fear was increased. Knowing the obstinacy of the Jews, in all matters of religion, he was afraid they would make a tumult in earnest; or, perhaps, he was himself more afraid than ever to take away his life, because he suspected it might be true. He doubtless remembered the miracles said to have been performed by Jesus, and therefore suspected that he really was the Son of God. For, it was well known, that the religion which the governor professed. directed him to acknowledge the existence of demi-gods and heroes, or men descended from gods. Nay, the heathen believed that their gods themselves appeared upon earth in the forms of men. Reflections of this kind induced Pilate to go again to the judgment hall, and ask Jesus from what father he sprung, and from what country he came? But our blessed Saviour gave him no answer, lest the governor should reverse his sentence, and absolutely refuse to crucify him. Pilate marveled greatly at his silence, and said unto Jesus, Why dost thou refuse to answer me? You can not be ignorant that I am invested with absolute power, either to release or crucify you. To which Jesus answered, I well know that you are Cæsar's servant, and accountable to him for your conduct. I forgive you any injury which, contrary to your inclination, the popular fury constrains you to do unto me. Thou hast thy power "from above," from the emperor; for which cause, the Jewish high priest, who hath put me into thy hands, and, by pretending that I am Cæsar's enemy, forces thee to condemn me; or, if thou refusest, will accuse thee as negligent of the emperor's interest: he is more guilty than thou. "He that delivered me unto thee hath the greater sin."

This sweet and modest answer made such an impression on Pilate, that he went out to the people, and declared his intention of releasing Jesus, whether they gave their consent or not. Upon which, the chief priests and rulers of Israel cried out, "If thou let this man go, thou art not Cæsar's friend: whosoever maketh himself a king, speaketh against Cæsar." If thou releasest the prisoner, who hath set himself up for a king, and has been accused of endeavoring to raise a rebellion in the country, thou art unfaithful to the interests of the emperor, thy master. This argument was weighty, and shook Pilate's resolution to the very basis. He was terrified at the thought of being accused to the emperor, who, in all affairs of government, always suspected the worst, and punished the most minute crimes relative thereto with death. The governor being thus constrained to yield, contrary to his inclination, was very angry with the priests for stirring up the people to such a pitch of madness, and determined to affront them.

He therefore brought Jesus out, a second time, into the pavement, wearing the purple robe and crown of thorns, and, pointing to him, said, "Behold your king!" ridiculing their national expectation of a Messiah. This sarcastical expression stung them to the quick, and they cried out, "Away with him! crucify him!" To which Pilate answered, with the same mocking air, "Shall I crucify your king? The chief priests answered, We have no king but Cæsar." Thus did they publicly renounce their hope of the Messiah, which the whole economy of their religion had been calculated to cherish; they also publicly acknowledged their subjection to the Romans, and, consequently, condemned themselves, when they afterward rebelled against the emperor.

CHAPTER XXX.

THE INNOCENT, IMMACULATE REDEEMER IS LED FORTH TO MOUNT CALVARY AND THERE IGNOMINIOUSLY CRUCIFIED BETWEEN TWO MALEFACTORS—A PHENOMENON APPEARS ON THE IMPORTANT OCCASION—OUR LORD ADDRESSES HIS FRIENDS FROM THE CROSS, AND GIVES UP THE GHOST.

THE solemn and awful period now approached, when the Son of God, the Redeemer of the world, was to undergo the oppressive burden of our sins, upon the tree, and submit unto death, even the death of the cross, that we might live at the right hand of God forever and ever.

Sentence being pronounced upon the blessed Jesus, the soldiers were ordered to prepare for his execution, a command which they readily obeyed; and, after clothing him in his own garments, led him away to crucify him. It is not said that they took the crown of thorns from his temples; probably he died wearing it, that the title placed over his head might be the better understood.

Being arrived at the place of execution, which was called Golgotha, or the Place of Skulls, from the criminal's bones which lay scattered there, some of our Redeemer's friends offered him a stupefying potion.

to render him insensible to the ignominy and excruciating pain of his punishment. But as soon as he tasted the potion, he refused to drink it, being determined to bear his sufferings, however sharp, not by intoxicating and stupefying himself, but by the strength of patience, fortitude, and faith. Jesus having refused the potion, the soldiers began to execute their orders, by stripping him quite naked, and in that condition began to fasten him to the cross. But while they were piercing his hands and his feet with nails, instead of crying out through the sharpness of the pain, he calmly, though fervently, prayed for them, and for all those who had any hand in his death; beseeching his heavenly Father to forgive them, and excusing them himself by the only circumstance that could alleviate their guilt — their ignorance. "Father," said the compassionate Redeemer of mankind, "forgive them; for they know not what they do." This was infinite meekness and goodness, truly worthy of the only begotten Son of God; an example of forgiveness, which, though it can never be equaled by any, should be imitated by all.

But, behold, the appointed soldiers dig the hole in which the cross is to be erected! — the cross is placed in the ground, the blessed Jesus lies on the bed of sorrows — they nail him to it — his nerves break — his blood distills — he hangs upon his wounds naked, a spectacle to heaven and earth! Thus was the only begotten Son of God, who came down from heaven to save the world, crucified by his own creatures; and, to render the ignominy still greater, placed between two thieves! "Hear, O heavens! O earth, earth, earth, hear! The Lord hath nourished and brought up children, and they have rebelled against him."

It was usual for the crimes committed by malefactors to be written on a white board, with black, and placed over their heads on the cross. In conformity to this custom, Pilate wrote a title in the Hebrew, Greek, and Latin languages, that all foreigners, as well as natives, might be able to read it, and fastened it to the cross, over the head of Jesus; and the inscription was, "This is the King of the Jews." But when the chief priests and elders had read this title, they were greatly displeased, because, as it represented the crime for which Jesus was condemned, it insinuated that he had been acknowledged for the Messiah. Besides, being placed over the head of one who was dying by the most infamous punishment, it implied that all who attempted to deliver the Jews should perish in the same manner. The faith and hope of the nation, therefore, being thus publicly ridiculed, it is no wonder that the priests thought themselves highly affronted, and accordingly came to Pilate, begging that the writing might be altered. But as he had intended the affront in revenge for their forcing him to crucify Jesus, contrary both to his judgment and inclination, he refused to grant their request: "What I have written," said he, "I have written."

When the soldiers had nailed the blessed Jesus to the cross, and erected it, they divided his garments among them. But his coat, or vesture, being without seam, woven from the top throughout, they agreed not to rend it, but to cast lots for it; by which the prediction of the prophet, concerning the death and sufferings of the Messiah, was fulfilled: "They parted my garments among them, and for my vesture did they cast lots." A sufficient indication that every circumstance of the death and passion of the blessed Jesus was perfectly known long before in the court of heaven; and accordingly, his being crucified between two malefactors was expressly foretold: "And he was numbered with the transgressors."

The common people, of the baser sort, whom the vile priests had incensed against the blessed Jesus, by the malicious falsehoods they had spread concerning him, and which they pretended to found on the deposition of witnesses; the common people, I say, seeing him hang in so infamous a manner upon the cross, and reading the inscription placed over his head, expressed their indignation at him by sarcastical expressions: "Ah! thou," said they, "that destroyest the temple, and buildest it in three days, save thyself, and come down from the cross!"

But the common people were not the only persons who mocked and derided the blessed Jesus, while he was suffering to obtain the remission of sins for all mankind. The rulers, who now imagined they had effectually destroyed his pretensions to the character of the Messiah, joined the populace in ridiculing him, and, with a meanness of soul which many infamous wretches would have scorned, mocked him, even while he was struggling with the agonies of death. They scoffed at the miracles by which he demonstrated himself to be the Messiah, and promised to believe on him, on condition of his proving his pretensions, by descending from the cross: "He saved others," said they, "himself he can not save; if he be the King of Israel, let him now come down from the cross, and we will believe on him." In the mean time, nothing could be more false and hypocritical than this pretension of the stiff-necked Jews; for they afterward continued in their unbelief, notwithstanding they well knew that he raised himself from the dead — a much greater miracle than his coming down from the cross would have been; a miracle attested by witnesses whose veracity they could could not call in question. It was told them by the soldiers, whom they themselves placed at the sepulchre to watch the body, and whom they were obliged to bribe largely to conceal the truth. It is therefore abundantly evident, that if the blessed Jesus had descended from the cross, the Jewish priests would have continued in their infidelity; and consequently, that their declaration was made with no other intention than to insult the Redeemer of mankind, thinking it impossible for him now to escape out of their hands.

The soldiers also joined in this general scene of mockery: "If thou be the King of the Jews," said they, "save thyself." If thou art the great Messiah expected by the Jews, descend from the cross by miracle, and deliver thyself from these excruciating torments. Nor did even one of the thieves forbear mocking the great Lord of heaven and earth, though laboring himself under the most racking pains, and struggling with the agonies of death. But the other exercised a most extraordinary faith, and at the time when our great Redeemer was in the highest affliction, mocked by men, and hanged on the cross, as the most ignominious of malefactors. This Jewish criminal seems to have entertained a more rational and exalted notion of the Messiah's kingdom, than even the disciples themselves. They expected nothing but a secular empire: he gave strong intimations of his having an idea of Christ's spiritual dominion; for, at the very time when Jesus was dying on the cross, he begged to be remembered by him when he came into his kingdom: "Lord," said he, "remember me when thou comest into thy kingdom." Nor did he make this request in vain: the great Redeemer of mankind answered him, "Verily, I say unto thee, to-day shalt thou be with me in Paradise."

But let us attentively consider the history of our blessed Saviour's passion, as it offers to our view events absolutely astonishing. For when we remember the perfect innocence of our great Redeemer, the uncommon love he bore to the children of men, and the many kind and benevolent offices he did for the sons and daughters of affliction; when we reflect on the esteem in which he was held all along by the common people, how cheerfully they followed him to the remotest corners of the country, nay, even into the desolate retreats of the wilderness, and with what pleasure they listened to his discourses; when we consider these particulars, I say, we can not help being astonished to find them at the conclusion rushing all of a sudden into the opposite extreme, and all, as it were, combined tc treat him with the most barbarous cruelty.

When Pilate asked the people, if they desired to have Jesus released, his disciples, though they were very numerous, and might have made a great appearance in his behalf, remained absolutely silent, as if they had been speechless or infatuated. The Roman soldiers, notwithstanding their general had declared him innocent, insulted him in the most inhuman manner. The scribes and Pharisees ridiculed him. The common people, who had received him with hosannas a few days before, mocked him as they passed by, and railed at him as a deceiver. Nay, the very thief on the cross reviled him. This sudden revolution in the humor of the whole nation may seem unaccountable. But if we could assign a proper reason for the silence of the disciples, the principles which influenced the rest might be discovered in their several speeches. The followers of the blessed Jesus had attached themselves to him in expectation of being raised to great wealth and power in his kingdom, which they expected would have been established long before this time; but seeing no appearance at all of what they had so long hoped for, they permitted him to be condemned, perhaps because they thought it would have obliged him to break the Roman yoke by a miracle.

With respect to the soldiers, they were angry that any one should pretend to royalty in Judea, where Cæsar had established his authority. Hence they insulted our blessed Saviour with the title of king, and paid him, in mockery, the honors of a sovereign. As for the common people, they seem to have lost their opinion of him, probably because he had neither convinced the council, nor rescued himself when they condemned him. They began, therefore, to consider the assertion of his destroying the temple, and building it in three days, as a kind of blasphemy, because it required a divine power to execute such an undertaking.

The priests and scribes were filled with the most implacable and diabolical malice against him; because he had torn off their mask of hypocrisy, and showed them to the people in their true colors. It is, therefore, no wonder that they ridiculed his miracles, from whence he derived his reputation. In short, the thief also fancied that he might have delivered both himself and them, if he had been the Messiah; but, as no such deliverance appeared, he upbraided him for making pretensions to that high character.

But now, my soul, take one view of thy dying Saviour, breathing out his spirit upon the cross! Behold his unspotted flesh lacerated with stripes, by which thou art healed! See his hands extended and nailed to the cross, those beneficent hands which were incessantly stretched out to unloose thy heavy burdens, and to impart blessings of every kind! Behold his feet riveted to the accursed tree with nails! those feet which always went about doing good, and traveled far and near to spread the glad tidings of everlasting salvation! View his tender temples encircled with a wreath of thorns, which shoot their keen afflicting points into his blessed head — that head which was ever meditating peace to poor, lost, and undone sinners, and spent many a wakeful night in ardent prayer for their happiness! See him laboring in the agonies of death! breathing out his soul into the hands of his Almighty Father, and praying for his cruel enemies! Was ever love like this? was ever benevolence so gloriously displayed?

But see, the sun, that glorious luminary of heaven, as it were, hides his face from this detestable action of mortals, and is wrapt in the pitchy mantle of chaotic darkness! This preternatural eclipse of the sun continued for three hours, to the great terror and astonishment of the people present at the crucifixion of our dear Redeemer. And surely nothing could be more proper than this extraordinary alteration in the face of nature, while the Son of righteousness was withdrawing his beams, not only from the promised land, but from the whole world; for it was at once a miraculous testimony, given by the Almighty himself, to the innocence of his Son, and a proper emblem of the departure of him who was the light of the world, at least, till his luminous rays, like beams of the morning, shone out anew with additional splendor in the ministry of his apostles.

Nor was the darkness which now covered Judea and the neighboring countries, beginning about noon and continuing till Jesus expired, the effect of an ordinary eclipse of the sun. It is well known that this phenomenon can only happen at the change of the moon; whereas the Jewish passover, at which our great Redeemer suffered, was always celebrated at the full. Besides, the total darkness of an eclipse of the sun never exceeds twelve or fifteen minutes; whereas this continued full three hours. Nothing, therefore, but the immediate hand of that Almighty Being which placed the sun in the center of the planetary system, could have produced this extraordinary darkness; nothing but Omnipotence, who first lighted this glorious luminary of heaven, could have deprived it of its cheering rays. Now, ye scoffers of Israel, whose blood ye have so earnestly desired, and wished it might fall upon you and your children, behold, all nature is dressed in the sable veil of sorrow, and, in a language that can not be mistaken, mourns the departure of its Lord and Master: weeps for your crimes, and deprecates the vengeance of Heaven upon your guilty heads. Happy for you that this suffering Jesus is compassion itself, and even in the agonies of death prays to his heavenly Father to avert from you the stroke of his justice.

This preternatural eclipse of the sun was considered

as a miracle by the heathens themselves; and one of them cried out, "Either the world is at an end, or the God of nature suffers." And well might he use the expression; for never since this planetary system was called from its primative chaos, was known such a deprivation of light in the glorious luminary of day. Indeed, when the Almighty punished Pharaoh for refusing to let the children of Israel depart out of his land, and the sable veil of darkness was for three days drawn over Egypt, the darkness was confined to a part of that kingdom; whereas this that happened at our Saviour's crucifixion was universal.

When the darkness began, the disciples naturally considered it as a prelude to the deliverance of their Master. For, though the chief priests, elders, and people had sarcastically desired him to descend from the accursed tree, his friends could not but be persuaded, that he who had delivered so many from incurable diseases, who had restored limbs to the maimed and eyes to the blind, who had given speech to the dumb, and called the dead from the chambers of the dust, might easily save himself, even from the cross. When, therefore, his mother, his mother's sister, Mary Magdalene, and the beloved disciple, observed the veil of darkness begin to extend over the face of nature, they drew near to the foot of the cross, probably in expectation that the Son of God was going to shake the frame of the universe, unloose himself from the cross, and take ample vengeance on his cruel and perfidious enemies. The blessed Jesus was now in the midst of his sufferings; yet, when he saw his mother and her companions, their grief greatly affected his tender breast especially the distress of his mother. The agonies of death, under which he was now laboring, could not prevent his expressing the most affectionate regard, both for her and for them. For, that she might have some consolation to support her under the greatness of her sorrows, he told her the disciple whom he loved would, for the sake of that love, supply his place to her after he was taken from them, even the place of a son; and, therefore, he desired her to consider him as such, and expect from him all the duties of a child. "Woman," said he, "behold thy son."

But now the moment, when he should resign his soul into the hands of his heavenly Father, approached, and he repeated part, at least, of the twenty-second Psalm, uttering with a loud voice, these remarkable words, "Eloi, eloi, lama sabacthani?" that is, "My God, my God, why hast thou forsaken me?"

Some believe that our blessed Saviour repeated the vhole Psalm; it having been the custom of the Jews, n making quotations, to mention only the first words of the Psalm or section which they cited. If so, as his Psalm contains the most remarkable particulars of our dear Redeemer's passion, being, as it were, a ummary of the prophecies relating to that subject, by epeating it on the cross, the blessed Jesus signified hat he was now accomplishing the things that were predicted concerning the Messiah. And as this Psalm s composed in the form of a prayer, by pronouncing t at this time, he also claimed of his Father the perormance of all the promises he had made, whether to im or to his people.

Some of the people who stood by, when they heard ur blessed Saviour pronounce the first words of the Psalm, misunderstood him, probably from their not hearing him distinctly, and concluded that he called for Elias. Upon which one of them filled a sponge with vinegar, put it on a reed, and gave it to him to drink; being desirous to keep him alive as long as possible, to see whether Elias would come to take him down from the cross. But as soon as Jesus had tasted the vinegar, he said, "It is finished;" that is, the work of man's redemption is accomplished; the great work, which the only begotten Son of God came into the world to perform, is finished. In speaking these words, he cried with an exceeding loud voice; and afterward addressed his Almighty Father, in words which form the best pattern of a recommendatory prayer at the hour of death, "Father, into thy hands I commend my spirit." And, having uttered these words, "he bowed his head, and yielded up the ghost."

But behold: at the very instant the blessed Jesus resigned his soul into the hands of his heavenly Father, the veil of the temple was miraculously rent from the top to the bottom, probably in the presence of the priest who burnt incense in the holy place, and who, doubtless, published the account when he came out for our blessed Saviour expired at the ninth hour, the very time of offering the evening sacrifice.

Nor was this the only miracle that happened at the death of the great Messiah: the earth trembled from its very foundation; the flinty rocks burst asunder and the sepulchres hewn in them were opened; and many bodies of saints deposited there, awaked, after his resurrection, from the sleep of death, left the gloomy chambers of the tomb, went into the city of Jerusalem, and appeared unto many.

CHAPTER XXXI.

ʼHE BLESSED JESUS TREATED WITH INDIGNITY AFTER HIS CRUCIFIXION — A PIOUS PERSON BEGS HIS BODY FROM PILATE IN ORDER FOR INTERMENT

IT was expressly forbidden by the law of Moses, that the bodies of those who were hanged should remain ll night on the tree. In conformity to this law, and ecause the Sabbath was at hand, the Jews begged the overnor that the legs of the three persons crucified night be broken, to hasten their death. To this request ilate readily consented; and, accordingly, gave the ecessary order to the soldiers to put it in execution. ut on perceiving that Jesus was already dead, the oldiers did not give themselves the trouble of breaking is legs, as they had done those of the two malefactors at were crucified with him. One of them, howevei, ither out of wantonness or cruelty, thrust a spear into is side, and out of the wound flowed blood and water. This wound, therefore, was of the greatest impor- nce to mankind, as it abundantly demonstrated the uth of our Saviour's death, and consequently pre- ented all objections that the enemies to our holy faith ould otherwise have raised against it. The evangelist dds, that the legs of our great Redeemer were not broken, but his side was pierced, that two particular prophecies might be fulfilled: "A bone of him shall not be broken;" and "They shall look on him whom they have pierced."

Among the disciples of Jesus, was one called Joseph of Arimathea, a person equally remarkable for his birth, fortune, and office. This man, who was not to be intimidated by the malice of his countrymen, went boldly to Pilate, and begged the body of his great Master. He had, indeed, nothing to fear from the Roman governor, who, during the whole course of our Saviour's trial, had shown the greatest inclination to release him; but he had reason to apprehend that this action might draw down upon him the malice of the rulers of the Jews, who had taken such great pains to get the Messiah crucified. However, the great regard he had for the remains of his Master, made him despise the malice of the Jews; being persuaded that Omnipotence would defend him, and cover his enemies with shame and confusion. And he well knew, that if no friend procured a grant of the body, it would be ignominiously cast out among the executed malefactors.

Pilate was at first surprised at the request of Joseph thinking it highly improbable that he should be dead in so short a time. He had, indeed, given orders for the soldiers to break the legs of the crucified persons but he knew it was common for them to live many hours after that operation was performed; for, though the pain they felt must have been exquisite to the last degree, yet, as the vital parts remained untouched, life would continue some time in the miserable body.

The governor, therefore, called the centurion, to know the truth of what Joseph had told him; and being convinced, from the answer of that officer, that Jesus had been dead some time, he readily gave the body to Joseph.

This worthy counselor having obtained his request, repaired to Mount Calvary; and being assisted by Nicodemus, took the body down from the cross. The latter was formerly so cautious in visiting Jesus, that he came to him by night. But, in paying the last duties to his Master, he used no art to conceal his design; he showed a courage far superior to that of any of his apostles, not only assisting Joseph in taking down the body of Jesus from the cross, but bringing with him a quantity of spices necessary in the burial of our Saviour. Accordingly, they wrapped the body with the spices, in fine linen, and laid it in a new sepulchre, which Joseph had hewn out of a rock for himself. This sepulchre was situated in a garden near Mount Calvary; and, in which having carefully deposited the body of the blessed Jesus, they fastened the door, by rolling to it a very large stone. "And when Joseph had taken the body, he wrapped it in a clean linen cloth, and laid it in his own new tomb, which he had hewn out in the rock: and he rolled a great stone to the door of the sepulchre, and departed." Matt. xxvii: 59, 60.

The women of Galilee, who had watched their Redeemer in his last moments, and accompanied his body to the sepulchre, observing that the funeral rites were performed in a hurry, agreed among themselves, as soon as the Sabbath was past, to return to the sepulchre, and embalm the body of our Saviour, by anointing and swathing him in the manner then common among the Jews. Accordingly, they retired to the city, and purchased the spices necessary for that purpose, Nicodemus having furnished only a portion of them.

During these transactions, the chief priests and Pharisees, remembering that Jesus had more than once predicted his own resurrection, came to the governor, and informed him of it; begging, at the same time, that a guard might be placed at the sepulchre, lest his disciples should carry away the body, and affirm that he was risen from the dead. This happened a little before it was dark in the evening, called the next day that followed, by the evangelist, because the Jewish day began at sunset.

This request being thought reasonable by Pilate, he gave them leave to take as many soldiers as they pleased out of the cohort, which, at the feast, came from the castle of Antonia, and kept guard of the porticoes of the temple. For, that they were not Jewish but Roman soldiers, whom the priests employed to watch the sepulchre, is evident from their asking them of the governor. Besides, when the soldiers returned with the news of our Saviour's resurrection, the priests desired them to report that his disciples had stolen him away while they slept; and, to encourage them to tell the falsehood boldly, promised, that if their neglect of duty came to the governor's ears, proper methods should be used to pacify him, and deliver them from any punishment: a promise which there was no need of making to their own servants.

The priests having thus obtained a guard of Roman soldiers, men long accustomed to military duties, and therefore the most proper for watching the body, set out with them to the sepulchre; and, to prevent these guards from combining with the disciples in carrying on any fraud, placed them at their post, and sealed the stone which was rolled to the door of the sepulchre.

Thus, what was designed to expose the mission and doctrine of Jesus, as rank falsehood and vile imposture, proved, in fact, the strongest confirmation of the truth and divinity of the same that could possibly be given; and placed what they wanted to refute (which was his resurrection from the dead) even beyond a doubt.

CHAPTER XXXII.

TWO PIOUS WOMEN GO TO VIEW THE SEPULCHRE OF THEIR CRUCIFIED LORD AND SAVIOUR—AN AWFUL PHENOMENON HAPPENS—A MINISTERING SPIRIT DESCENDS—THE REDEEMER BURSTS THE CHAINS OF DEATH, AND RISES FROM THE TOMB.

VERY early in the morning, after the Sabbath, Mary Magdalene, and the other Mary, came to visit the sepulchre, in order to embalm our Lord's body; for the performance of which they had, in concert with several other women from Galilee, brought ointments and spices. But before they reached the sepulchre, there was a great earthquake preceding the most memorable event that ever happened among the children of men, the resurrection of the Son of God from the dead. "For the angel of the Lord descended from heaven, and came and rolled back the stone from the door of the sepulchre, and sat upon it; his countenance was like lightning, and his raiment white as snow; and for fear of him, the keepers did shake, and became as dead men:" they fled into the city, and the Saviour of the world rose from the dead.

The angel, who had till then sat upon the stone, quitted his station, and entered into the sepulchre. In the mean time, Mary Magdalene, and the other Mary, were still on their way to the place, together with Salome, who joined them on the road. As they proceeded on their way, they consulted among themselves, with regard to the method of putting their design of embalming the body of their Master into execution; particularly with respect to the enormous stone which they had seen placed there, with the utmost difficulty, two days before, "Who," said they, "shall roll away the stone from the door of the sepulchre?" But, in the midst of this deliberation, about removing this great and sole obstacle to their design, (for it does not appear they knew anything of the guard,) they lifted up their eyes, and perceived it was already rolled away.

Alarmed at so extraordinary and unexpected a circumstance, Mary Magdalene concluded, that the stone could not have been rolled away without some design; and that those who rolled it away could have no other intent than that of removing our Lord's body. Imagining, by appearances, that they had really done so, she ran immediately to acquaint Peter and John of what she had seen, and what she suspected; leaving Mary and Salome there, that if the other women should arrive during her absence, they might acquaint them with their surprise, at finding the stone removed, and of Mary Magdalene's running to inform the apostles of it.

In the mean time, the soldiers, who were terrified at seeing an awful messenger from on high roll away the stone from the door of the sepulchre, and open it in quality of a servant, fled into the city, and informed the Jewish rulers of these miraculous appearances. This account was highly mortifying to the chief priests, as it was a proof of our Saviour's resurrection that could not be denied: they therefore resolved to stifle it immediately; and accordingly bribed the soldiers to conceal the real fact, and to publish every where, that his disciples had stolen the body out of the sepulchre.

While Mary Magdalene was going to inform the disciples that the stone was rolled away from the mouth of the sepulchre, and the body taken away, Mary and Salome continued advancing toward the place, and at their arrival found what they expected — the body of their beloved Master gone from the sepulchre, where it had been deposited by Nicodemus and Joseph of Arimathea; but at the same time beheld, to their great astonishment, a beautiful young man in shining raiment, very glorious to behold, sitting on the right side of the sepulchre.

Matthew tells us, that it was the angel who had rolled away the stone, and frightened away the guards from the sepulchre. It seems he had now laid aside the terrors in which he was then arrayed, and assumed the form and dress of a human being, in order that these pious women, who had accompanied our Saviour during the greatest part of the time of his public ministry, might be as little terrified as possible.

But, notwithstanding his beauty and benign appearance, they were greatly affrighted, and on the point of turning back, when the heavenly messenger, to banish their fears, told them, in a gentle accent, that he knew their errand. "Fear not," said he, "for I know that ye seek Jesus who was crucified. He is not here; for he is risen, as he said:" and then invited them to come down into the sepulchre, and view the place where the Son of God had lain; that is, to look on the linen clothes, and the napkin that had been about his head, and which he had left behind him when he arose from the dead; for, to look at the place in any other view, would not have tended to confirm their faith of his resurrection. The women, greatly encouraged by the agreeable news, as well as the peculiar accent with which this blessed messenger from the heavenly Canaan delivered his speech, went down into the sepulchre, when, behold, another of the angelic choir appeared. They did not, however, yet seem to give sufficient credit to what was told them by the angel; and therefore the other gently reproved them for seeking the living among the dead, with an intention to do him an office due only to the latter, and for not believing what was told them by a messenger from heaven, or rather for not remembering the words which their great Master himself had told them with regard to his own resurrection: "Why seek ye the living among the dead? He is not here, but is risen; remember how he spake unto you when he was yet in Galilee, saying, The Son of Man must be delivered into the hands of sinful men, and be crucified, and the third day rise again."

When the women had satisfied their minds by looking at the place where the Lord had lain, and where nothing was to be found but the linen clothes, the angel who first appeared to them resumed the discourse, and bade them go and tell his disciples, particularly Peter, the glad tidings of his Master's resurrection from the dead: that he was going before them to Galilee; and that they should there have the pleasure of seeing him.

The reason why the disciples were ordered to go into Galilee, to meet their great and beloved Master, seems to be this: they were most of them at Jerusalem, celebrating the passover; and it may be easily imagined that, on receiving the news of their Lord's resurrection, many, if not all would resolve to tarry at Jerusalem, in expectation of meeting him there: a thing that must have proven of great detriment to them at that time of the year, when the harvest was about to begin, the sheaf of first-fruits being always offered on the second day of the passover week. In order, therefore, to prevent their staying so long from home, the message was sent directing them to return into Galilee, with full assurance that they should there have the pleasure of seeing their Lord and Master: and by that means have all their doubts removed, and be fully convinced that he had patiently undergone all his sufferings for the sins of mankind. The women, highly elated with the news of their Lord's resurrection, left the sepulchre immediately, and ran to carry the disciples the glad tidings.

During these transactions at the sepulchre, Peter and John, having been informed by Mary Magdalene that the stone was rolled away, and the body of Jesus not to be found, were hastening to the grave, and missed the women who had seen the appearance of angels.

The disciples being astonished at what Mary Magdalene had told them, and desirous of having their doubts cleared up, made all possible haste to the sepulchre; and John, being younger than Peter, arrived at the place first, but did not go in, contenting himself with stooping down, and seeing the linen clothes lying, which had been wrapped about the Saviour's body. Peter soon arrived, and went to the sepulchre, where he saw the linen clothes, and the napkin that was about his head not lying with the linen clothes, but wrapped together in a place by itself. Our Lord left the grave-clothes in the sepulchre, probably, to show that his body was not stolen away by his disciples, who, in such a case, would not have taken time to have stripped it. Besides, the circumstance of the grave-clothes induced the disciples themselves to believe, when the resurrection was related to them. But at that time they had no suspicion that he was risen from the dead.

These two disciples having thus satisfied themselves that what Mary Magdalene had told them was really true, returned to their respective habitations; but Mary, who had returned, continued weeping at the door of the sepulchre. She had, it seems, followed Peter and John to the garden, but did not leave it with them, being anxious to find the body. Accordingly, stepping down into the place to examine it once more, she saw two angels sitting, the one at the head and the other at the feet, where the body of Jesus had lain. They were now in the same position as when they appeared to the other women; but had rendered themselves invisible while Peter and John were at the sepulchre. Mary, on beholding these heavenly messengers dressed in the robes of light, was greatly terrified. But they, in the most endearing accent, asked her, "Woman, why weepest thou? To which she answered, Because they have taken away my Lord, and I know not where they have laid him." On pronouncing these words, she turned herself about, and saw Jesus standing near her; but the terror she was in, and the garments in which he was now dressed, prevented her from knowing him for some time. Jesus repeated the same question used before by the angel, "Woman, why weepest thou?" To which Mary, who now supposed him to be the gardener, answered, Sir if his body be troublesome in the sepulchre, and thou hast removed him, tell me where he is deposited, and I will take him away. But our blessed Saviour, willing to remove her anxiety, called her by name, with his usual tone of voice; on which she immediately knew him, and falling down before him, would have embraced his knees, according to that modesty and reverence with which the women of the east saluted the men, especially those who were their superiors in station. But Jesus refused this compliment, telling her that he was not going immediately into heaven. He was often to show himself to the disciples before he ascended; so that she would have frequent opportunities of testifying her regard to him. And, at the same time, said to her, "Go to my brethren, and say unto them, I ascend to my Father and your Father, and to my God and your God. Thus did the blessed Jesus contemplate, with a singular pleasure, the work of redemption he had just finished. The happy relation between God and man, which had been long canceled by sin, was now renewed.

The women, on their arrival, told as many of the disciples as they could find, that they had seen at the sepulchre the appearance of angels, who assured them that Jesus was risen from the dead. This new information astonished the disciples exceedingly; and as they had before sent Peter and John to examine into the truth of what Mary Magdalene had told them, concerning the body being removed out of the sepulchre, so they now judged it highly proper to send some of of their number to see the angels, and learn from them the joyful tidings of that great transaction, of which the women had given them an account. That this was really the case, appears from what the disciples, in their journey to Emmaus, told their great Lord and

Master; namely, that when the women came and told them that they had seen the angels, certain of their number went to the sepulchre, and found it even as the women had said, but him they saw not.

The second deputation from the apostles did not go alone; for, as Mary Magdalene returned with Peter and John, who were sent to examine the truth of her information, so the women who brought an account of the appearance of angels, in all probability returned with those who were sent to be witnesses of the truth of their report. Besides curiosity, they had an errand thither: the angels had expressly ordered them to tell the news to Peter in particular; for which reason, when they understood that he was gone to the sepulchre, it is natural to think they would return with the disciples to seek him. About the time that the disciples and women set out from the sepulchre, Peter and John reached the city; but passing through a different street, did not meet their brethren. The disciples having a great desire to reach the place, soon left the women behind; and, just as they arrived, Mary Magdalene, having seen the Lord, was coming away. But they did not meet her, because they entered the the garden at one door, while she was coming out at another. When they came to the sepulchre, they saw the angels, and received from them the news of their blessed Master's resurrection; for St. Luke tells us, "They found it even as the women had said." Highly elated with what they saw, they departed, and ran back to the city, with such expedition, that they gave an account of what they had seen in the hearing of the two disciples, before Mary Magdalene arrived.

In the mean time, the company of women, who

followed the disciples, happened to meet Peter and John. But they had not gone far from the sepulchre, before Jesus himself met them, and said, "All hail!" On which they approached their great Lord and Master, held him by the feet, and worshiped him. The favor of embracing his knees, Jesus had before refused to Mary Magdalene, because it was not then necessary; but he granted it to the women, because the angels' words having strongly impressed their minds with the notion of his resurrection, they might have taken his appearance for an illusion of their own imagination, had he not permitted them to touch him, and convince themselves, by the united reports of their senses, that he was their great Lord and Master, who was then risen from the dead, after having suffered on the cross for the sins of mankind.

This company of pious women having tarried some time with Jesus on the road, did not arrive with the joyful tidings of their great Master's resurrection, till some time after Peter and John; and perhaps were overtaken by Mary Magdalene on the road, unless we suppose that she arrived a few minutes before them.

The disciples were now lost in astonishment at what the women had related; they considered the account they had before given them, of their having seen the angels, as an improbability, and now they seem to have considered this as something worse; for the evangelist tells us, that they "believed not."

Peter, indeed, to whom the angel had sent the message, was disposed, by his sanguine temper, to give a little more credit to their words than the rest; possibly, because the messengers from the heavenly Canaan had done him the honor of naming him in particular.

Elated with the respect thus paid him, he immediately repaired again to the sepulchre; hoping, in all probability, that his Master would appear to him; or at least, the angel who had so particularly distinguished him from the rest of his disciples. As soon as Peter arrived at the sepulchre, he stooped down, and seeing the linen clothes lying in the same manner as before, he viewed their position, the form in which they were laid, and returned, wondering greatly in himself at what had happened.

CHAPTER XXXIII.

JESUS APPEARS ON DIVERS OCCASIONS, TO DIFFERENT DISCIPLES — REPROVES AND CONVINCES THOMAS OF HIS UNBELIEF — SHOWS HIMSELF TO A GREAT NUMBER OF HIS FOLLOWERS IN GALILEE.

SOON after the women's first return to the disciples with the news of their having seen the appearance of angels, who told them that Jesus had risen from the dead, two of the disciples departed on their journey to a village called Emmaus, about two miles distant from Jerusalem. The concern they were in, on account of the death of their great and beloved Master, was sufficiently visible in their countenances; and, as they pursued their journey, talking one with another, and debating about the things that had lately happened among them, concerning the life and doctrine, the sufferings and death of the holy Jesus, and of the report that was just spread among his disciples, of his being that very morning risen from the dead, Jesus himself overtook them, and joined company with them.

As he appeared like a stranger, they did not in the least suspect that their fellow-traveler was no other than the great Redeemer of the sons of men. He soon entered into discourse with them, by inquiring what event had so closely engaged them in conversation, and why they appeared so sorrowful and dejected, as if they had met with some heavy disappointment? One of them, whose name was Cleophas, being surprised at the question, replied, Is it possible that you can be so great a stranger to the affairs of the world, as to have been at Jerusalem, and not have heard the surprising events that have happened there? Events that have astonished the whole city, and are now the constant topic of conversation among all the inhabitants? Jesus asked, what surprising events he meant. To which Cleophas replied, The transactions which have happened concerning Jesus of Nazareth, who appeared as a great prophet and teacher sent from God; and accordingly was highly venerated among the people, for the excellency of his doctrine, his humility of life, and the number, benefit, and greatness of his miracles. Our chief priests and elders, therefore, envying him as one who lessened their authority over the people, apprehended him, and found means to put him to death. But we firmly believed he would have proved himself the Messiah, or great Deliverer; and this persuasion we a long time supported; nor were we willing to abandon it, even when we saw him put to death. But it is now three days since these things were done; and, therefore, we begin to fear we were mistaken. This very morning, indeed, a thing happened, which extremely surprised us, and we were very solicitous with regard to it. Some women, who had entertained the same hopes and expectations as we, going early in the morning to pay the last duties to their Master, by embalming his body, returned with great haste to the city, and informed us, that they had been at the sepulchre, but were disappointed in not finding the body; and to increase our surprise, they added, that they had seen the appearance of angels, who had told them that Jesus was risen from the dead. This relation seemed, at first, to us not probable, nay, altogether incredible; but, two of the company going immediately after to the sepulchre, found every thing exactly as the women had reported: they saw the angels, but heard not anything of the body; so that we are still in doubt and perplexity with regard to this wonderful event.

In reply, Jesus said, Why are ye so very averse to believe all that the prophets have, with one voice, predicted of the Messiah? Is it not clearly and very expressly foretold, in all the prophetic writings, that it was appointed by the counsel of Omnipotence for the Messiah to suffer in this manner; and that, after sustaining the greatest indignities, reproaches, and contempt, from the malice and perverseness of mankind, and even undergoing an ignominious and cruel death, he should be exalted to a glorious and eternal kingdom? Having said this, he began at the writings of Moses, and explained to them, in order, all the principal passages, both in the books of that great legislator, and the writings of the other prophets, relating to his own sufferings, death, and glorious resurrection.

And this he did with such surprising plainness, clearness, and strength, that the two disciples, not yet suspecting who he was, were as much amazed to find a stranger so well acquainted with all that Jesus did and suffered, as they at first wondered at his appearing to be so totally ignorant of these transactions. They were also astonished to hear him interpret and apply the Scriptures to their present purpose, with such readiness and convincing clearness of argument, as carried with it a strange and unusual authority and efficacy. When, therefore, they came to the village whither they were going, and Jesus seemed as if he would have passed on, and traveled farther, they, desirous of his company, pressed him, in the strongest manner, to tarry with them that night, as it was then late. To this request the great Redeemer of mankind consented; and when they were sat down to supper, he took bread, and gave thanks to God, and brake it, and gave it to them in the same manner he used to do, while he conversed with them upon earth, before his death. This engaged their attention, and looking steadfastly on him, they perceived it was their great and beloved Master. But they had then no time to express their joy and astonishment to their benevolent Redeemer; for he immediately vanished out of their sight.

As soon as they found their Master was departed, they said one to another, How slow and stupid were we before, not to know him upon the road, while he explained to us the Scriptures; when, besides the affability of his discourse, and the strength and clearness of his argument, we perceived such an authority in what he said, and such a powerful efficacy attending his words, and even striking our hearts with affection, that we could not but have known him (if we had not been remarkably stupid) to have been the very same that used to acccompany his teaching, and was peculiar to it! This surprising event would not permit them to stay any longer in Emmaus. They returned that very night to Jerusalem, and found the apostles, with several other disciples, discoursing about the resurrection of their Master; and, on their entering the room, the disciples accosted them, saying, "The Lord is risen indeed, and hath appeared unto Simon."

They had given little credit to the reports of the women, supposing they were occasioned more by imagination than reality. But when a person of Peter's capacity and gravity declared he had seen the Lord, they began to think that he was really risen from the dead. And their belief was greatly confirmed by the arrival of the two disciples from Emmaus, who declared to their brethren, how Jesus appeared to them on the road, and how they discovered him to be their Master, by the circumstances before related. While the disciples from Emmaus were thus describing the manner of the appearance of Jesus to them, and offering arguments to convince those who doubted the truth of it, their great Master himself put an end to the debate, by standing in the midst of them, and saying, "Peace be unto you."

This appearance of our blessed Saviour greatly terrified the disciples, who supposed they had seen a spirit; for, having secured the doors of the house where they were assembled, for fear of the Jews, and Jesus having opened the locks by his miraculous power, without the knowledge of any in the house, it was natural for them to think that a spirit only could enter. The circumstance, therefore, of the doors being shut, is very happily mentioned by St. John; because it suggests a reason why the disciples took their Master for a spirit, notwithstanding many of them were convinced that he was really risen from the dead, and were at that moment conversing about his resurrection. But to dispel their fears and doubts, Jesus came forward and spoke to tnem in the most endearing manner, showed them his hands and feet, and desired them to handle him, in order to convince themselves, by the united powers of their different senses, that it was he himself, and no spectre or apparition. "Why are ye troubled," said the benevolent Redeemer of mankind, "and why do thoughts arise in your hearts? Behold my hands and my feet, that it is I myself: handle me and see, for a spirit hath not flesh and bones as ye see me have." These infallible proofs sufficiently convinced the disciples of the truth of their Lord's resurrection, and they received him with rapture and exultation. But their joy and wonder had so great an effect upon their minds, that some of them, sensible of the great commotion they were in, suspended their belief, till they had considered the matter more calmly. Jesus, therefore, knowing their thoughts, called for meat, and ate with them, in order to prove more fully the truth of his resurrection from the dead, and the reality of his presence with them on this occasion.

After giving this farther ocular demonstration of his having vanquished the power of death, and opened the tremendous portals of the grave, he again repeated his salutation, "Peace be unto you:" adding, "The same commission that my Father hath given unto me, I give unto you: go ye therefore into every part of the world, and preach the gospel to all the children of men." Then breathing on them he said, Receive ye the Holy Ghost, to direct and assist you in the execution of your commission. Whosoever embraces your doctrine, sincerely repents, and believes on me, ye shall declare unto him the free forgiveness of his sins, and your declaration shall be ratified and confirmed in the courts of heaven. And whosoever either obstinately rejects your doctrine, disobeys it, or behaves himself unworthily after he hath embraced it, his sins shall not be forgiven him; but the censure ye shall pass upon him on earth, shall be confirmed in heaven.

Thomas, otherwise called Didymus, was absent at the meeting of the apostles; nor did this happen without the special direction of Providence, that the particular and extraordinary satisfaction which was afterward granted him, might be an abundant and undeniable testimony of the truth of our blessed Saviour's resurrection to all succeeding generations. The rest of the apostles, therefore, told him, that they had seen the Lord, and repeated to him the words he had delivered in their hearing. But Thomas replied, This event is of such great importance, that unless, to prevent all possibility of deception, I see him with mine own eyes, and feel him with mine own hands, putting my fingers into the print of the nails, whereby he was fastened to the cross, and thrust my hand into his side, which the soldiers pierced with the spear, I will not believe that he is really and truly risen from the dead.

Eight days after the resurrection of our great Redeemer, the blessed Jesus showed himself again to his disciples, while Thomas was with them, and upbraided that disciple for his unbelief; but knowing that it did not, like that of the Pharisees, proceed from a wicked mind, but from an honest heart, and a sincere desire of being satisfied of the truth, he thus addressed himself to his doubting disciple: "Thomas," said he, "since thou wilt not be contented to rely on the testimony of others, but must be convinced by the experience of thine own senses, behold the wounds in my hands, and reach hither thy hand, and thrust it into my side, and doubt no longer of the reality of my resurrection." Thomas was immediately induced to believe, by the invitation of his dear Master, and being fully satisfied, he cried out, "I am abundantly convinced; thou art, indeed, my Lord, the very same that was crucified; and I acknowledge thine Almighty power in having triumphed over death, and worship thee as my God." To which the blessed Jesus replied, "Because thou hast seen me, Thomas, thou hast believed that I am really risen from the dead. But blessed are they who, without such evidence of the senses, shall, upon credible testimony, be willing to believe and embrace a doctrine which tends so greatly to the glory of God, and the salvation of the sons of men."

St. John adds, that the blessed Jesus appeared, on several other occasions, to his disciples, after his resurrection; and, by many clear and infallible proofs, (not mentioned by the evangelist,) fully convinced them that he was alive after his passion. But those which are mentioned are abundantly sufficient to excite men to believe that Jesus was the Son of God, the great Messiah so often foretold by the ancient prophets; and, by means of that belief they may attain everlasting life in the happy regions of the heavenly Canaan.

Our blessed Saviour having, first by the angels, and afterward in person, ordered his disciples to repair to their respective habitations in Galilee, it is reasonable to think they would leave Jerusalem as soon as possible. This they accordingly did, and on their arrival at their respective places of abode, applied themselves to their usual occupations; and the apostles returned to their old trade of fishing, on the lake of Tiberias.

Here they were toiling with their nets very early in the morning, and saw Jesus standing on the shore, but did not then know him to be their Master, as it was somewhat dark, and they at a considerable distance from him. He, however, called to them, and asked if they had taken any fish? To which they answered, they had caught nothing. He then desired them to let down their net on the right side of the boat, and they should not be disappointed. The disciples, imagining that he might be acquainted with the places proper for fishing, did as he directed them, and inclosed in their net such a prodigious multitude of fishes, that they were not able to draw it into the boat, but were forced to drag it after them toward the shore.

It seems, they had toiled all the preceding night to no purpose; and, therefore, such remarkable success could not fail of causing various conjectures among them, with regard to the stranger on the shore, who had given them such happy advice. Some of the apostles declared they could not imagine who he was; but others were persuaded that this person was no other than their great and beloved Master. John was fully convinced of his being the Lord, and accordingly told his thoughts to Simon Peter, who, making no doubt of it, girded on his fisher's coat, and leaped into the sea, in order to get ashore sooner than the boat could be brought to land, dragging after it a net full of large fishes.

When the disciples came ashore, they found a fire kindled, and on it a fish broiling, and near it some bread. But neither being sufficient for the company, Jesus bade them bring some of the fish they had now caught, and invited them to eat with him. Thus did the blessed Jesus prove again to his disciples the reality of his resurrection; not only by eating with them, but by working a miracle like that which, at the beginning of his ministry, had made such an impression upon them, as disposed them to be his constant followers. This was the third time that Jesus appeared publicly to a great number of his disciples in a body besides showing himself several times to particular persons, upon special occasions.

When they had eaten, Jesus reminded Peter how diligent and zealous he ought to be in order to wipe off the stain of his denying him when he was carried before the high priest: "Simon, son of Jonas," said our blessed Saviour to him, "Art thou more zealous and affectionate in thy love toward me than the rest of my disciples?" To which Peter answered, "Yea, Lord, thou knowest that I love thee." He was taught modesty and diffidence by his late fall; and therefore would not compare himself with others, but humbly appealed to his Master's omniscience, for the sincerity of his regard to him. Jesus answered, "Express then thy love toward me by the care of my flock committed to thy charge. 'Feed my lambs; feed my sheep.' Show thy love to me, by publishing the great salvation I have accomplished, and feeding the souls of faithful believers with that food which never perishes, but endures forever and ever. I well know, indeed," continued the blessed Jesus, "that thou wilt continue my faithful shepherd, even until death. For the time will come, when thou, who now girdest on thy fisher's coat voluntarily, and stretchest out thy hand to come to me, shalt, in thine old age, be girt by others, and forced to stretch out thy hands against thy will, in a very different manner, for the sake of thy constant profession of my religion."

By these last words, Jesus signified the manner of Peter's death, and that he should finally suffer martyrdom, for the glory of God, and testimony of the truth of the Christian religion.

The time being now come when the disciples were to meet their great Lord and Master, according to the messages he had sent them by the women, and, in all probability, appointed at some former appearance not mentioned by the evangelists, the brethren set out for the mountain in Galilee, perhaps that on which he was transfigured. Here five hundred of them were gathered together, expecting the joyful sight of their great Master, after he had triumphed over death and the grave; some of them not having yet seen him after his resurrection.

They did not wait long before Jesus appeared, on which they were seized with rapture, their hearts overflowed with gladness, they approached their kind, their benevolent Master, and worshiped him. Some few, indeed, doubted; it being natural for men to be afraid to believe what they vehemently wished, lest they should indulge themselves in false joys, which vanish like a morning cloud. But Jesus afterward appeared frequently to them, and gave them full satisfaction, and instructed them in many things relating to their preaching the gospel, establishing the church, and spreading it through the whole earth.

CHAPTER XXXIV.

OUR BLESSED LORD INSTRUCTS HIS DISCIPLES IN WHAT MANNER THEY SHOULD CONDUCT THEMSELVES IN ORDER TO PROPAGATE THE DOCTRINES OF THE GOSPEL — GIVES THEM HIS FINAL BLESSING, AND ASCENDS INTO HEAVEN — GENERAL REVIEW OF THE LIFE AND DOCTRINES OF THE GREAT REDEEMER.

A FEW days before the feast of Pentecost, or the "feast of weeks," the disciples went up to Jerusalem, where the blessed Jesus made his last appearance to them; and, after instructing them in many particulars concerning the kingdom of God, and the manner they were to behave themselves in propagating the doctrines of the gospel, he put them in mind, that, during his abode with them in Galilee, he had often told them that all things written in the law, the prophets, and the Psalms, concerning him, were to be exactly accomplished. At the same time, "he opened their understandings" by divine illumination, he removed their prejudices by the operation of his Spirit, cleared their doubts, improved their memories, strengthened their judgments, and enabled them to discern the true meaning of the Scriptures.

Having thus qualified them for receiving the truth, he again assured them, that both Moses and the prophets had foretold that the Messiah was to suffer in the very manner he had suffered; that he was to rise from the dead on the third day, as he had done; and that repentance and remission of sins were to be preached in the Messiah's name among all nations, beginning with the Jews in Jerusalem.

He next delivered unto them their commission to preach the doctrine of repentance and remission of sins, in his name, among all nations, and to testify unto the world the exact accomplishment, in him, of all things foretold concerning the Messiah; and, to enable them to perform this important work, promised to bestow on them the gift of the Holy Spirit, which he called the promise of his Father—because the Almighty had promised it by his prophets.

Having thus strengthened them for the important work they were going to undertake, he led them on to the Mount of Olives, as far as Bethany; where, standing on a hill above the town, he told them that he was going to ascend to his Father; for which reason they might go courageously through all the world, and preach the gospel to every rational creature: that they who believed should be admitted into his church by the rite of baptism, in the name of the Father, the Son, and the Holy Ghost; and be taught, in consequence of their baptism, to obey all the precepts he had enjoined upon them: that such baptized believers should receive the pardon of their sins, together with eternal life in the happy mansions of his Father's kingdom; but such as refused to embrace the doctrines of the gospel, should be forever excluded from those happy regions, and have their portion in the lake that burneth with fire and brimstone: that while they were employed in this work he would be constantly with them, to assist them by his Spirit, and protect them by his providence. Finally, that those who should, through their preaching, be induced to believe, should themselves work most astonishing miracles, by which the gospel should be propagated with the greatest rapidity.

When the blessed Jesus had spoken these things, he lifted up his hands, and blessed them. And in the action of blessing them, he was parted from them, in the midst of the day a shining cloud received him out of their sight; that is, this brilliant cloud encompassed him about, and carried him up to heaven, not suddenly, but at leisure, that they might behold him departing, and see the proofs of his ascending into heaven, as he had promised them. The cloud in which the blessed Jesus ascended, was more bright and pure than the clearest lambent flame, being, as is supposed, no other than the shechinah, or glory of the Lord; the visible symbol of the divine presence, which had so often appeared to the patriarchs of old; which filled the temple at its dedication, and which, in its greatest splendor, could not be beheld with mortal eyes; for which reason it is called the light inaccessible. As he ascended, the flaming cloud that surrounded him marked his passage through the air, but gradually lost its magnitude in the eyes of those who stood below, till it at last vanished, together with their beloved Master, out of their sight.

We shall conclude this chapter with a few observations on the general conduct of our blessed Redeemer, during his abode with men on earth.

The human character of the blessed Jesus, as it results from the account given of him by the evangelists, (for they have not formally drawn it up,) is entirely different from that of all other men whatsoever; for whereas they have selfish passions deeply rooted in their breasts, and are influenced by them in almost everything they do, Jesus was so entirely free from them, that the most severe scrutiny can not furnish one single action in the whole course of his life, wherein he consulted his own interest only. No; he was influenced by very different motives: the present happiness, and eternal welfare of sinners, regulated his conduct; and while others followed their respective occupations, Jesus had no other business than that of doing the will of his Father, and promoting the happiness of the sons of men. Nor did he wait till he was solicited to extend his benevolent hand to the distressed; "he went about doing good," and always accounted it "more blessed to give than to receive;" resembling God rather than man. Benevolence was the very life of his soul; he not only did good to objects presented to him for relief, but he industriously sought them out, in order to extend his compassionate assistance.

It is common for persons of the most exalted faculties to be elated with success, and applause, or dejected by censure and disappointments; but the blessed Jesus was never elated by the one, or depressed by the other. He was never more courageous than when he met with the greatest opposition and cruel treatment; nor more humble, than when the sons of men worshiped at his feet.

He came into the world inspired with the grandest purpose that ever was formed: that of saving from eternal perdition, not a single nation, but the whole world; and in the execution of it went through the longest and heaviest train of labors that ever was sustained, with a constancy and resolution, on which no disadvantageous impression could be made by any accident whatever. Calumny, threatenings, bad success, with many other evils constantly attending him, served only to quicken his endeavors in this glorious enterprise, which he unceasingly pursued, even till he had finished it by his death.

The generality of mankind are prone to retaliate injuries received, and all seem to take a satisfaction in complaining of the cruelties of those who oppress them, whereas the whole of Christ's labors breathed nothing but meekness, patience, and forgiveness, even to his bitterest enemies, and in the midst of the most excruciating torments. The words, "Father, forgive them, for they know not what they do," uttered by him when his enemies were nailing him to the cross, fitly express the temper which he maintained through the whole course of his life, even when assaulted by the heaviest provocation. He was destined to sufferings here below, in order that he might raise his people to honor, glory, and immortality, in the realms of bliss above; and therefore patiently, yea joyfully, submitted to all that the malice of earth and hell could inflict. He was vilified that we might be honored; he died that we might live forever and ever.

To conclude: the greatest and best men have discovered the degeneracy and corruption of human nature, and shown them to have been nothing more than men; but it was otherwise with Jesus. He was superior to all the men that ever lived, both with regard to the purity of his manners, and the perfection of his holiness. He was holy, harmless, undefiled, and separate from sinners.

Whether we consider him as a teacher, or as a man, "he did no sin, neither was guile found in his mouth." His whole life was perfectly free from spot or weakness; at the same time, it was remarkable for the greatest and most extensive exercises of purity and goodness. But never to have committed the least sin in word or deed: never to have uttered any sentiment that could be censured, upon the various topics of religion and morality, which were the daily subjects of his discourses; and that through the course of a life filled with action, and led under the observation of many enemies, who had always access to converse with him, and who often came to find fault, is a pitch of perfection evidently above the reach of human nature; and consequently he who possessed it must have been divine.

Such was the person who is the subject of the evangelical history. If the reader, by reviewing his life, doctrine, and miracles, as they are here represented to him, united in one series, has a clearer idea of these things than before; or observes a beauty in his actions thus linked together, which, taken separately, do not appear so fully; if he feels himself touched by the character of Jesus in general, or with any of his sermons or actions in particular, thus simply delineated in writing, whose principal charms are the beauties of truth; above all, if his dying so generously for men strikes him with admiration, or fills him with hope, in the prospect of that pardon which is thereby purchased for the world, let him seriously consider with himself what improvements he ought to make of the divine goodness.

Jesus, by his death, hath set open the gate of immortality to the sons of men; and by his word, spirit, and example, graciously offers to make them meet for the glorious rewards in the kingdom of the heavenly Canaan, and to conduct them into the inheritance of the saints in light. Let us therefore, remember, that being born under the dispensations of his gospel, we have, from our earliest years, enjoyed the best means of securing to ourselves an interest in that favor of God which is life, and that loving kindness which is better than life.

We have been called to aspire after an exaltation to the nature and felicity of the Almighty, exhibited to mortal eyes in the man Christ Jesus, to fire us with the noblest ambition. His gospel teaches us that we are made for eternity; and that our present life is, to our future existence, as infancy to manhood. But, as in the former many things are to be learned, many hardships to be endured, many habits to be acquired, and that by a course of exercises, which, in themselves, though painful, and possibly useless to the child, yet are necessary to fit him for the business and enjoyments of manhood; so, while we remain in this infancy of human life, things are to be learned, hardships to be endured, and habits to be acquired by a laborious disipline, which, however painful, must be undergone, because necessary to fit us for the employments and pleasures of our riper existence in the realms above; always remembering, that whatever our trials may be in this world, if we ask for God's assistance, he has promised to give it. Inflamed, therefore, with the love of immortality and its joys, let us submit ourselves to our heavenly teacher, and learn of him those lessons which alone can render life pleasant, death desirable, and fill our hearts with ecstatic joy.

CHAPTER XXXV.

REMARKS ON THE PECULIAR NATURE OF THE CHRISTIAN RELIGION, THE PRINCIPLES IT INCULCATES, AND ITS FITNESS TO RENDER MEN HOLY AND HUMBLE HERE, AND HAPPILY GLORIFIED HEREAFTER.

WE can not close this delightful scene of the life of our dear Lord and Saviour more comfortably, than by considering the benefits resulting from a due attendance to his doctrines by all who shall, by faith, receive and embrace the same. Probably none have been greater enemies to the progress of religion, than those who delineate it in a gloomy and terrifying form; nor any guilty of a more injurious calumny against the gospel, than those who represent its precepts as rigorous impositions and unnecessary restraints.

True religion is the perfection of human nature, and the foundation of uniform exalted pleasure, of public order, and private happiness. Christianity is the most excellent, and the most useful institution, having the "promise of the life that now is, and of that which is to come." It is the voice of reason; it is also the language of Scripture, "The ways of wisdom are ways of pleasantness, and all her paths are peace;" and our blessed Saviour himself assures us, that his precepts are easy, and the burden of his religion light.

The Christian religion is a rational service, a worship "in spirit and truth," a worship worthy of the majesty of the Almighty to receive, and of the nature of man to pay. It comprehends all we ought to believe, and all we ought to practice; its positive rites are few, of plain and easy significancy, and manifestly adapted to establish a sense of our obligation to God. The gospel places religion, not in abstruse speculation, and metaphysical subtleties; nor in outward show, and tedious ceremony; not in superstitious austerities, and enthusiastic visions; but in purity of heart, and holiness of life. The sum of our duty, according to our great Master himself, consists in the love of God and of our neighbor; according to St. Paul, in denying ungodliness and worldly lusts, and in living soberly, righteously, and godly, in this present evil world; according to St. James, in visiting the fatherless and widows in affliction, and in keeping ourselves unspotted from the world. This is the constant strain and tenor of the gospel. This it inculcates most earnestly, and on this it lays the greatest stress.

But is the Christian system only a republication of the law of nature, or merely a refined system of morality? No, certainly; it is a great deal more. It is an act of grace, a stupendous plan of Providence, designed for the recovery of mankind from a state of degradation and ruin, and to the favor of the Almighty, and to the hopes of a happy immortality, through a Mediator.

Under this dispensation, true religion consists in "repentance toward God," and in "faith in the Lord Jesus Christ," as the person appointed by the supreme authority of heaven and earth to reconcile apostate man to his offended Creator; as a Sacrifice for Sin;

our vital Head, and governing Lord. This is religion, as we are Christians. And what hardship, what exaction is there in all this? Surely, none. Nay, the practice of religion is much easier than the servitude of sin.

Our rational powers, all will readily agree, are dreadfully impaired, and the soul weakened, by sin. The animal passions are strong and corrupt, and oppose the dictates of the Spirit of God; objects of sense make powerful impressions on the mind. We are, in every situation, surrounded with many snares and temptations. In such a disordered state of things, we cannot please God, till created anew in Christ Jesus unto good works. We must be born again—born from above.

The God of all grace has planted in the human breast a quick sense of good and evil; a faculty which strongly dictates right and wrong: and though, by the strength of appetite and warmth of passion, men are often hurried into immoral practices, yet, in the beginning, especially when there has been the advantage of a good education, it is usually with reluctance and opposition of mind. What inward struggles precede! what bitter pangs attend their sinful excesses! what guilty blushes and uneasy fears! what frightful prospects and pale reviews! "Terrors are upon them, and a fire not blown consumeth them." To make a mock of sin, and to commit iniquity without remorse, is, in some instances, an attainment that requires length of time, and much painful labor; more labor than is requisite to attain that salvation which is the glory of the man, the ornament of the Christian, and the chief of his happiness. The soul can no more be reconciled to acts of wickedness and injustice, than the body to excess, but by suffering many bitter pains and cruel attacks. The mouth of conscience may, indeed, be stopped for awhile by false principles; its sacred whispers may be drowned by the noise of company, and stifled by the entertainments of sense; but this principle of conscience is so deep-rooted in human nature, and, at the same time, her voice is so clear and strong, that the sinner's arts will be unable to lull her into a lasting security. When the hour of calamity arrives, when sickness seizeth, and death approaches the sinner, conscience then constrains him to listen to her accusation, and will not suffer the temples of his head to take any rest. "There is no peace to the wicked;" the foundations of peace are subverted; they are at utter enmity with their reason, with their conscience, and with their God.

Not so is the case of true religion. For when religion, pure and genuine, forms the temper and governs the life, conscience applauds, and peace takes her residence in the breast. The soul is in its proper state. There is order and regularity both in the faculties and actions. Conscious of its own integrity, and secure of the divine approbation, the soul enjoys a calmness not to be described. But why do I call this happy frame mere calmness; the air may be calm, and the day overcast with thick mists and dark clouds. The pious and virtuous mind resembles a serene day enlightened and enlivened with the brightest rays of the sun. Though all without may be clouds and darkness, there is light in the heart of a devout man: "He is satisfied with favor, and filled with peace and joy in believing." In the concluding scene, the awful moment of dissolution, all is peaceful and serene. The immortal part quits its tenement of clay, with the well-grounded hope of ascending to happiness and glory.

Nor does the gospel enjoin any duty but what is fit and reasonable. It calls upon all its professors to practice reverence, submission, love, and gratitude to God; justice, truth, and universal benevolence to men; and to maintain the government of our minds. And what has any one to object against this? From the least to the greatest commandment of our dear Redeemer, there is not one which impartial reason can find fault with. "His law is perfect; his precepts are true and righteous altogether." Not even those excepted which require us "to love our enemies, to deny ourselves," and to "take up our cross." To forgive an injury is more generous and manly than to revenge it; to control a licentious appetite, than to indulge it; to suffer poverty, reproach, and even death itself, in the sacred cause of truth and integrity, is much wiser and better than by base compliances to make "shipwreck of faith and a good conscience." Thus in a storm on sea, or a conflagration on the land, a man with pleasure abandons his slumber to secure his jewels. Piety and virtue are the wisest and most reasonable things in the world, vice and wickedness the most irrational and absurd.

The all-wise Author of our being hath so framed our natures, and placed us in such relations, that there is nothing vicious but what is injurious, nothing virtuous but what is advantageous to our present interest, both with respect to body and mind. Meekness and humility, patience, and universal charity, and grace, give a joy "unknown to transgressors."

The divine virtues of truth and equity are the only

bands of friendship, the only supports of society. Temperance and sobriety are the best preservatives of health and strength; but sin and debauchery impair the body, consume the substance, reduce to poverty, and form the direct path to an immediate and untimely death. Now this is the chief excellency of all laws and what will always render their burden pleasant and delightful is, that they enjoin nothing unbecoming or injurious. Besides, to render our duty easy, we have the example, as well as the commands, of the blessed Jesus. The masters of morality among the heathen gave excellent rules for the regulation of men's manners; but they wanted either the honesty or the courage to try their own arguments upon themselves. It was a strong presumption that the yoke of the scribes and Pharisees was grievous, when they laid "heavy burdens upon men's shoulders," which they themselves refused to touch with one of their fingers. Not thus our great lawgiver, Jesus Christ the righteous. His behaviour was, in all respects, conformable to his doctrine. His devotion toward God, how sublime and ardent! benevolence toward men, how great and diffusive! He was in life an exact pattern of innocence; for he "did no sin, neither was guile found in his mouth." In the Son of God, incarnate, is exhibited the brightest, the fairest resemblance of the Father, that earth or heaven ever beheld; an example peculiarly persuasive, calculated to inspire resolution, and to animate us to use our utmost endeavors to imitate the divine pattern, the example of "the author and finisher of our faith," of him "who loved us, and gave himself for us." Our profession and character, as Christians, oblige us to make his example the model of our lives. Every motive of decency, gratitude, and interest, constrains us to tread the paths he trod before us.

We should also remember that our burden is easy; because God, who "knoweth whereof we are made, who considereth that we are but dust," is ever ready to assist us. The heathen sages themselves, had some notion of this assistance, though guided only by the glimmering lamp of reason. But what they looked upon as probable, the gospel clearly and strongly asserts. We there hear the apostles exhorting, "Let us come boldly to the throne of grace, that we may obtain mercy, and find grace to help in time of need." We there hear the blessed Jesus himself arguing in this convincing manner: "If ye, being evil, know how to give good gifts unto your children, how much more shall your heavenly Father give the Holy Ghost to them that ask him?"

Another particular, which renders the Christian religion delightful, is its leading us to the perfect, eternal life of heaven. It can not be denied, but that we may draw from the light of nature strong presumptions of a future state. The present existence does not look like an entire scene; but rather like the infancy of human nature, which is capable of arriving at a much higher degree of maturity. But whatever solid foundation the doctrine of a future state may have in nature and reason, certain it is, through the habitual neglect of reflection, and the force of irregular passions, this doctrine was, before the coming of our blessed Saviour, very much disfigured, and, in a great measure, lost among the sons of men.

In the heathen world, a future state of rewards and

punishments was a matter of mere speculation and uncertainty; sometimes hoped for, sometimes doubted of, and sometimes absolutely denied. The law of Moses, though of divine origin, is chiefly enforced by promises of temporal blessings; and, even in the writings of the prophets, a future immortality is very sparingly mentioned, and obscurely represented; but the doctrine of our Saviour hath "brought life and immortality to light." In the gospel we have a distinct account of another world, attended with many engaging circumstances, about which the decisions of reason were dark and confused. We have the testimony of the Author of our religion, who was raised from the dead, and who afterward, in the presence of his disciples, ascended into heaven. In the New Testament, it is expressly declared, that good men, "when absent from the body, are present with the Lord." Here we are assured of the resurrection of the body in a glorious form, clothed with immortal vigor, suited to the active nature of the animating spirit, and assisting its most enlarged operations and incessant progress toward perfection. Here we are assured, that "the righteous shall go into life everlasting;" that they shall enter into the kingdom of the heavenly Canaan, where no ignorance shall cloud the understanding, no vice disturb the will. In these regions of perfection, nothing but love shall possess the soul, nothing but gratitude employ the tongue; there the righteous shall be united to an innumerable company of angels, and to the general assembly and church of the first-born; there they shall see their exalted Redeemer at the right hand of Omnipotence, and sit down with him on his throne; there they shall be admitted into the immediate presence of the supreme Fountain of life and happiness, and, beholding his face, be changed into the same image from glory to glory. Here language, here imagination fails me! It requires the genius, the knowledge, and the pen of an angel, to paint the happiness and blissful scene of the New Jerusalem, which human eyes can not behold, till this mortal body shall be purified from its corruption, and dressed in the robes of immortality: "eye hath not seen, nor ear heard, neither hath it entered into the heart to conceive, the joys which God hath prepared for those that love him."

What is the heaven of the heathen, compared with the heaven of the Christian? The hope, the prospect of this is sufficient to reconcile us to all the difficulties that may attend our progress, sweeten all our labors, alleviate every grief, and silence every murmur.

But why, says the libertine, in the gayety of his heart, should there be any difficulties or restraint at all? God hath made nothing in vain. The appetites he hath planted in the human breast are to be gratified. To deny or restrain them, is ignominous bondage; but to give full scope to every desire and passion of the heart, without check or control, is true, manly freedom.

In opposition to this loose and careless way of reasoning, let it be considered, that the liberty of a rational creature doth not consist in an entire exemption from all control, but in following the dictates of reason, as the governing principle, and in keeping the various passions in due subordination. To follow the regular notion of those affections which the wise Creator hath implanted within us, is our duty; but as our natural desires, in this state of trial, are often irregular, we are bound to restrain their excesses, and not to indulge them, but in a strict subserviency to the integrity and peace of our minds, and to the order and happiness of human society established in the world. Those who allow the supreme command to be usurped by sensual and brutal appetites, may "promise themselves liberty," but are truly and absolutely the "servants of corruption." To be vicious, is to be enslaved. We behold with pity those miserable objects that are chained in the galleys, or confined in dark and loathsome dungeons: but much more abject and vile is the slavery of the sinner! No slavery of the body is equal to the bondage of the mind; no chains press so closely, or gall so cruelly, as the fetters of sin, which corrode the very substance of the soul, and fret every faculty.

It must, indeed, be confessed, that there are some profligates, so hardened by custom, as to be past all feeling; and, because insensible of their bondage, boast of this insensibility as a mark of their native freedom, and of their happiness. Vain men! they might extol, with equal propriety, the peculiar happiness of an apoplexy, or the profound tranquillity of a lethargy.

Thus have we endeavored to place, in a plain and conspicuous light, some of the peculiar excellences of the Christian religion; and from hence many useful reflections will naturally arise in the mind of every attentive reader. It is the religion of Jesus that hath removed idolatry and superstition, and brought immortality to light, when concealed under the veil of darkness almost impenetrable. This hath set the great truths of religion in a clear and conspicuous point of view, and proposed new and powerful motives to influence our minds, and to determine our conduct. Nothing is enjoined to be believed but what is worthy of God; nothing to be practiced but what is friendly to man. All the doctrines of the gospel are rational and consistent; all its precepts are truly wise, just, and good. The gospel contains nothing grievous to an ingenious mind; it debars us from nothing, but doing harm to ourselves, or to our fellow creatures; and permits us to range anywhere, but in the paths of danger and destruction. It only requires us to act up to its excellent commands, and to prefer to the vanishing pleasures of sin, the smiles of a reconciled God, and "an eternal weight of glory." And is this a rigorous exaction, a heavy burden not to be endured? How can sinful mortals harbor so unworthy a thought!

Surely no man, who is a real friend to the cause of virtue, and to the interest of mankind, can ever be an enemy to Christianity, if he truly understands it, and seriously reflects on its wise and useful tendency. It conducteth us to our journey's end by the plainest and securest path; where the "steps are not straitened, and where he that runneth stumbleth not." Let us who live under this last and most gracious dispensation of God to mankind, "count all things but loss, for the excellency of the knowledge of Christ Jesus our Lord;" and not suffer ourselves, by the slight cavils of unbelievers, to be "moved away from the hope of the gospel." Let us demonstrate that we believe the superior excellency of the Christian dispensation, by conforming to its precepts. Let us show that we are Christians in deed and in truth; not by endless disputes about trifles, and the transports of a blind zeal, but by abounding in those "fruits of righteousness, which are, through Christ, to the praise and glory of God."

From what has been said, we may clearly perceive how groundless all these prejudices are, which some conceive against religion, as if it were a peevish, morose scheme, burdensome to human nature, and inconsistent with the true enjoyment of life. Such sentiments are too apt to prevail in the heat of youth, when the spirits are brisk and lively, and the passions warm and impetuous; but it is wholly a mistake, and a mistake of the most dangerous tendency. The truth is, there is no pleasure like that of a good conscience; no real peace but what results from the sense of the divine favor. This ennobles the mind, and can alone support it under all the various and unequal scenes of the present state of trial. This lays a sure foundation of an easy, comfortable life, of a serene and peaceful death, and of eternal joy and happiness hereafter; whereas vice is ruinous to all our most valuable interests; spoils the native beauty, and subverts the order of the soul; renders us the scorn of man, the rejected of God, and, without timely repentance, will rob us of a happy eternity. Religion is the health, the liberty, and the happiness of the soul; sin is the disease, the servitude, and destruction of it.

If this be not sufficient to convince you, let me lead you into the chamber of an habitual rioter, the lewd debauchee, worn out in the cause of iniquity, "his bones full of the sins of his youth," that from his own mouth, as he lies on his expiring bed, you may learn that "the way of transgressors is hard;" and that, however sweet sin may be in the commission, "it stings like a serpent, and bites like an adder."

I am going, reader, to represent to you the last moments of a person of high birth and spirits; of great parts and strong passions; every way accomplished, but unhappily attached to those paths which lead to vice and destruction:

His unkind treatment was the cause of the death of a most amiable wife; and his monstrous extravagance, in effect, disinherited his only child. And surely the deathbed of a profligate is next in horror to that abyss to which it leads! It has the most of hell that is visible upon earth; and he that hath seen it, hath more than faith to confirm him in his creed. I see now, (says the worthy divine, from whom I shall borrow this relation,) for who can forget it? Are there in it no flames and furies? You are ignorant, then, of what a scared imagination can figure! what a guilty heart can feel! How dismal it is! The two great enemies of soul and body, Sickness and Sin, sink and confound his friends; silence and darkness are the dismal scene. Sickness excludes the light of heaven, and sin its blessed hope. Oh! double darkness, more than Egyptian! actually to be felt!

The sad evening before the death of the noble youth, whose last hours suggested these thoughts, I was with him. No one else was there but his physician and an intimate acquaintance, whom he loved, and whom he had ruined. At my coming he said, "You and the physician are come too late: I have neither life nor hope. You both aim at miracles. You would raise the dead!" "Heaven," I said, "was merciful." "Or I could not," answered he, "have been thus guilty. What has it not done to bless and to save me? I have been too strong for Omnipotence. I plucked down ruin." I said, "The blessed Redeemer"— "Hold, hold," said he, "you wound me! This is the rock on which I have split! I denied his name!" Refusing to hear anything from me, or take anything from his physician, he lay silent, as far as sudden darts of pain would permit, till the clock struck. Then he cried out, with vehemence, "Oh, time! time! it is fit thou shouldst strike thy murderer to the heart. How art thou fled forever!—A month!—Oh! for a single week! I ask not for years, though an age were too little for the much I have to do." On my saying to him, "We could not do too much; that heaven was a blessed place:" "So much the worse," replied he, "'t is lost! 't is lost! Heaven is to me the severest part of hell!" Soon after, I proposed prayer. To which he answered, "Pray, you that can? I never pray. I can not pray. My conscience is too much wounded. I have deserted my benevolent Maker, and my soul is enveloped in the deepest horrors."

His friend, being much troubled, even to tears, at this, (for who could forbear?—I could not,) he, with the most affectionate look, said, "Keep those tears for thyself, I have undone thee. Dost thou weep for me? That is cruel. What can pain me more?" Here his friend, too much affected, would have left him. "No," said he, "stay. You still may hope; therefore hear me. How madly have I talked! how madly hast thou listened and believed! But look on my present state as a full answer to thee and to myself. This body is all weakness and pain; but my soul, as if stung up by torment to greater strength and spirit, is full powerful to reason, full mighty to suffer; and that which thus triumphs within the jaws of mortality, is, doubtless, immortal. And, as for a Deity, nothing less than an Almighty could inflict the pains I feel."

I was about to congratulate this passive, involuntary confession, in his asserting the two prime articles of his creed, extorted by the rack of nature; when he thus very passionately added, "No, no! let me speak on. I have not long to speak. My much injured friend! My soul, as my body, lies in ruins, in scattered fragments of broken thoughts. Remorse for the past throws my thoughts on the future; worse dread of the future strikes it back on the past. I turn, and turn, and find no ray. Didst thou feel half the mountain that is on me, thou wouldst struggle with the martyr for his stake, and bless Heaven for the flame—that is not an everlasting flame, that is not an unquenchable fire!"

How were we struck! yet, soon after, still more. With an eye of distraction, with a face of despair, he cried out, "My principles have poisoned my friend; my extravagance beggared my boy; my unkindness murdered my wife!—And is there another hell? Oh! thou blasphemed, yet most indulgent Lord God! Hell itself is a refuge, if it hides me from thy frown." Soon after, his understanding failed; his terrified imagination uttered horrors not to be repeated, or ever forgotten; and, before the sun (which I hope has seen few like him) arose, this gay, young, noble, ingenuous, accomplished, and most wretched mortal expired.

It will, perhaps, be said, that the sons of vice and riot have pleasure in sensual indulgences. Allowed; but it is altogether of the lower kind, empty, fleeting, and transient: "like the crackling of thorns under a pot, so is the mirth of the wicked." It makes a noise and a blaze for the present, but soon vanishes away into smoke and vapor.

On the other hand, the pleasure of religion is solid and lasting; and will attend us through all, even the last stages of life. When we have passed the levity of youth, and have lost our relish for the gay entertainments of sense; when old age steals upon us, and stoops us toward the grave, this will cleave fast to us, and give us relief. It will be so far from terminating at death, that it then commences perfect, and continu ally improves, with new additions.

Clad in this immortal robe, we need not fear the awful summons of the king of terrors, nor regret our retiring into the chambers of the dust. Our immortal part will wing its way to the arms of its Omnipotent Redeemer, and find rest in the heavenly mansions of the Almighty. And though our earthly part, this tabernacle of clay, returns to its original dust and is dissolved, our joy, our consolation, our confidence is, that "we have a building of God, an house not made with hands, eternal in the heavens."

THE

LIVES OF THE APOSTLES.

St. PETER.

ST. PETER was born at Bethsaida, a city of Galilee, situate on the banks of the lake of Gennesareth, called also the sea of Galilee, from its being situated in that country, and the lake of Tiberias, from that city being built on its banks. The particular time of this great apostle's birth can not be known; the evangelist and other writers among the primitive Christians, having been silent with regard to this particular. It is, however, pretty certain, that he was at least ten years older than his Master; the circumstances of his being married, and in a settled course of life, when he first became a follower of the great Messiah, and that authority and respect the gravity of his person procured him among the rest of the apostles, sufficiently declare this conjecture to be just.

As he was a descendant of Abraham, he was circumcised according to the rites of the Mosaic law, and called by his parents, Simon or Simeon, a name common at that time among the Jews. But after his becoming a disciple of the blessed Jesus, the additional title of Cephas was conferred upon him by his Master, to denote the firmness of his faith; the word Cephas, in the Syriac, the common language of the Jews at that time, signifying a stone or rock; and thence he is called, in Greek, *Petros*, and by us Peter, which implies the same thing.

With regard to the parents of St. Peter, the evangelists have also been silent, except in telling us that his father's name was Jonah, who was highly honored by our blessed Saviour, who chose two of his sons, Andrew and Peter, to be his apostles, and preachers of the glad tidings of salvation to the children of men.

St. Peter, in his youth, was brought up to the trade of fishing on the lake of Bethsaida, famous for different kinds of fish, which excelled all others in the fineness of their taste.

Here he followed the trade of fishing, but afterward removed to Capernaum, where he settled; for we find he had a house there when our Saviour began his public ministry, and there he paid tribute. Nicephorus tells us, that Helen, the mother of Constantine, erected a beautiful church over the ruins of St. Peter's house, in honor of that apostle.

Sacred history hath not ascertained of what sect the apostle was. We know, indeed, that his brother Andrew was a follower of John the Baptist, that preacher of repentance; and it is very unlikely that he, who was ready to carry his brother the early tidings of the Messiah, that the "sun of righteousness" was already risen in those parts, should not be equally solicitous to bring him under the discipline and influence of John the Baptist, the day-star which appeared to usher in the appearance of the Son of God.

He became acquainted with the immaculate Lamb of God, in the following manner: The blessed Jesus having spent thirty years in the solitude of a private life, had lately been baptized by John, in Jordan, and there owned by the solemn attestation of heaven to be the Son of God; whereupon he was immediately hurried into the wilderness, and there for forty days maintained a personal contest with the devil. But, having conquered this great enemy of mankind, he returned to "the place beyond Jordan," where John was baptizing his proselytes and endeavoring to answer the Jews, who had sent a deputation to him to inquire concerning this new Messiah that appeared among them. To satisfy these curious inquirers of Israel, John faithfully related everything he knew concerning him, gave him the greatest character, and soon after pointed him out to his disciples; upon which two of them followed the great Redeemer of mankind, one of whom was Andrew, Simon's brother.

Nor did he conceal the joyful discovery he had made; for early in the morning he hastened to inform his brother Simon that he had found the Messiah.

Simon, who was one of those who waited for the redemption of Israel, ravished with the joyful news, and impatient of delay, presently followed his brother to the place; and on his arrival our blessed Saviour immediately gave him a proof of his divinity; saluting him at first sight by his name, and telling him both who he was, his name and kindred, and what title should be conferred upon him.

From this time Peter and his companions became the inseparable and constant disciples of the great Messiah, living under the rules of his discipline and institutions.

The blessed Jesus, having entered upon his important mission, thought proper to select some peculiar persons from among his followers, to be constant witnesses of his miracles and doctrine; and who, after his departure, might be entrusted with the care of building his church, and planting that religion in the world, for which he himself left the mansions of heaven, and put on the veil of mortality. In order to this, he withdrew privately, in the evening, to a solitary mountain, where he spent the night in solemn addresses to his Almighty Father, for rendering the great work he was going to undertake, prosperous and successful.

Early the next morning, the disciples came to him, out of whom he made a choice of twelve, to be his apostles and the attendants on his person. These he afterward invested with the power of working miracles, and sent them into different parts of Judea, in order to carry on with more rapidity the great work which he himself had so happily begun.

We have no further account of St. Peter in particular, till the night after our Saviour's miraculously feeding the multitude in the wilderness. Jesus had ordered his disciples to take ship, and pass over to the other side, while he sent the multitude away. But, a violent storm arising, they were in great danger of their lives, when their Master came unto them, walking on the surface of the boisterous billows, with the same ease as if it had been dry ground. At his approach the disciples were greatly terrified, supposing they had seen a spirit. But their compassionate Mas ter soon dispelled their fears, by telling them it was ne himself, and therefore they had no reason to be terrified.

Peter, who was always remarkable for bold resolutions, desired his Master to give him leave to come to him on the water; and, on obtaining permission, he left the ship, and walked on the sea to meet his Saviour. But when he heard the deep roar around him, and the waves increase, he began to be afraid; and as his faith declined, his body sunk in the water; so that in the greatest agony he called for assistance to him who was able to save. Nor was his cry in vain; the compassionate Redeemer of mankind stretched out his hand, and again placed him on the surface of the water, with this gentle reproof, "O thou of little faith, wherefore didst thou doubt?" And no sooner was the blessed Jesus and his disciple entered into the ship, than the winds ceased, the waves subsided, and the ship was at the land whither they were going.

Some time after, the great Redeemer of the souls of men, being to receive a specimen of his future glorification, took with him three of his most intimate apostles, Peter and the two sons of Zebedee, and went up into a very high mountain; and, while they were employed in earnest addresses to the Almighty, he was transfigured before them, darting such luster from his face, as exceeded the meridian rays of the sun in brightness; and such beams of light issued from his garments, as exceeded the light of the clearest day; an evident and sensible representation of that state when the "just shall walk in white robes, and shine as the sun in the kingdom of their father."

In the mean time Peter and the two apostles were fallen asleep; but, on their waking, were strangely surprised to see the Lord surrounded with so much glory, and the two great persons conversing with him. They, however, remained silent till those visitants from the courts of heaven were going to depart, when Peter, in rapture and ecstacy of mind, addressed himself to his Master, declared their infinite pleasure and delight in being favored with this glorious spectacle; and desired his leave to erect three tabernacles, one for him, one for Moses, and one for Elias. But while he was speaking, a bright cloud overshadowed these two great prophets, and a voice came from it, uttering these remarkable words, "This is my beloved Son, in whom I am well pleased; hear ye him." On which the apostles were seized with the utmost consternation, and fell upon their faces to the ground; but Jesus touching them, bid them dismiss their fears, and look up with confidence; they immediately obeyed, but saw their Master only.

After this heavenly scene our blessed Lord traveled through Galilee, and at his return to Capernaum, the tax-gatherers came to Peter and asked whether his Master was not obliged to pay tribute. When our blessed Saviour was informed of this demand, rather than give offence, he wrought a miracle to pay it. Our great Redeemer was now going, for the last time, to Jerusalem; and he ordered two of his disciples, probably Peter and John, to fetch him an ass, that he might enter into the city on it, as had been foretold. The disciples obeyed their Master, and brought the ass to Jesus, who, being mounted thereon, entered the city amidst the hosannas of a numerous multitude, with palm branches in their hands, proclaiming at once both the majesty of a prince, and the triumph of a Saviour.

The blessed Jesus proceeded from Jerusalem to Bethany, from whence he sent two of his disciples, Peter and John, to make preparation for his celebrating the passover. Every thing being ready, our blessed Saviour and his apostles entered the house, and sat down to the table. But their great Master, who often taught them by example as well as precept, arose from his seat, laid aside his upper garment, took the towel, and, pouring water into a basin, began to wash his disciples' feet, to teach them humility and charity, by his own example. But on his coming to Peter, he would by no means permit his Master to perform so mean and condescending an office. What, the Son of God stoop to wash the feet of a sinful mortal! A thought which shocked the apostle, who strenuously declared, "Thou shalt never wash my feet." But the blessed Jesus told him, that if he washed him not, he could have no part with him; intimating, that this action was mystical, and signified the remission of sins, and the purifying virtue of the Spirit of the Most High, to be poured upon all true Christians. This answer sufficiently removed the scruples of Peter, who cried out, "Lord, not my feet only, but also my hands and my head." Wash me in every part, rather than let me lose my portion in thee.

The blessed Jesus, having set this pattern of humility, began to reflect on his approaching sufferings, and on the person who should betray him into the hands of wicked and cruel men; telling them, that not a stranger, or an enemy, but one of his friends, one of his apostles, and even one of them who sat at the table, would betray him. This declaration exceedingly affected them all in general, and Peter in particular, who made signs to St. John to ask him particularly who it was. Jesus complied with this request, and gave them to understand that it was Judas Iscariot.

Our great Redeemer now began the institution of his supper, that great and solemn institution which he resolved to leave behind him to be constantly celebrated in his church, as a standing monument of his love in dying for mankind; telling them, at the same time, that he himself was now going to leave them, and that "whither he went they could not come."

Supper being now ended, they sung a hymn, and departed to the Mount of Olives; where Jesus again put them in mind how greatly the things he was going to suffer would offend them. To which Peter replied, that "though all men should be offended because of him, yet he himself would never be offended."

They now repaired to the garden of Gethsemane; and leaving the rest of the apostles near the entrance, our blessed Saviour, taking with him Peter, James, and John, retired into the most solitary part of the garden, to enter on the preparatory scene of the great tragedy that was now approaching. Here the blessed Jesus labored under the bitterest agony that ever human nature suffered, during which he prayed with the utmost fervency to his Father, "offering up prayers and supplications with strong crying and tears; and his sweat was as it were great drops of blood falling down to the ground."

While our blessed Redeemer was thus interceding with the Almighty, his three disciples were fallen asleep, though he had made three several visits to them, and calling to Peter, asked him if he could not watch one hour with him. Advising them all to watch and pray, that they might not enter into temptation, adding, "the spirit indeed is willing, but the flesh is weak."

While he was discoursing with them, a band of soldiers, from the chief priests and elders, preceded by the traitor Judas, to conduct and direct them, rushed into the garden, and seized the high priest of our profession. Peter, whose ungovernable zeal would admit of no restraint, drew his sword, and, without the least order from his Master, struck at one of the persons who seemed to be remarkably busy in binding Jesus, and cut off his right ear. This wild and unwarrantable zeal was very offensive to his Master, who rebuked Peter, and entreated the patience of the soldiers while he miraculously healed the wound. But now the fidelity of the apostles, which they had urged with so much confidence, was put to the trial. They saw their Master in the hands of a rude and inconsiderate band of men; and therefore should have exerted their power to release him, or at least have been the companions of his sufferings, and endeavored by every kind, endearing action, to have lessened his grief. But alas! instead of assisting or comforting their great Master, they forsook him and fled.

The soldiers after binding Jesus, led him away, and delivered him to the chief priests and elders, who carried him from one tribunal to another, first to Annas, and then to Caiaphas, where the Jewish sanhedrim were assembled, in order to try and condemn him. In the mean time, Peter, who had followed the other disciples in their flight, recovered his spirits, and being encouraged by his companion, St. John, returned to seek his Master. Seeing him leading to the high priest's hall, he followed at a distance to know the event: but on his coming to the door, was refused admittance, till one of the disciples, who was acquainted there, came out, and prevailed upon the servant who kept the door, to let him in. Peter, being admitted, repaired to the fire, burning in the middle of the hall, round which the officers and servants were standing; where, being observed by the maid-servant who let him in, she charged him with being one of Christ's disciples; but Peter publicly denied the charge, declaring that he did not know him, and presently withdrew into the porch, where, being secluded from the people, the reflection of his mind awakened his conscience into a quick sense of his duty, and the promise he had a few hours before made to his Master. But alas! human nature, when left to itself, is remarkably frail and inconstant. This Peter sufficiently experienced; for, while he continued in the porch, another maid met him, and charged him with being one of the followers of Jesus of Nazareth, which Peter firmly denied, and, the better to gain belief, ratified it with an oath. About an hour after this, the servant of the high priest, he whose ear Peter had cut off, charged him with being a disciple of Christ, and that he himself had seen him in the garden with him: adding that his very speech sufficiently proved that he was a Galilean. Peter, however, still denied the fact; and, to his sin, ratified it not only by an oath, but a solemn curse and execration, that "he was not the person," and that "he knew not the man." But no sooner had he uttered this denial, (which was the third time,) than the "cock crew;" at which his Master turned about, and earnestly looked upon him in a manner that pierced him to the heart, and brought to his remembrance what his Saviour had more than once foretold, namely, that he would basely and shamefully deny him. Peter was now no longer able to conceal his sorrow: he flew from the palace of the high priest, and "wept bitterly," passionately bewailing his folly, and the aggravation of his sin.

It is certain, from various circumstances, that Peter, after the crucifixion of his Lord and Master, stayed at Jerusalem, or at least in the neighborhood; for when Mary Magdalene returned from the sepulchre to inform the disciples that the stone was rolled away from the door, and the body not to be found, Peter and John set out immediately toward the garden. John, who was the younger, arrived at the sepulchre first, looked into it, but did not enter, either out of fear or reverence to our Saviour. Peter came soon after, and resolutely went into the sepulchre, where he found the linen clothes lying together in one place, and the napkin that was about his head wrapped together in another, a sufficient indication that the body was not stolen away; for had that been the case, so much care and order would not have been observed in disposing of the linen clothes. But Peter did not wait long in suspense, with regard to his great Lord and Master; for the same day Jesus appeared to him; and, as he was the first of the disciples who had made a signal confession of the divinity of the Messiah's mission, so it was reasonable he should first see him, after his resurrection, and, at the same time, to convince him that the crime he had been guilty of, in denying him, was pardoned, and that he was come, like the good Samaritan, to pour oil into the wounded conscience.

Soon after the apostles prepared to obey the command of their great Master, of retiring into Galilee; and we find that Peter, Nathaniel, the two sons of Zebedee, and two other disciples, returned to their old trade of fishing in the lake. One morning early, as they were laboring at their employment, having spent the whole night to no purpose, they saw on the shore a grave person, who called to them, and asked them if they had any meat? To which they answered, No. Cast then, replied he, the net on the right side of the ship, and ye shall find. They followed his directions, and caught a prodigious number of large fish. Astonished at such remarkable success, the disciples looked upon one another for some time, till St. John told Peter that the person on the shore was, doubtless, their great Lord and Master, whom the winds, the sea and the inhabitants of the watery region, were ready to obey. Peter no sooner heard the beloved disciple declare his opinion concerning the stranger, than his zeal took fire, and, notwithstanding the coldness of the season, he girt on his fisher's coat, threw himself into the sea, and swam to shore; his impatience to be with his dear Lord and Master not suffering him to stay the few minutes necessary to bring the ship to land.

As soon as the disciples came on shore, they found a fire kindled, and a fish laid upon it, either immediately created by the power of their divine Master, or which came ashore of its own accord, and offered itself to his hand. But notwithstanding there were fish already on the shore, he ordered them to bring those they had now caught, and dress them for their repast, he himself eating with them; both to give them an instance of mutual love and friendship, and also to assure them of the truth of his human nature, since he was risen from the dead. When the repast was ended, our blessed Saviour addressed himself particularly to Peter, urging him to the utmost diligence in the care of souls: and because he knew that nothing but a sincere love to him could support him under the trouble and dangers of so laborious and difficult an employment, he inquired of him, whether he loved him more than the rest of the apostles: mildly reproving him for his over-confident resolution. Peter, whom fatal experience had taught humility, modestly answered, that none knew so well as himself the integrity of his affections. Thou knowest the hearts of all men, nothing is hid from thee, and therefore, thou knowest that I love thee. The question was three several times repeated by our blessed Saviour, and as oftentimes answered by the apostle; it being but just, that he, who by a threefold denial, had given so much reason to question his affection, should now by a threefold confession, give more than common assurance of his sincere love to his Master; and to each of these confessions our great Redeemer added this signal trial of his affection, "Feed my sheep." Instruct and teach them with the utmost care, and the utmost tenderness.

Not long after, our blessed Saviour appeared to his disciples at Jerusalem, to take his last farewell of them who had attended him during his public ministry among the sons of men. He led them out as far as Bethany, a small village on the Mount of Olives, where he briefly told them that they were the persons he had chosen to be the witnesses, both of his death and resurrection; a testimony which they should publish in every part of the world. In order to which, he would, after his ascension into heaven, pour out his Spirit upon them, in an extraordinary manner, that they might be the better enabled to struggle with that violent rage and fury, with which the doctrine of the gospel would be opposed by men and devils. Adding, that in the mean time, they would return to Jerusalem, and there wait till those miraculous powers were given them from on high.

Having finished this discourse, he laid hands upon them, and gave them his solemn benediction; during which he was taken from them, and received up into the regions of the heavenly Canaan. The apostles, who beheld their Master visibly ascend into heaven were filled with a greater sense of his glory than they had ever been while he conversed with them familiarly on earth. And having performed their solemn adoration to him, they returned to Jerusalem with great joy, there to wait for the accomplishment of their great Master's promise.

The apostles, though deprived of the personal presence of their dear Lord and Master, were indefatigable in fulfilling the commission they had received from him. The first object that engaged their attention, after their return to Jerusalem, was to fill up the vacancy in their number, lately made by the unhappy fall and apostacy of Judas. In order to this, they called together the church, and entered into "an upper room," when Peter, as president of the assembly, proposed to them the choice of a new apostle.

He put them in mind that Judas, one of the disciples of their great and beloved Master, being betrayed by his covetous and insatiable temper, had lately fallen from the honor of his place and ministry. That this was no more than what the prophet had long since foretold should come to pass, and that the care of the church, which had been committed to him, should devolve upon another; that therefore it was highly necessary that some person who had been familiarly conversant with the blessed Jesus, from first to last, and consequently, a competent witness both of his doctrine and miracles, his death, resurrection, and ascension, should be substituted in his room.

After filling up the vacancy in the apostolic number, they spent their time in prayer and meditation, till the feast of Pentecost; when the promise of their great Master in sending the Holy Ghost was fulfilled. The Christian assembly were met as usual to perform the public services of their worship, when suddenly a sound, like that of a mighty wind, rushed in upon them; representing the powerful efficacy of that divine spirit which was now to be communicated to them. Upon this they were all immediately filled with the Holy Ghost, which, in an instant, enabled them to speak fluently several languages they had never learned, and probably never heard.

The report of so sudden and strange an action, was soon spread through every part of Jerusalem, which at that time was full of Jewish proselytes, "devout men of every nation under heaven, Parthians, Medes, Elamites, the dwellers in Mesopotamia and Judea, Cappadocia, Pontus, and Asia, Phrygia and Pamphylia, Egypt, the parts of Lybia and Cyrene," from

Rome, from Crete, and from Arabia. These no sooner heard of this miraculous effusion of the Holy Spirit, than they flocked in prodigious numbers to the Christian assembly, where they were amazed to hear these Galileans speaking to them in their own native languages, so various, and so very different from one another.

This surprising transaction had different effects on the minds of the people: some attributing it to the effect of a miracle, and others to the power and strength of "new wine." Upon which the apostles all stood up, and Peter, in the name of the rest, undertook to confute this injurious calumny. The effect of his discourse was equally wonderful and surprising; for great numbers of those, who before ridiculed the religion of Jesus, now acknowledged him for their Saviour, and flew to him for refuge from the impending storm: and St. Luke tells us, that there were that day added to the church no less than three thousand souls, who were all baptized and received into the flock of the great Shepherd of Israel, the bishop of our souls.

Soon after this wonderful conversion, Peter and John, going up to the temple about three in the afternoon, near the conclusion of one of the solemn hours of prayer, saw a poor impotent cripple, near forty years of age, who had been lame from his birth, lying at the "beautiful gate of the temple," and asking alms of those who entered the sacred edifice. This miserable object moved their compassion; and Peter beholding him with attention, said, The riches of this world, the silver and gold so highly coveted by the sons of men, are not in my power to bestow; but I possess the power of restoring life and health, and am ready to assist thee. Then taking the man by the hand, he commanded him in the name of "Jesus of Nazareth, to rise up and walk." Immediately the nerves and sinews were strengthened, and the several parts of the diseased members performed their natural functions. Upon which the man accompanied them into the temple, walking, exulting, and praising God.

So strange and extraordinary a cure filled the minds of the people with admiration, and their curiosity drew them around the apostle, to view the man who had performed it. Peter, seeing the multitude gathering round them, took the opportunity of speaking to them in the following manner: "Men and brethren, this remarkable cure should not excite your admiration of us, as if we had performed it by our own power. It was wrought in the name of Jesus of Nazareth, our crucified Master, by the power of that very Christ, that holy and just person, whom you yourselves denied and delivered to Pilate."

While Peter was speaking to the people in one part of the temple, John was, in all probability, doing the same in the other; and the success plainly indicated how powerful the preaching of the apostles was; five thousand persons embracing the doctrines of the gospel, and acknowledging the crucified Jesus for their Lord and Saviour.

The labors of the apostles were crowned with abundant success, and it seems that such was the aversion of the inveterate Jews to those who became converts to the faith of Christ, that they were deprived of business, in their respective callings; for we find that the professors of the religion of the holy Jesus sold their effects, and brought the money to the apostles, that they might deposit it in one common treasury, and from thence supply the several exigences of the church.

The Christian doctrine had been propagated hitherto without much violence or opposition, in Jerusalem; but now a storm commenced with the death of the protomartyr Stephen; nor did it end but with the dispersion of the disciples, except the apostles, by which means the glad tidings of the gospel, which had till now been confined to Judea, was preached to the Gentile world, and an ancient prophecy fulfilled, which says, "Out of Sion shall go forth the law, and the word of the Lord from Jerusalem." Thus does the Almighty bring good out of evil, and cause the malicious intentions of the wicked to redound to his praise.

The storm, though violent, being at length blown over, the church enjoyed a time of calmness and security; during which, St. Peter went to visit the churches lately planted in those parts, by the disciples whom the persecution had dispersed. And at his arrival at Lydda, he miraculously healed Æneas, who had been afflicted with the palsy, and confined to his bed eight years; but on Peter's bidding him arise in the name of Jesus, he was immediately restored to perfect health. Nor was the success of his miracle confined to Æneas and his family; the fame of it was blazed through all neighboring country, and many believed in the doctrine of the Son of God. It was even known at Joppa, a sea-port town about six miles from Lydda, and the brethren immediately sent for Peter, on the following melancholy occasion: Tabitha, whose Greek name was Dorcas, a woman venerable for her piety and extensive charity, was lately dead, to the great loss of mankind, who loved genuine benevolence, especially the poor and afflicted, who were supported by her charity. At Peter's arrival, he found her dressed for funeral solemnity, and surrounded by mournful widows, who showed the coats and garments wherewith she had clothed them, the monuments of her liberality. But Peter put them all out, and kneeling down, prayed with the utmost fervency; then turning to the body, he commanded her to arise, and taking her by the hand, presented her in perfect health to her friends and others, who were assembled to pay their last duties to so good a woman. This miracle confirmed those who had newly embraced the doctrine of Jesus, and converted many more to the faith. After which he stayed a considerable time at Joppa, lodging in the house of one Simon, a tanner.

Peter, after having finished his visitation to the newly-planted churches, returned to Jerusalem, and was indefatigable in instructing the converts in the religion of Jesus, and preaching the glad tidings of salvation to the descendants of Jacob. But he did not long continue in this pleasing course; Herod Agrippa, in order to ingratiate himself into the favor of the Jews, put the apostle James to death, and finding the action was highly acceptable to that stiff-necked people, he resolved to extend his cruelty to Peter, and accordingly cast him into prison. But the churches were incessant in their prayers to God for his safety; and what have mortals to fear, when guarded by the hand of Omnipotence? Herod was persuaded he should soon accomplish his intention, and sacrifice Peter to the insatiable cruelty of the Jews. But the night before this intended execution, a messenger from the court of heaven visited the gloomy horrors of the dungeon, where he found Peter asleep between his keepers. The angel raised him up, took off his chains, and ordered him to gird on his garments and follow him. Peter obeyed, and having passed through the first and second watch, they came to the iron gate leading to the city, which opened to them of its own accord. The angel also accompanied him through one of the streets, and then departed from him; on which Peter came to himself, and perceived that it was no vision, but that his great and beloved Master had really sent a messenger from above, and released him from prison. In the morning the officers came from Herod to the prison, with orders to bring Peter out to the people, who were gathered together to behold his execution. But when they came to the prison, the keepers informed them that the apostle had made his escape; which so exasperated Herod, that he commanded those who were entrusted with the care of the prisoner, to be put to death.

As we have now related the principal transactions of this apostle, that are founded on Scripture authority, we shall have recourse to ancient historians for the residue of his life.

Toward the latter end of the reign of Nero, when Peter was in Rome, orders were given by that emperor for apprehending him, together with his companion, Paul. St. Ambrose tells us, that when the people perceived the danger to which St. Peter was now exposed, they prayed him to quit Rome, and repair for awhile to some secure retreat, that his life might be preserved for the benefit of the church. Peter, with great reluctance, yielded to their entreaties, and made his escape by night: but as he passed the gate, he was met by a person in the form of his great and beloved Master, and on his asking him whither he was going, answered, "To Rome, to be crucified a second time:" which Peter taking for a reproof of his cowardice, returned again into the city, and was soon after apprehended, and cast, together with St. Paul, into the Mamertine prison. Here they were confined eight or nine months; but spent their time in the exercise of religion, especially in preaching to the prisoners, and those who resorted to them. And during this confinement, it is generally thought, St. Peter wrote the second epistle to the dispersed Jews, wherein he endeavors to confirm them in the belief and practice of Christianity, and to fortify them against those poisonous and pernicious principles and actions which even then began to break in upon the Christian church.

Nero at last returning from Achaia, entered Rome in triumph; and soon after his arrival, resolved that the apostles should fall as victims and sacrifices to his cruelties and revenge. While the fatal stroke was daily expected, the Christians in Rome were continually offering up their prayers to heaven to protect these two holy persons. But the Almighty was now willing to put an end to their sorrows; and after sealing the truth they had preached with their own blood, to receive them into the regions of eternal bliss and happiness, and exchange their crowns of martyrdom for crowns of glory. Accordingly, they were both condemned by the cruel emperor of Rome: and St. Peter, having taken his farewell of the brethren, especially of St. Paul, was taken from the prison and led to the top of the Vatican mount near the Tiber, where he was sentenced to surrender up his life on the cross.

At his coming to the place of execution, he begged the favor of the officers, that he might not be crucified in the common manner, but with his head downward; affirming that he was unworthy to suffer in the same posture in which his Lord had suffered before him. This request was accordingly complied with; and the great apostle St. Peter surrendered up his soul into the hands of his great and beneficent Master, who came down from heaven to ransom mankind from destruction, and open for them the gates of the heavenly Canaan.

His body being taken down from the cross, is said to have been embalmed by Mercellinus, the presbyter, after the manner of the Jews, and then buried in the Vatican, near the Appian way, two miles from Rome.

St. PAUL.

This great apostle of the Gentiles was a descendant from the ancient stock of Abraham. He belonged to the tribe of Benjamin, the youngest son of Jacob. Tarsus, the place of his nativity, was the metropolis of Cilicia, and situated about three hundred miles distant from Jerusalem; it was exceedingly rich and populous, and a Roman municipium, or free corporation, invested with the privileges of Rome by the two first emperors, as a reward for the citizens' firm adherence to the Cæsars, in the rebellion of Crassus. St. Paul was therefore born a Roman citizen, and he often pleads this privilege on his trials.

It was common for the inhabitants of Tarsus to send their children into other cities for learning and improvement, especially to Jerusalem, where they were so numerous, that they had a synagogue of their own, called the synagogue of Cilicians. To this capital our apostle was also sent, and brought up at the school of that eminent rabbi, Gamaliel, in the most exact knowledge of the law of Moses. Nor did he fail to profit by the instructions of that great Master; for he so diligently conformed himself to precepts, that, without boasting, he asserts of himself, that, touching the righteousness of the law, he was blameless, and defied even his enemies to allege anything to the contrary, even in his youth. He joined himself to the sect of the Pharisees, the most strict order of the Jewish religion, but, at the same time, the proudest, and the greatest enemies to Christ and his holy religion.

With regard to his double capacity, of Jewish extraction and Roman freedom, he had two names, Saul and Paul; the former Hebrew, and the latter Latin We must also consider his trade of tent-making as a part of his education; it being a constant practice of the Jews to bring up their children to some honest calling, that, in case of necessity, they might provide for themselves by the labor of their own hands.

The first action we find him engaged in, was the disputation he and his countrymen had with the martyr Stephen, with regard to the Messiah. The Christian was too hard for them in the dispute: but they were too powerful for him in their civil interests: for being enraged at his convincing arguments, they carried him before the high priest, who, by false accusations, condemned him to death. How far Saul was concerned in this cruel action, it is impossible to say; all we know is, that he "kept the raiment of those that slew him."

The storm of persecution against the church being thus begun, it increased prodigiously, and the poor Christians of Jerusalem were miserably harassed and dispersed. In this persecution our apostle was a principal agent, searching all the adjacent parts for the afflicted saints, beating some in the synagogue, inflicting other cruelties, confining some in prison, and procuring others to be put to death.

But it was the will of Providence that he should be employed in a work of a very different nature; and accordingly, he was stopped in his journey. For, as he was traveling between Jerusalem and Damascus, to execute the commission of the Jewish sanhedrim, a refulgent light, far exceeding the brightness of the sun, darted upon him; at which both he and his companions were terribly amazed and confounded, and immediately fell prostrate on the ground. While they lay in this state, a voice was heard, in the Hebrew language, saying, "Saul, Saul, why persecutest thou me?" To which Saul replied, "Who art thou, Lord?" And was immediately answered, "I am Jesus, whom thou persecutest: It is hard for thee to kick against the pricks." As if the blessed Jesus had said, All thy attempts to extirpate the faith in me will prove abortive; and, like kicking against the spikes, wound and torment thyself.

In the meantime our blessed Saviour appeared in a vision to Ananias, a very devout and religious man, highly esteemed by all the inhabitants of Damascus. "And the Lord said unto him, Arise, and go into the street which is called Straight, and inquire in the house of Judas for one called Saul, of Tarsus: for behold, he prayeth, and hath seen in a vision a man named Ananias, coming in and putting his hand on him, that he might receive his sight." Ananias, who was ever ready to obey the commands of the Most High, started at the name, having heard of the bloody practices of Saul at Jerusalem, and what commission he had come to execute in Damascus. He, therefore, suspected that his conversion was nothing more than a snare, artfully laid by him against the Christians. But our blessed Saviour soon removed his apprehensions, by telling him that his suspicions were entirely destitute of foundation; and that he had now taken him, as a chosen vessel, to preach the Gospel both to the Jews and Gentiles, and even before the greatest monarchs of the earth. "Go thy way," said he, "for he is a chosen vessel unto me, to bear my name before the Gentiles, and kings, and the children of Israel." At the same time he acquainted him with the great persecutions he should undergo for the sake of the gospel: "For I will show him how great things he must suffer for my name's sake." This quieted the fears of Ananias, who immediately obeyed the heavenly vision, repaired to the house of Judas, and, laying his hands upon Saul, addressed him in words to this effect: "That Jesus," said he, "who appeared to thee in the way, has sent me to restore thy sight, and by the infusion of his Spirit to give thee the knowledge of those truths which thou hast blindly and ignorantly persecuted; but who is willing to receive thee by baptism into his church, and make thee a member of his body."

This speech was no sooner pronounced, than there fell from his eyes thick films, resembling scales, and he received his sight: and after baptism conversed with the Christians of Damascus. Nor did he only converse with them, he also, to the great astonishment of the whole church, preached the gospel to those Christians he came with an intention to destroy, at the same time boldly asserting, "that Jesus was the Christ, the Son of God;" and proving it to the Jews, with such demonstrative evidence that they were confounded, and found it impossible to answer him.

The miraculous convert, at the instance of the divine command, retired into Arabia Petræa, where he received a full revelation of all the mysteries of Christianity: for he himself declares that he conversed not with flesh and blood. Having preached in several parts of that country for some time, he returned again to Damascus, applying himself, with the utmost assiduity, to the great work of the ministry, frequenting the synagogues there, powerfully confuting the objections commonly made by the descendants of Jacob against Jesus of Nazareth, and converting great numbers of Jews and Gentiles.

He was, indeed, remarkably zealous in his preaching, and blessed with a very extraordinary method of reasoning, whereby he proved the fundamental points of Christianity, beyond exception. This irritated the Jews to the highest degree; and at length, after two or three years' continuance in those parts, they found means to prevail on the governor of Damascus to have him put to death. But they knew it would be difficult to take him, as he had so many friends in the city; they therefore kept themselves in a continual watch, searched all the houses where they supposed he might conceal himself, and also obtained a guard from the governor, to observe the gates, in order to prevent his escaping from them. In this distress his Christian friends were far from deserting him: they tried every method that offered, to procure his escape, but finding it impossible for him to pass through either of the gates of the city, they let him down from one of their houses, through a window, in a basket, over the wall, by which means the cruel designs of his enemies were rendered abortive.

During this interval, he was remarkably assiduous in preaching the gospel of the Son of God, and confuting the Hellenist Jews with the greatest courage and resolution. But snares were laid for him; as malice can as easily cease to be, as to remain inactive. Being warned by God in a vision, that his testimony would not be received at Jerusalem, he thought proper to depart, and preach the gospel to the Gentiles. Accordingly, being conducted by his brethren to Cesarea Philippi, he set sail for Tarsus, his native city: from whence he was soon after brought, by Barnabas, to Antioch, to assist him in propagating Christianity in that city. Soon after their arrival, they entered the synagogue of the Jews on the Sabbath-day, and, after the reading of the law, Paul, being invited by the rulers of the synagogue, delivered an address so powerful, that it obtained from the converted Gentiles a request that it should again be delivered the ensuing Sabbath, when almost the whole city flocked to hear the apostle; at which the Jews were filled with envy, and contradicted Paul, uttering many blasphemous expressions against the name of Jesus of Nazareth.

From Antioch they went to Iconium, and preached with much success in the synagogue; but excited the malice of the Jews, so that they prevailed on the multitude to stone them. But the apostles, having notice of their design, fled from the city and traveled to Lystra, where they preached the gospel to the inhabitants and those who dwelt in the adjacent country. Among the converts at Lystra, was a man who had been lame from his mother's womb, and never had walked. But Paul, perceiving that he had faith to be saved, thought proper to add the cure of his body to that of his soul, knowing that it would not only be beneficial to him, but to all the rest of the believers, by confirming their faith. And that the miracle might be wrought in the most conspicuous manner, he, in the midst of the congregation, said, in an audible voice, to the man, "Stand upright on thy feet." And the words were no sooner pronounced than his strength was at once restored, and he leaped up, and walked.

The apostles indefatigably persevered in the execution of their important commission, declaring, whereever they went, the glad tidings of salvation, through repentance unto life, and faith in the Lord Jesus Christ. But the malice of the Jews still pursued them; for some of these bigoted Israelites coming from Antioch and Iconium, exasperated and stirred up the multitude, so that those very persons who could hardly be restrained from offering sacrifice to them, now used them like slaves, stoning them in so cruel a manner that Paul was thought to be dead, and as such they dragged him out out of the city; but, while the Christians of Lystra were attending on the body, probably in order to carry him to the grave, he arose, and returned with them into the city, and the next day departed with Barnabas to Derbe, where they preached the gospel, and converted many; no danger being able to terrify them from the work of the ministry, and publishing the glad tidings of salvation in every place.

They did not, however, long continue at Derbe, but returned to Lystra, Iconium, Antioch, and Pisidia, confirming the Christians of those places in the faith, earnestly persuading them to persevere, and not to be discouraged with those troubles and persecutions which they must expect would attend the profession of the gospel. And that the affairs of the church might be conducted with more regularity, they ordained elders and pastors, to teach, to instruct, and to watch over them; and then left them to the protection of the Almighty, to whose care they recommended them by prayer and fasting. After leaving Antioch, they passed through Pisidia, and came to Pamphilia; and after preaching the gospel at Perga, they went down to Attalia.

Having thus finished the circuit of their ministry, they returned back to Antioch, in Syria, from whence they at first departed. Here they summoned the church, and gave them an account of their ministry, the success it had met in different parts, and how great a door had thus been opened for the conversion of the Gentile world.

The controversy concerning the observation of Jewish ceremonies in the Christian church, being decided in favor of St. Paul, he and his companions returned back to Antioch; and soon after Peter himself came down. On reading the decretal epistle in the church, the converts conversed freely and inoffensively with the Gentiles, till some of the Jews coming thither from Jerusalem, Peter withdrew his conversation, as if it had been a thing unwarrantable and unlawful. By such a strange method of proceeding, the minds of many were dissatisfied, and their consciences very uneasy. St. Paul with the greatest concern observed it, and publicly rebuked Peter, with that sharpness and severity his unwarrantable practice deserved.

Soon after this dispute, Paul and Barnabas resolved to visit the churches they had planted among the Gentiles, and Barnabas was desirous of taking with them his cousin Mark; but this Paul strenuously opposed, as he had left them in their former journey. This trifling dispute arose to such a height, that these two great apostles and fellow-laborers in the gospel parted; Barnabas taking Mark with him, repaired to Cyprus, his native country; and Paul having made choice of Silas, and recommended the success of his undertaking to the care of Divine Providence, set forward on his intended journey.

They first visited the churches of Syria and Cilicia, confirming the people in the faith, by their instructions and exhortations. Hence they sailed to Crete, where Paul preached the gospel, and constituted Titus to be the first bishop and pastor of the island. From hence Paul and Silas returned back to Cilicia, and came to Lystra, where they found Timothy—whose father was a Greek, but his mother a Jewish convert, and by her he had been brought up under all the advantages of a pious and religious education. This person St. Paul designed for the companion of his travels, and a special instrument in the ministry of his gospel. But knowing that his being uncircumcised would prove a stumbling-block to the Jews, he caused him to be circumcised; being willing, in lawful and indifferent matters, to conform himself to the tempers and apprehensions of men, in order to save their souls.

Everything being ready for their journey, St. Paul and his companion departed from Lystra, passed through Phrygia, and the country of Galatia, where the apostle was entertained with the greatest kindness and veneration, the people looking upon him as an angel sent immediately from heaven; and, being by revelation forbidden to go into Asia, he was commanded by a second vision to repair to Macedonia, to preach the gospel. Accordingly our apostle prepared to pass from Asia into Europe.

Here St. Luke joined them, and became, ever after, the inseparable companion of St. Paul; who, being desirous of finding the speediest passage into Macedonia, took ship with his companions, Silas, Luke, and Timothy, and came to Samothracia, an island in the Ægean sea, not far from Thrace; and the next day he went to Neapolis, a port of Macedonia. Leaving Neapolis, they repaired to Philippi, the metropolis of that part of Macedonia, and a Roman colony, where they stayed some days.

In this city, Paul, according to his constant practice, preached in a proseucha, or oratory of the Jews, which stood by the river side, at some distance from the city, and was much frequented by the devout women of their religion, who met there to pray, and hear the law. And after several days, as they were repairing to the same place of devotion, there met them a damsel who possessed a spirit of divination, by whom her masters acquired a very great advantage.

This woman followed Paul and his companions, crying out, "These men are the servants of the Most High God, which show unto us the way of salvation!" Paul, at first, took no notice of her, not being willing to multiply miracles without necessity. But, when he saw her following them several days together, he began to be troubled, and commanded the spirit, in the name of Jesus, to come out of her. The evil spirit with reluctance obeyed, and left the damsel that very instant. This miraculous cure proving a great loss to her masters, who acquired large gains from her soothsayings, they were filled with envy and malice against the apostles; and, by their instigation, the multitude arose and seized upon Paul and his companions, hurried them before the magistrates and governors of the colony, accusing them of introducing many innovations which were prejudicial to the state, and unlawful for them to comply with, as being Romans.

The magistrates being concerned for the tranquillity of the state, and jealous of all disturbances, were very forward to punish the offenders, against whom great numbers testified; and therefore commanded the officers to strip them, and scourge them severely as seditious persons. This was accordingly executed; after which the apostles were committed to close custody, the gaoler receiving more than ordinary charge to keep them safely; and he accordingly thrust them into the inner prison, and made their feet fast in the stocks. But the most obscure dungeon, or the pitchy mantle of the night, can not intercept the beams of divine joy and comfort from the souls of pious men. Their minds were all serenity; and at midnight they prayed and sang praises so loud, that they were heard in every part of the prison. Nor were their prayers offered to the throne of grace in vain: an earthquake shook the foundations of the prison, opened the doors, loosed the chains, and set the prisoners at liberty.

This convulsion of nature roused the gaoler from his sleep; and concluding from what he saw, that all his prisoners were escaped, he was going to put a period to his life; but Paul, observing him, hastily cried, "Do thyself no harm, for we are all here." The keeper was now as greatly surprised at the goodness of the apostles, as he was before terrified at the thoughts of their escape: and calling for a light, he came immediately into the presence of the apostles, fell down at their feet, and took them from the dungeon, brought them to his house, washed their stripes, and begged of them to instruct him in the knowledge of that God who was so mighty to save. St. Paul readily granted his request, and replied, That, if he believed in Jesus Christ, he might be saved with his whole house; accordingly, the gaoler, with all his family, were, after a competent instruction, baptized, and received as members of the church of Christ.

As soon as it was day, the magistrates either hearing what had happened, or reflecting on what they had done as too harsh and unjustifiable, sent their sergeant to the gaoler, with orders to discharge the apostles. The gaoler joyfully delivered the message, and bid them "depart in peace;" but Paul, that he might make the magistrates sensible what injury they had done them, and how unjustly they had punished them, without examination or trial, sent them word, that, as they had thought proper to scourge and imprison Romans, contrary to the laws of the empire, he expected they should come themselves and make them some satisfaction. The magistrates were terrified at this message; well knowing how dangerous it was to provoke the formidable power of the Romans, who never suffered any freeman to be beaten uncondemned; they came therefore to the prison, and very submissively entreated the apostles to depart without any further disturbance. This small recompense for the cruel usage they had received, was accepted by the meek followers of the blessed Jesus; they left the prison, and retired to the house of Lydia, where they comforted their brethren with an account of their deliverance, and departed.

During the stay of the apostles at Thessalonica, they lodged in the house of a certain Christian named Jason, who entertained them very courteously. But the Jews would not suffer the apostles to continue at rest. They refused to embrace the gospel themselves, and therefore envied its success, and determined to oppose its progress. Accordingly, they gathered together a great number of lewd and wicked wretches, who beset the house of Jason, intending to take Paul, and deliver him up to an incensed multitude. But in this they were disappointed; Paul and Silas being removed from thence by the Christians, and concealed in some other part of the city, and finally sent away by night to Beræa, a city about fifty miles south of Thessalonica, but out of the power of their enemies. Here also Paul's great love for his countrymen, the Jews, and his earnest desire of their salvation, excited him to preach to them in particular; accordingly, he entered into their synagogue, and explained the gospel unto them, proving, out of the scriptures of the Old Testament, the truth of the doctrines he advanced.

Paul leaving Beræa, under the conduct of certain guides, it was said he designed to retire by sea out of Greece, that his restless enemies might cease their persecution; but the guides, according to Paul's order, brought him to Athens, and left him there, after receiving from him an order for Silas and Timotheus to repair to him as soon as possible. While St. Paul continued at Athens, expecting the arrival of Silas and Timothy, he walked up and down, to take a more accurate survey of the city, which he found miserably overrun with superstition and idolatry. Their superstitious practices grieved the spirit of the apostle; accordingly he exerted all his strength for their conversion; he disputed on the Sabbath days in the synagogues of the Jews, and at other times took all opportunities of preaching to the Athenians the coming of the Messiah to save the world.

During St. Paul's stay at Athens, Timothy, according to the order he had received, came to him, out of Macedonia, and brought an account that the Christians at Thessalonica were under persecution from their fellow citizens, ever since his departure: at which St. Paul was greatly concerned, and at first inclined to visit them in person, to confirm them in the faith they had embraced; but being hindered by the enemies of the gospel, he sent Timothy to comfort them, and put them in mind of what they had at first heard, namely, that persecution would be the constant attendant on their profession. On Timothy's departure, St. Paul left Athens, and traveled to Corinth, a very populous place, and famous for its trade.

During his stay at Corinth, he wrote his second epistle to the Thessalonians, to supply his absence. In this epistle he again endeavors to confirm their minds in the truth of the gospel, and prevent their being shaken with those troubles which the wicked and unbelieving Jews would be continually raising against them.

St. Paul, on his leaving the church at Corinth, took ship at Cenchrea, the port of Corinth, for Syria, taking with him Aquila and Priscilla; and on his arrival at Ephesus, he preached awhile in the synagogue of the Jews, promising to return to them, after keeping the passover at Jerusalem. Accordingly, he again took ship, and landed at Cesarea, and from thence traveled to Jerusalem, where he kept the feast, visited the church, and then repaired to Antioch. Here he staid some time, and then traversed the countries of Galatia and Phrygia, confirming the newly-converted Christians, till he came to Ephesus, where he fixed his abode for three years, bringing with him Gaius of Derbe, Aristarchus, a native of Thessalonica, Timotheus and Erastus of Corinth, and Titus.

After this, he entered into the Jewish synagogues, where, for the first three months, he contended and disputed with the Jews, endeavoring, with great earnestness and resolution, to convince them of the truth of the Christian religion. But when, instead of success, he met with nothing but obstinacy and infidelity, he left the synagogue, and taking those with him whom he had converted, instructed them and others who resorted to him, in the school of one Tyrannus, a place where scholars used to be instructed.

About this time the apostle wrote his epistle to the Galatians; for he had heard that, since his departure, corrupt opinions had crept in among them, with regard to the necessity of observing the legal rites.

Soon after the great tumult at Ephesus, about the goddess Diana, Paul called the Christians together, and took his leave of them with the most tender expressions of love and affection. He had now spent almost three years at Ephesus, and founded there a very considerable church, of which he had ordained Timothy the first bishop. He first traveled about two hundred miles northward, to Troas, before he took ship, expecting to meet Titus there. But missing him, he proceeded on his voyage to Macedonia. On his arrival there, he preached the gospel in several places, even as far as Illyricum, now called Sclavonia. During this journey he met with many troubles and dangers; "without were fightings, and within were fears."

During the stay of Titus in Macedonia, Paul wrote his second epistle to the Corinthians, and sent it to them by Titus and Luke. About this time, also, he wrote his first epistle to Timothy, whom he left at Ephesus.

During his stay in Greece, he went to Corinth, where he wrote his famous epistle to the Romans, which he sent by Phœbe, a deaconess of the church at Cenchrea, near Corinth.

St. Paul being now determined to return into Syria, in order to convey the contributions to the brethren at Jerusalem, set out on his journey; but being informed that the Jews had formed a design of killing and robbing him by the way, he returned back into Macedonia, and came to Philippi, from whence he went to Troas, where he staid seven days. Here he preached to them on the Lord's day, and continued his discourse till midnight, being himself to depart in the morning. The night being thus spent in holy exercises, St. Paul took his leave of the brethren in the morning, traveling on foot to Assos, a sea-port town, whither he had before sent his companions by sea. From thence they sailed to Mytilene, a city in the Isle of Lesbos. They next sailed from thence, and came over against Chios, and the day following landed at Trogyllium, a promontory of Ionia, near Samos. The next day they came to Miletus, not putting in at Ephesus, because the apostle was resolved, if possible, to be at Jerusalem on the day of Pentecost.

On his arrival at Miletus, he sent to Ephesus, to summon the elders of the church, and, on their coming, reminded them of the manner in which he had conversed among them, how faithfully and affectionately he had discharged the offices of his ministry, and how incessantly he had labored for the good of the souls of men.

Paul, with his companions, now departed from Miletus, and arrived at Coös, from whence they sailed the next day to Rhodes, a large island in the Ægean sea. Leaving this place, they came to Patara, the metropolis of Lycia, where they went on board another vessel bound for Tyre, in Phœnicia. On his arrival, he visited the brethren there, and continued with them a week, and was advised by some of them, who had the gift of prophecy, not to go up to Jerusalem. But the apostle would by no means abandon his design, or refuse to suffer any thing, provided he might spread the gospel of his Saviour. Finding all persuasions were in vain, they jointly accompanied him to the shore, where he kneeled down and prayed with them; and after embracing them with the utmost affection, he went on board, and came to Ptolemais, and the next day to Cesarea

During their stay in this place, Agabus, a Christian prophet, came thither from Judea, who, taking Paul's girdle, bound his own hands and feet with it, signifying, by this symbol, that the Jews would bind Paul in that manner, and deliver him over to the Gentiles. Whereupon, both his own companions and the Christians of Cesarea earnestly besought him that he would not go up to Jerusalem. But the apostle asked them, if they intended by these passionate dissuasives to add more affliction to his sorrow. "For I am ready," continued he, "not only to be bound, but also to die at Jerusalem, for the name of the Lord Jesus."

When the disciples found that his resolution was not to be shaken, they importuned him no further, leaving the event to be determined according to the pleasure of the Most High. And all things being ready, Paul and his companions set forward on their journey, and were kindly and joyfully received by the Christians on their arrival at Jerusalem.

Our apostle soon after his arrival, encountered Tertullus, who, in a short, but eloquent speech, began to accuse him, charging him with sedition, heresy, and the profanation of the temple. The orator having finished his charge against the apostle, Felix told St. Paul that he was now at liberty to make his defence, which he did in the following manner:

"I answer this charge of the Jews with the greatest satisfaction before thee, because thou hast for many years been a judge of this nation. About twelve days since, I repaired to Jerusalem, to worship the God of Jacob. But I neither disputed with any man, or endeavored to stir up the people in the synagogues or the city. Nor can they prove the charge they have brought against me. This, however, I readily confess: that after the way which they call heresy, so worship I the God of my fathers, and according to this faith, I am careful to maintain a clear and quiet conscience, both toward God and man."

Felix having thus heard both parties, refused to pass any final sentence, till he had more fully advised about it, and consulted Lysias, the governor of the castle, who was the most proper person to give an account of the sedition and tumult.

Some time after St. Paul had appealed unto Cæsar, king Agrippa, who succeeded Herod in the tetrarchate of Galilee, and his sister Bernice, came to Cesarea to visit the new governor. Festus embraced this opportunity of mentioning the case of our apostle to king Agrippa, together with the remarkable tumult this affair had occasioned among the Jews, and the appeal he had made to Cæsar. This account excited the curiosity of king Agrippa, and he was desirous of hearing himself what St. Paul had to say in his own vindication.

Accordingly, the next day, the king and his sister, accompanied with Festus the governor, and several other persons of distinction, came into the court with a pompous and splendid retinue, where the prisoner was brought before them. On his appearing, Festus informed the court, how greatly he had been importuned by the Jews, both at Cesarea and Jerusalem, to put the prisoner to death as a malefactor.

Festus having finished his speech, Agrippa told Paul, he was now at liberty to make his own defence: and silence being made, he delivered himself in the following manner, addressing his speech particularly to Agrippa:

"I consider it as a peculiar happiness, king Agrippa, that I am to make my defence against the accusations of the Jews before thee: because thou art well acquainted with all their customs, and the questions commonly debated among them: I therefore beseech thee to hear me patiently. All the Jews are well acquainted with my manner of life, from my youth; the greatest part of it having been spent with my own countrymen at Jerusalem. They also know that I was educated under the institutions of the Pharisees, the strictest sect of our religion, and am now arraigned for a tenet believed by all our fathers; a tenet sufficiently credible in itself, and plainly revealed in the Scriptures, I mean, the resurrection of the dead. Why should any mortal think it either incredible or impossible, that God should raise the dead? I, indeed, formerly thought myself indispensably obliged to oppose the religion of Jesus of Nazareth. Nor was I satisfied with imprisoning and punishing with death itself the saints I found at Jerusalem; I even persecuted them in strange cities, whither my implacable zeal pursued them; having procured authority for that purpose from the chief priests and elders. Accordingly I departed for Damascus, with a commission from the sanhedrim: but as I was traveling toward that city, I saw at midday, O king, a light from heaven, far exceeding the brightness of the sun, encompassing me and my companions. On seeing this awful appearance, we all fell to the earth, and I heard a voice which said to me, in the Hebrew language, 'Saul, Saul, why persecutest thou me? It is hard for thee to kick against the pricks.' To which I answered, 'Who art thou, Lord?' and he replied, 'I am Jesus, whom thou persecutest.'

But be not terrified, arise from the earth: for I have appeared unto thee, that thou mightest be both a witness of the things thou hast seen, and also of others which I will hereafter reveal unto thee. My power shall deliver thee from the Jews and Gentiles, to whom now I send thee to preach the gospel; to withdraw the veil of darkness and ignorance; to turn them from falsehood unto truth, 'and from the power of Satan unto God.' Accordingly, king Agrippa, I readily obeyed the heavenly vision; I preached the gospel first to the inhabitants of Damascus, then to those of Jerusalem and Judea, and afterward to the Gentiles; persuading them to forsake iniquities, and, by sincere repentance, turn to the living God. These endeavors to save the souls of sinful mortals exasperated the Jews, who caught me in the temple, and entered into conspiracy to destroy me. But, by the help of Omnipotence, I still remain a witness to all the human race, preaching nothing but what Moses and all the prophets foretold, namely, That the Messiah should suffer, be the first that should rise from the chambers of the grave, and publish the glad tidings of salvation, both to the Jews and Gentiles."

While the apostle thus pleaded for himself, Festus cried out, "Paul, thou art mad; too much study hath deprived thee of thy reason." But Paul answered, "I am far, most noble Festus, from being transported with idle and distracted ideas; the words I speak are dictated by truth and sobriety; and I am persuaded that king Agrippa himself is not ignorant of these things." To which Agrippa answered, "Thou hast almost persuaded me to embrace the Christian faith." Paul replied, "I sincerely wish that not only thou, but also all that hear me, were not almost, but altogether, the same as I myself, except being prisoners."

It being now finally determined, that Paul should be sent to Rome, he was, with several other prisoners of consequence, committed to the care of Julius, commander of a company belonging to the legion of Augustus; and was accompanied in his voyage by St. Luke, Aristarchus, Trophimus, and some others, not mentioned by the sacred historian.

In the month of September, they embarked on board a ship of Adramyttium, and sailed to Sidon, where the centurion courteously gave the apostle leave to go on shore to visit his friends and refresh himself. After a short stay they sailed for Cyprus, and arrived opposite the Fair-Havens, a place near Myra, a city of Lycia. Here the season being far advanced, and Paul foreseeing it would be a dangerous voyage, persuaded them to put in and winter there. But the Roman centurion preferring the opinion of the master of the ship, and the harbor being at the same time incommodious, resolved, if possible, to reach Phœnice, a port of Crete, and winter there. But they soon found themselves disappointed; for the fine southerly gale which had favored them for some time, suddenly changed into a stormy and tempestuous wind at north-east, which blew with such violence, that the ship was obliged to sail before it; and to prevent her sinking they threw overboard the principle part of her lading. In this desperate and uncomfortable condition they continued fourteen days, and on the fourteenth night the mariners discovered they were near some coast, and, therefore, to avoid the rocks, thought proper to come to an anchor, till the morning might give them better information.

The country near which they were, was, as Paul had foretold, an island called Melita, now Malta, situated in the Lybian sea, between Syracuse and Africa. Here they landed, and met with great civility from the people, who treated them with humanity, and entertained them with every necessary accommodation.

After three months' stay on this island, the centurion, with his charge, went on board the Castor and Pollux, a ship of Alexandria, bound to Italy. They put in at Syracuse, where they tarried three days; then they sailed to Rhegium, and from thence to Puteoli, where they landed; and finding some Christians there, staid, at their request, a week with them, and then set forward on their journey to Rome. The Christians of this city, hearing of the apostle's coming, went to meet him as far as the distance of about thirty miles from Rome, and others as far as the Appii-forum, fifty-one miles distant from the capital. They kindly embraced each other, and the liberty he saw the Christians enjoy at Rome greatly tended to enliven the spirits of the apostle.

Having refreshed himself after the fatigue of his voyage, the apostle sent for the heads of the Jewish consistory at Rome, and related to them the cause of his coming, in the following manner: "Though I have been guilty of no violence of the laws of our religion, yet I was delivered by the Jews at Jerusalem to the Roman governors, who more than once would have acquitted me as innocent of any capital offence: but, by the perverseness of my persecutors, I was obliged to appeal unto Cæsar; not that I had anything to accuse my nation of: I had recourse to this metlted merely to show my own innocence."

For two whole years Paul dwelt at Rome, in a house he had hired for his own use; wherein he assiduously employed himself in preaching and writing for the good of the church.

St. Paul afterward lived about three years at Ephesus, preaching the gospel to the numerous inhabitants of that city, and was therefore well acquainted with the state and condition of the place: so that taking the opportunity of Tychicus's going thither, he wrote his epistle to the Ephesians, wherein he endeavors to countermine the principles and practices both of the Jews and Gentiles, to confirm them in the belief and practices of the Christian doctrine, and to instruct them fully in the great mysteries of the gospel.

Having thus discharged his ministry, both by preaching and writing, in Italy, St. Paul, accompanied by Timothy, prosecuted his long-intended journey into Spain; and, according to the testimony of several writers, crossed the sea and preached the gospel in Britain. He continued there eight or nine months, and then returned again to the east, visited Sicily, Greece, and Crete, and then repaired to Rome.

Here he met with Peter, and was, together with him, thrown into prison, doubtless in the general persecution raised against the Christians, under pretence that they had set fire to the city. How long he remained in prison is uncertain; nor do we know whether he was scourged before his execution. He was, however, allowed the privilege of a Roman citizen, and therefore beheaded.

Being come to the place of execution, which was the Aquiæ Salviæ, three miles from Rome, he cheerfully, after a solemn preparation, gave his neck to the fatal stroke, and, from this vale of misery, passed to the blissful regions of immortality, to the kingdom of his beloved Master, the great Redeemer of the human race.

He was buried in the Via Ostiensis, about two miles from Rome; and about the year 317, Constantine the Great, at the instance of Sylvester, bishop of Rome, built a stately church over his grave, adorned it with an hundred marble columns, and beautified it with the most exquisite workmanship.

St. ANDREW.

This apostle was born at Bethsaida, a city of Galilee, built on the banks of the lake of Gennesareth, and was son to John, or Jonas, a fisherman of that town. He was brother to Simon Peter, but whether older or younger is not certainly known, though the generality of the ancients intimate that he was the younger. He was brought up to his father's trade, at which he labored till our blessed Saviour called him to be a fisher of men, for which he was, by some preparatory instructions, qualified even before the appearance of the Messiah.

John the Baptist had lately preached the doctrine of repentance, and was, by the generality of the Jews, from the impartiality of his precepts and the remarkable strictness and austerity of his life, held in great veneration. In the number of his followers was our apostle, who accompanied him beyond Jordan, when the Messiah, who had some time before been baptized, came that way. Upon his approach, the Baptist pointed him out as the Messiah, styling him the Lamb of God, the true sacrifice that was to expiate the sins of the world. As soon as the Baptist had given this character of Jesus, Andrew, and another disciple, probably St. John, followed the Saviour of mankind to the place of his abode.

Something more than a year after, Jesus, passing through Galilee, found Andrew and Peter fishing on the sea of Galilee, where he fully satisfied them of the greatness and divinity of his person, by a miraculous draught of fishes, which they took at his command.

After the ascension of the blessed Jesus into heaven, and the descent of the Holy Ghost on the apostles, to qualify them for their great undertaking, St. Andrew, according to the generality of ancient writers, was chosen to preach the gospel in Scythia, and the neighboring countries.

Accordingly he departed from Jerusalem, and first traveled through Cappadocia, Galatia, and Bythnia, instructing the inhabitants in the faith of Christ, and continued his journey along the Euxine sea, into the deserts of Scythia. An ancient author tells us, that he first came to Amnysus, where, being entertained by a Jew, he went into the synagogue, preached to them concerning Jesus, and, from the prophecies of the Old Testament, proved him to be the Messiah, and Saviour of the world.

He went next to Trapezium, a maritime city on the Euxine sea; from whence, after visiting many other places, he came to Nice, where he stayed two years.

preaching and working miracles with great success. After leaving Nice, he passed to Nicodemia, and from thence to Chalcedon, whence he sailed through the Propontis, came by the Euxine sea to Heraclea, and afterward to Amastris.

He next came to Synope, a city situated on the same sea, and famous both for the birth and burial of king Mithridatis; here he met with his brother Peter, and stayed with him a considerable time.

Departing from Synope, he returned to Jerusalem; but he did not continue long in that neighborhood. He returned again to the province allotted him for the exercise of his ministry, which greatly flourished through the power of the divine grace that attended it. He traveled over Thrace, Macedonia, Thessaly, Achaia, and Epirus, preaching the gospel, propagating Christianity, and then confirming the doctrine he taught with signs and miracles. At last he came to Petrea, a city of Achaia, where he gave his last and greatest testimony to the gospel of his divine Master, sealing it with his blood.

Ægenas, proconsul of Achaia, came at this time to Petrea, where, observing that multitudes had abandoned the heathen religion, and embraced the gospel of Christ, he had recourse to every method, both of favor and cruelty, to reduce the people to their old idolatry. The apostle observed to him, that if he would renounce his idolatries, and heartily embrace the Christian faith, he should, with him and the members who had believed in the Son of God, receive eternal happiness in the Messiah's kingdom. The proconsul answered, that he himself should never embrace the religion he mentioned. The apostle replied, that he saw it was in vain to endeavor to persuade a person incapable of sober counsels, and hardened in his own blindness and folly. Ægenas could hold no longer; and after treating him with very opprobrious language, and showing him the most distinguished marks of contempt, he passed sentence upon him that he should be put to death. He first ordered the apostle to be scourged, and seven lictors successively whipped his naked body; but seeing his invincible patience and constancy, he commanded him to be crucified; but to be fastened to the cross with cords instead of nails, that his death might be more lingering and tedious.

On his coming near the cross, he saluted it in the following manner: "I have long desired and expected this happy hour. The cross has been consecrated by the body of Christ hanging on it, and adorned with his members as with so many inestimable jewels."

After offering up his prayers to the throne of grace, and exhorting the people to constancy and perseverance in the faith he had delivered to them, he was fastened to the cross, on which he hung two whole days, teaching and instructing the people in the best manner his wretched situation would admit, being sometimes so weak and faint as scarce to have the power of utterance.

In the mean time great interest was made to the proconsul to spare his life: but the apostle earnestly begged of the Almighty that he might now depart, and seal the truth of his religion with his blood. His prayers were heard, and he expired on the last day of November, but in what year is uncertain.

His body having been taken down from the cross, was decently and honorably interred by Maximillia, a lady of great quality and estate, and who, Nicephorus tells us, was wife to the proconsul.

Constantine the Great, afterward removed his body to Constantinople, and buried it in the great church he had built to the honor of the apostles.

ST. JAMES THE GREAT.

THIS apostle, (who was surnamed the Great, by way of distinction from another of that name,) was the son of Zebedee, and by trade a fisherman, to which he applied himself with remarkable assiduity, and was exercising his employment, when the Saviour of the world passing by the Sea of Galilee, saw him with his brother in the ship, and called them both to be his disciples.

Soon after this he was called from the station of an ordinary disciple to the apostolic office, and even honored with some particular favors beyond most of the apostles, being one of the three whom our Lord made choice of as his companions in the more intimate transactions of his life, from which the rest were excluded. Thus, with Peter and his brother John, he attended his Master when he raised the daughter of Jairus from the dead; he was admitted to Christ's glorious transfiguration on the mount; and when the holy Jesus was to undergo his bitter agonies in the garden, as preparatory sufferings to his passion, James was one of the three taken to be a spectator of them.

When our Lord was determined on his journey to Jerusalem, he sent some of his disciples before him to make preparations for his coming; but, on their entering a village of Samaria, they were rudely rejected, from the old grudge that subsisted between the Samaritans and Jews, and because the Saviour, by going up to Jerusalem, seemed to slight their place of worship on Mount Gerizim. This piece of rudeness and inhumanity was so highly resented by St. James and his brother, that they came to Jesus, desiring to know if he would not imitate Elias, by calling fire down from heaven to consume this barbarous, inhospitable people?

Herod, who was a bigot to the Jewish religion, as well as desirous of acquiring the favor of the Jews, began a violent persecution of the Christians, and his zeal animated him to pass sentence of death on St. James immediately. As he was led to the place of execution, the officer who guarded him to the tribunal, or rather his accuser, having been converted by that remarkable courage and constancy shown by the apostle at the time of his trial, repented of what he had done, came and fell down at the apostle's feet, and heartily begged pardon for what he had said against him. The holy man, after recovering from the surprise, tenderly embraced him. "Peace," said he, "my son, peace be unto thee, and pardon of thy faults." Upon which the officer publicly declared himself a Christian, and both were beheaded at the same time. Thus fell the great apostle St. James, taking cheerfully that cup of which he had long since told his Lord he was ready to drink.

St. JOHN THE EVANGELIST.

From the very minute and circumstantial accoun this evangelist gives of John the Baptist, he is supposed to have been one of his followers, and is thought to be that other disciple who, in the first chapter of his gospel, is said to have been present with Andrew, when John declared Jesus to be "the Lamb of God," and thereupon to have followed him to the place of his abode. He was by much the youngest of the apostles, yet he was admitted into as great a share of his Master's confidence as any of them. He was one of those to whom he communicated the most private transactions of his life: one of those whom he took with him when he raised the daughter of Jairus from the dead: one of those to whom he displayed a specimen of his divinity, in his transfiguration on the mount: one of those who were present at his conference with Moses and Elias, and heard that voice which declared him "the beloved Son of God;" and one of those who were companions in his solitude, most retired devotions, and bitter agonies in the garden.

After the ascension of the Saviour of the world, when the apostles made a division of the provinces among themselves, that of Asia fell to the share of St. John, though he did not immediately enter upon his charge, but continued at Jerusalem till the death of the blessed Virgin, which might be about fifteen years after our Lord's ascension. Many churches of note and eminence were of his foundation, particularly those of Smyrna, Pergamus, Thyatira, Sardis, Philadelphia, Laodicea, and others; but his chief place of residence was at Ephesus, where St. Paul had many years before founded a church, and constituted Timothy bishop.

After spending several years at Ephesus, he was accused to Domitian, who had begun a persecution against the Christians, as an eminent asserter of atheism and impiety, and a public subverter of the religion of the empire; so that by his command the proconsul sent him bound to Rome, where he met with the treatment that might have been expected from so barbarous a prince, being thrown into a caldron of boiling oil. But the Almighty, who reserved him for further service in the vineyard of his Son, restrained the heat, as he did in the fiery furnace of old, and delivered him from this seemingly unavoidable destruction. And surely one would have thought that so miraculous a deliverance should have been sufficient to have persuaded any rational man, that the religion he taught was from God, and that he was protected from danger by the hand of Omnipotence. But miracles themselves were not sufficient to convince this cruel emperor, or abate his fury. He ordered St. John to be transported to an almost desolate island in the Archipelago, called Patmos, where he continued several years, instructing the poor inhabitants in the knowledge of the Christian faith; and here, about the end of Domitian's reign, he wrote his book of Revelations, exhibiting by visions and prophetical representations, the state and condition of Christianity in the future periods and ages of the church.

Upon the death of Domitian, and the succession of Narva, who repealed all the odious acts of his predecessor, and, by public edicts, recalled those whom the fury of Domitian had banished, St. John returned to Asia, and fixed his seat again at Ephesus; the rather because the people of that city had lately martyred Timothy the bishop.

In this manner St. John continued to labor in the vineyard of his great Master, until death put a period to all his toils and sufferings; which happened in the beginning of Trajan's reign, in the ninety-eighth year of his age; and, according to Eusebius, his remains were buried near Ephesus.

The greatest instance of our apostle's care for the souls of men is in the writings he left to posterity; the first of which in time, though placed last in the sacred canon, is his Apocalypse, or Book of Revelations, which he wrote during his banishment at Patmos.

Next to the Apocalypse, in order of time, are his three epistles; the first of which is catholic, calculated for all times and places, containing the most excellent rules for the conduct of a Christian life, pressing to holiness and pureness of manners, and not to be satisfied with a naked and empty profession of religion. The other two epistles are but short, and directed to particular persons; the one to a lady of great quality, the other to the charitable and hospitable Gaius, the kindest friend and most courteous entertainer of all indigent Christians.

Before he undertook the task of writing the gospel, he caused a general fast to be kept by all the Asiatic churches, to implore the blessing of heaven on so great and momentous an undertaking. When this was done, he set about the work, and completed it in so excellent and sublime a manner, that the ancients generally compared him to an eagle soaring aloft among the clouds, whither the weak eye of man was not able to follow him.

Such is the character given of the writings of this great apostle and evangelist, who was honored with the endearing title of being the beloved disciple of the Son of God: a writer so profound as to deserve by way of eminence, the character of "St. John the Divine."

St. PHILIP.

This apostle was a native of Bethsaida, "the city of Andrew and Peter." He had the honor of being first called to be a disciple of the great Messiah, which happened in the following manner: Our blessed Saviour, soon after his return from the wilderness, where he had been tempted by the devil, met with Andrew and his brother Peter, and after some discourse parted from them. The next day, as he was passing through Galilee, he found Philip, whom he presently commanded to follow him, the constant form he made use of in calling his disciples and those that inseparably attended him.

It cannot be doubted, that notwithstanding St. Philip was a native of Galilee, yet he was excellently skilled in the law and the prophets. Metaphrastes assures us, that he had, from his childhood, been excellently educated; that he frequently read over the books of Moses, and attentively considered the prophecies relating to the Messiah.

Nor was our apostle idle after the honor he had received of being called to attend the Saviour of the world; he immediately imparted the glad tidings of the Messiah's appearance to his brother Nathanael, and conducted him to Jesus.

After his being called to the apostleship, we have very little record of him by the evangelists. It was, however, to him that our Saviour proposed the question, where they should find bread sufficient to satisfy the hunger of so great a multitude. Philip answered that it was not easy to procure so great a quantity; not considering that it was equally easy for Almighty power to feed double the number, when it should be his divine will.

The compassionate Jesus had been fortifying their minds with proper considerations against his departure from them, and had told them that he was going to prepare for them a place in the mansions of the heavenly Canaan; that he was "the way, the truth, and the life;" and that no man could come to the Father but by him.

Philip, not thoroughly understanding the force of his Master's reasonings, begged of him, that he would "show them the Father." Our blessed Lord gently reproved his ignorance, that after attending so long to his instructions, he should not know that he was the image of his Father, the express character of his infinite wisdom, power, and goodness, appearing in him; that he said and did nothing but by his Father's appointment; which, if they did not believe, his miracles were a sufficient evidence: that such demands were, therefore, unnecessary and impertinent; and that it was an indication of great weakness in him, after three years' education under his discipline and instruction, to appear so ignorant with regard to these particulars.

The ancients tell us, that in the distribution, made by the apostles, of the several regions of the world, the Upper Asia fell to his share, where he labored with an indefatigable diligence and industry.

After several years successfully exercising his apostolical office in all those parts, he came at last to Hierapolis, in Phrygia, a city remarkably rich and populous, but at the same time overrun with the most enormous idolatry. St. Philip being grieved to see the people so wretchedly enslaved by error and superstition, continually offered his addresses to heaven, till, by his prayers, and often calling on the name of Christ, he procured the death, or at least the vanishing, of an enormous serpent, to which they paid adoration.

Having thus demolished their deity, he demonstrated to them how ridiculous and unjust it was for them to pay divine honors to such odious creatures: showed them that God alone was to be worshiped as the great parent of all the world, who in the beginning made man after his own glorious image, and, when fallen from that innocent and happy state, sent his own Son into the world to redeem him. This discourse roused them from their lethargy; they were ashamed of their late idolatry, and great numbers embraced the doctrines of the gospel.

This provoked the great enemy of mankind, and he had recourse to his old methods, cruelty and persecution. The magistrates of the city seized the apostle, and, having thrown him into prison, caused him to be scourged. When this preparatory cruelty was over, he was led to execution, and, being bound, was hanged against a pillar; or, according to others, crucified. The apostle being dead, his body was taken down by St. Bartholomew, his fellow laborer in the gospel, and Mariamne, St. Philip's sister, the constant companion of his travels, and decently buried; after which, they confirmed the people in the faith of Christ, and departed from them.

St. BARTHOLOMEW.

This apostle is mentioned among the twelve immediate disciples of our Lord under the appellation of Bartholomew, though it is evident, from divers passages of Scripture, that he was also called Nathanael: we shall, therefore, in our account of his life, consider the names of Nathanael and Bartholomew as belonging to one and the same person.

With regard to his descent and family, some are of opinion that he was a Syrian, and that he was descended from the Ptolemies of Egypt. But it is plain from the evangelical history, that he was a Galilean; St. John having expressly told us that Nathanael was of Cana, in Galilee.

The Scripture is silent with regard to his trade and manner of life, though, from some circumstances, there is room to imagine that he was a fisherman. He was, at his first coming to Christ, conducted by Philip, who told him they had now found the long-expected Messiah, so often foretold by Moses, and the prophets, "Jesus of Nazareth, the son of Joseph." And when he objected that the Messiah could not be born at Nazareth, Philip desired him to come and satisfy himself that he was the Messiah.

At his approach, our blessed Saviour saluted him with this honorable character, that he was an "Israelite indeed, in whom there was no guile;" not in an absolute, but restricted sense; for perfection can not be attached to human nature, but in the character of the blessed Jesus, of whom it is said, with peculiar propriety, that he was "holy, harmless, undefiled, and separate from *sinners;*" also, that he "knew no sin, neither was guile," that is, fraud or deception, found in his tongue. He was greatly surprised at our Lord's salutations, wondering how he could know him at first sight, as if imagining he had never before seen his face.

Our apostle having his peculiar spot allotted him for the promulgation of the gospel of his blessed Master, (who had now ascended into heaven, and sent his Holy Spirit to fit and qualify his disciples for the important work,) visited different parts of the world to preach the gospel, and penetrated as far as the hither India.

After spending considerable time in India, and the eastern extremities of Asia, he returned to the northern and western parts, and we find him at Hierapolis, in Phrygia, laboring in concert with St. Philip to plant Christianity in those parts; and to convince the blind idolaters of the evil of their ways, and direct them in the paths that lead to eternal salvation. This enraged the bigoted magistrates, and he was, together with St. Philip, designed for martyrdom, and in order to this, fastened to a cross; but their consciences pricking them for a time, they took St. Bartholomew down from the cross and set him at liberty.

From hence he retired to Lycaonia, and St. Chrysostom assures us that he instructed and trained up the inhabitants in the Christian discipline. His last remove was to Albanople, in Great Armenia, a place overrun with idolatry, from which he labored to reclaim the people. But his endeavors to "turn them from darkness unto light, and from the power of Satan unto God," were so far from having the desired effect, that it provoked the magistrates, who prevailed on the governor to put him to death, which he cheerfully underwent, sealing the truth of the doctrine he had preached with his blood.

St. MATTHEW.

St. Matthew, called also Levi, though a Roman officer, was a true Hebrew, and probably a Galilean. His trade was that of a publican or tax-gatherer to the Romans, an office detested by the generality of the Jews, on two accounts; first, because having farmed the customs of the Romans, they used every method of oppression to pay their rents to them; secondly, because they demanded tribute of the Jews, who considered themselves as a free people, having received that privilege from God himself.

Our blessed Saviour having cured a person long afflicted with the palsy, retired out of Capernaum, to walk by the seaside, where he taught the people that flocked after him. Here he saw Matthew sitting in his office, and called him to follow him. The man was rich, had a large and profitable employment, was a wise and prudent person, and doubtless understood what would be his loss to comply with the call of Jesus. He was not ignorant that he must exchange wealth for poverty, a custom-house for a prison, and rich and powerful masters for a naked and despised Saviour. But he overlooked all these considerations, left all his interest and relations, to become our Lord's disciple, and to embrace a more spiritual way of life.

After St. Matthew's election to the apostleship, he continued with the rest till the ascension of his great and beloved Master; but the evangelical writers have recorded nothing particular concerning him during that period.

After our blessed Saviour's ascension into heaven, St. Matthew, for the first eight years, at least, preached in different parts of Judea; but afterward he left the country of Palestine, to convert the Gentile world. After his leaving Judea, he traveled into several parts, especially Ethiopia, but the particular places he visited are not known with any certainty.

However, after laboring indefatigably in the vineyard of his Master, he suffered martyrdom at a city of Ethiopia, called Nadabar: but by what kind of death is not absolutely known, though the general opinion is, that he was slain with a halberd.

St. Matthew was a remarkable instance of the power of religion, in bringing men to a better temper of mind. If we reflect upon his circumstances while he continued a stranger to the great Redeemer of mankind, we shall find that the love of the world had possessed his heart.

His contempt of the world appeared in his exemplary temperance and abstemiousness from all delights and pleasures; nay, even from the ordinary conveniences and accommodations of it. He was mean and modest in his own opinion, always preferring others to himself; for whereas the other evangelists, in describing the apostles by pairs, constantly place him before St. Thomas, he modestly places him before himself. The rest of the evangelists are careful to mention the honor of his apostleship, but speak of his former sordid, dishonest, and disgraceful course of life, only under the name of Levi; while he himself sets it down with all the circumstances under his own proper and common name.

The last thing we shall remark in the life of this apostle, is his Gospel, written at the entreaty of the Jewish converts, while he abode in Palestine; but at what time is uncertain; some believe it to have been written eight, some fifteen, and some thirty years after our Lord's ascension. It was originally written in Hebrew, but soon after translated into Greek by one of the disciples. After the Greek translation was admitted, the Hebrew copy was chiefly owned and used by the Nazarei, a middle sect between Jews and Christians; with the former they adhered to the rites and ceremonies of the Mosaic law, and with the latter they believed in Christ, and embraced his religion; and hence it has been styled "The Gospel according to the Hebrew" and "The Gospel of the Nazarenes."

St. THOMAS.

Evangelical history is entirely silent with regard either to the country or kindred of Thomas. It is, how ever, certain that he was a Jew, and in all probability a Galilean.

He was, like the rest, called to the apostleship; and, not long after, gave an eminent instance of his being ready to undergo the most melancholy fate that might attend him. For when the rest of the apostles dissuaded their Master from going into Judea, at the time of Lazarus' death, because the Jews lately endeavored to stone him, Thomas desired them not to hinder his journey thither, though it might cost them all their lives.

When the holy Jesus, a little before his sufferings, had been speaking to them of the joys of heaven, and had told them that he was going to prepare mansions for them, that they might follow him, and that they knew both the place whither he was going, and the way thither, our apostle replied, that they knew not whither he was going, much less the way that would lead them thither. To which our Lord returned this short but satisfactory answer, "I am the way;" I am the person whom the Father has sent into the world to show mankind the paths that lead to eternal life, and therefore you can not miss the way, if you follow my example.

After the disciples had seen their great Master expire on the cross, their minds were distracted by hopes and fears concerning his resurrection, about which they were not then fully satisfied; which engaged him the sooner to hasten his appearance, that by the sensible manifestations of himself, he might put the matter beyond all possibility of dispute. Accordingly, the very day in which he rose from the dead, he came into the house where they were assembled, while the doors about them were close shut, and gave them sufficient assurance that he was risen from the dead.

At this meeting Thomas was absent, having probably never rejoined their company since their dispersion in the garden, where every one's fears prompted him to consult his own safety. At his return they told him that the Lord had appeared to them; but he obstinately refused to give credit to what they said, or believe that it was really he, presuming it rather a specter or apparition, unless he might see the very print of the nails, and feel the wounds in his hands and side.

But our compassionate Saviour would not take the least notice of his perverse obstinacy, but on that day seven-night, came again to them, as they were solemnly met at their devotions, and calling to Thomas, bade him look upon his hands, put his fingers into the prints of the nails, and thrust his hand into his side, to satisfy his faith by a demonstration from the senses. Thomas was soon convinced of his error and obstinacy, confessing that he now acknowledged him to be his Lord and Master, saying, "My Lord and my God."

Our great Redeemer having, according to promise before his ascension, poured an extraordinary effusion of the Holy Ghost upon the disciples, to qualify them for the great work of preaching the gospel, St. Thomas as well as the rest preached the gospel in several parts of Judea; and after the dispersion of the Christian church in Jerusalem, repaired into Parthia, the province assigned him for his ministry. After which, as Sempronius and others inform us, he preached the gospel to the Medes, Persians, Carminians, Hyrcani, Bactrians, and the neighboring nations.

Leaving Persia, he traveled into Ethiopia, preaching the glad tidings of the gospel, healing their sick, and working other miracles to prove he had his commission from on high. And after traveling through these countries, he entered India.

When the Portuguese first visited these countries after their discovery of a passage by the Cape of Good Hope, they received the following particulars, partly from ancient monuments, and partly from constant and uncontroverted traditions preserved by the Christians in those parts; namely, that St. Thomas came first to Socotora, an island in the Arabian sea, and thence to Cranganor, where having converted many from the error of their ways, he traveled further into the east; and having successfully preached the gospel, returned back to the kingdom of Coromandel, where, at Maliapur, the metropolis of that kingdom, not far from the mouth of the Ganges, he began to erect a place for divine worship, till prohibited by the idolatrous priests, and Sagamo, prince of that country. But after performing several miracles, the work was suffered to proceed, and Sagamo himself embraced the Christian faith, whose example was soon after followed by great numbers of his friends and subjects.

This remarkable success alarmed the brahmins, who plainly perceived that their religion would soon be extirpated, unless some method could be found of putting a stop to the progress of Christianity; and therefore resolved to put the apostle to death. At a small distance from the city was a tomb, whither St. Thomas often retired for private devotions. Hither the brahmins and their armed followers pursued him, and while he was at prayer, they first shot at him with a shower of darts, after which one of the priests ran him through with a lance.

His body was taken up by his disciples, and buried in the church he had so lately erected, and which was afterward improved into a fabric of grea magnificence.

St. JAMES THE LESS.

It has been doubted by some, whether this was the same with that St. James who was afterward bishop of Jerusalem, two of this name being mentioned in the sacred writings, namely, St. James the Great, and St. James the Less, both apostles. The ancients mention a third, surnamed the Just, which they will have to be distinct from the former, and bishop of Jerusalem. But this opinion is built on a sandy foundation, for nothing is plainer than that St. James the apostle (whom St. Paul calls "our Lord's brother," and reckons, with Peter and John, one of the pillars of the church) was the same who presided among the apostles, doubtless by virtue of his episcopal office, and determined the causes in the synod of Jerusalem. It is reasonable to think that he was the son of Joseph, afterward the husband of Mary, by his first wife, whom St. Jerome styles Escha, and adds, that she was the daughter of Aggi, brother to Zacharias, the father of John the Baptist. Hence he was reputed our Lord's brother.

After the resurrection, he was honored by the particular appearance of our Lord to him, which, though passed over in silence by the evangelists, is recorded by St. Paul.

Some time after this appearance, he was chosen bishop of Jerusalem, and preferred before all the rest for his near relation to Christ.

When St. Paul came to Jerusalem after his conversion, he applied to St. James, and was honored by him with "the right hand of fellowship." And it was to St. James that Peter sent the news of his miraculous deliverance out of prison. "Go," said he, "show these things unto James and to the brethren;" that is, to the whole church, especially to St. James the pastor of it.

He performed every part of his duty with all possible care and industry, omitting no particular necessary to be observed by a diligent and faithful guide of souls, strengthening the weak, instructing the ignorant, reducing the erroneous, and reproving the obstinate. But a person so careful, so successful in his charge, could not fail of exciting the spite and malice of his enemies; a sort of men to whom the apostle has given too true a character, that "they please not God, and are contrary to all men." They were vexed to see St. Paul had escaped their hands, by appealing unto Cæsar; and therefore turned their fury against St. James; but being unable to effect their design under the government of Festus, they determined to attempt it under the procuratorship of Albinus his successor, Ananus the younger, of the sect of the Sadducees, being high priest.

In order to this a council was summoned, and the apostle, with others, arraigned and condemned as violators of the law. But, that the action might appear more plausible and popular, the scribes and Pharisees, masters in the art of dissimulation, endeavored to ensnare him; and, at their first coming, told him that they had all placed the greatest confidence in him; that the whole nation as well as they, gave him the title of a just man, and one that was no respecter of persons; that they therefore desired that he would correct the error and false opinion the people had conceived of Jesus, whom they considered as the Messiah, and take this opportunity of the universal confluence to the paschal solemnity, to set them right in their opinions in this particular, and would go with them to the top of the temple, where he might be seen and heard by all.

The apostle readily consented; and being advantageously placed on a pinnacle of the temple, they addressed him in the following manner: "Tell us, O Justus, for we have all the reason in the world to believe that the people are thus generally led away with the doctrine of Jesus whom they crucified; tell us, what is this institution of the crucified Jesus?" To which the apostle answered, with an audible voice, "Why do you inquire of Jesus the Son of Man? He sits in heaven, at the right hand of the Majesty on high, and will come again in the clouds of heaven." The people below hearing this, glorified the blessed Jesus, and openly proclaimed, "Hosanna to the Son of David."

The scribes and Pharisees now perceived that they had acted foolishly; that instead of altering, he had confirmed the people in their belief; and that there was no way left but to dispatch him immediately, in order to warn others by his sufferings, not to believe in Jesus of Nazareth. Accordingly they suddenly cried out, That James himself was seduced, and become an impostor: and they immediately threw him from the pinnacle on which he stood, into the court below; but not being killed on the spot, he recovered himself so far as to rise on his knees, and pray fervently to heaven for his murderers. But malice is too diabolical to be pacified with kindness, or satisfied with cruelty. Accordingly his enemies, vexed that they had not fully accomplished their work, poured a shower of stones upon him, while he was imploring their forgiveness at the throne of grace; and one of them, more merciful than the rest, put an end to his misery with a fuller's club.

Thus did this great and good man finish his course, in the ninety-sixth year of his age, and about twenty-four years after our blessed Saviour's ascension into heaven. His death was lamented by all good men, even by the sober and just persons among the Jews, as Josephus himself confesses.

St. SIMON THE ZEALOT.

St. Simon, in the catalogue of the apostles, is styled "Simon the Canaanite," whence some conjecture he was born in Cana of Galilee, and others will have him to have been the bridegroom mentioned by St. John, at whose marriage our blessed Saviour turned the water into wine. But this word has no relation to his country, or the place of his nativity, being derived from the Hebrew word "knah," which signifies "zeal," and denotes a warm and sprightly temper. What some of the evangelists therefore call "Canaanite," others, rendering the Hebrew by the Greek word, style "Zealot;" not from his great zeal, his ardent affection to his Master, and his desire of advancing his religion in the world, but from his warm, active temper, and zealous forwardness in some particular sect of religion before his coming to our Saviour.

St. Simon continued in communion with the rest of the apostles and disciples at Jerusalem; and at the feast of Pentecost received the same miraculous gift of the Holy Ghost; so that as he was qualified with the rest of his brethren for the apostolic office, in propagating the gospel of the Son of God, we can not doubt of his exercising his gifts with the same zeal and fidelity, though in what part of the world is uncertain. Some say he went into Egypt, Cyrene, and Africa, preaching the gospel to the inhabitants of those remote and barbarous countries. And others add, that after he had passed through those burning wastes, he took ship, and visited the frozen regions of the north, preaching the gospel to the inhabitants of the western parts, and even in Britain: where, having converted great multitudes and sustained the greatest hardships and persecutions, he was at last crucified, and buried in some part of Great Britain, but where, is unknown.

St. JUDE.

This apostle is mentioned by three several names in the evangelical history: namely, Jude or Judas, Thaddeus, and Lebbeus.

He was brother to St. James the Less, afterward bishop of Jerusalem, being the son of Joseph the reputed father of Christ, by a former wife. It is not known when or by what means he became a disciple of our blessed Saviour, nothing being said of him, till we find him in the catalogue of the twelve apostles; nor afterward, till Christ's last supper, when discoursing with them about his departure, and comforting them with a promise, that he would return to them again, (meaning after his resurrection,) though the "world should see him no more," our apostle said to his Master, "Lord, how is it that thou wilt manifest thyself to us, and not unto the world?"

Paulinus tells us that the province which fell to the share of St Jude, in the apostolic division of the provinces, was Lybia; but he does not tell us whether it was the Cyrenian Lybia, which is thought to have received the gospel from St. Mark, or the southern parts of Africa. But however that be, in his first setting out to preach the gospel, he traveled up and down Judea and Galilee; then through Samaria unto Idumea, and to the cities of Arabia and the neighboring countries, and afterward to Syria and Mesopotamia. Nicephorus adds, that he came at last to Edessa, where Abagarus governed, and where Thaddeus, one of the seventy, had already sown the seeds of the gospel. Here he perfected what the other had begun; and having by his sermons and miracles established the religion of Jesus, he died in peace; but others say that he was slain at Berytus, and honorably buried there. The writers of the Latin Church are unanimous in declaring that he traveled into Persia, where, after great success in his apostolical ministry for many years, he was at last, for his freely and openly reproving the superstitious rites and customs of the Magi, cruelly put to death.

St. Jude left only one epistle, which is placed the last of those seven, styled catholic, in the sacred canon. It was some time before this epistle was generally received in the church. The author, indeed, like St. James, St. John, and sometimes St. Paul himself, does not call himself an apostle, styling himself only "the servant of Christ." But he has added what is equivalent, "Jude the brother of James," a character that can belong to no other but our apostle. And surely the humility of a follower of Jesus should be no objection against his writings.

St. MATTHIAS.

As Matthias was not an apostle of the first election, immediately called and chosen of the Son of God himself, it can not be expected that any account of him can be found in the evangelical history. He was one of our Lord's disciples, probably one of the seventy, that had attended on him the whole time of his public ministry, and after his death was elected into the apostleship, to supply the place of Judas, who, after betraying his great Lord and Master, laid violent hands on himself.

The defection of Judas having made a vacancy in the apostolical college, two persons were proposed, Joseph, called Barsabas, and Matthias, both duly qualified for the important office. The method of election was by lot; and this course seems to have been taken by the apostles because the Holy Ghost was not yet given, by whose immediate dictates and inspirations they were afterward chiefly guided. The prayer being ended, the lots were drawn, by which it appeared that Matthias was the person, and he was accordingly numbered among the twelve apostles.

St. Matthias spent the first year of his ministry in Judea, where he reaped a very considerable harvest of souls, and then traveled into different parts of the world, to publish the glad tidings of salvation to a people who had never before heard of a Saviour; but the particular parts he visited are not certainly known.

It is uncertain by what kind of death he left the regions of mortality, and sealed the truth of the gospel he had so assiduously preached, with his blood. Dorotheus says, he finished his course at Sebastople, and was buried there, near the temple of the sun. An ancient martyrology reports him to have been seized by the Jews, and, as a blasphemer, to have been stoned and then beheaded. But the Greek offices, supported herein by several ancient breviaries, tell us that he was crucified.

St. MARK.

St. Mark was descended from Jewish parents, of the tribe of Levi. The ancients generally considered him as one of the seventy disciples; and Epiphanius expressly tells us, that he was one of those who, taking exception at our Lord's discourse of "eating his flesh and drinking his blood, went back and walked no more with him." But there appears no manner of foundation for these opinions, nor likewise for that of Nicephorus, who will have him to be the son of St. Peter's sister.

Eusebius tells us, that St. Mark was sent into Egypt by St. Peter, to preach the gospel, and accordingly planted a church in Alexandria, the metropolis of it. He did not, however, confine himself to Alexandria, and the oriental parts of Egypt, but removed westward to Lybia, passing through the countries of Marmacia,

Pentapolis, and others adjacent, where, though the people were both barbarous in their manners, and idolatrous in their worship, yet by his preaching and miracles he prevailed on them to embrace the tenets of the gospel; nor did he leave them till he had confirmed them in the faith.

After this long tour he returned to Alexandria, where he preached with the greatest freedom, ordered and disposed of the affairs of the church, and wisely provided for a succession, by constituting governors and pastors of it. But the restless enemy of the souls of men would not suffer our apostle to continue in peace and quietness; for while he was assiduously laboring in the vineyard of his Master, the idolatrous inhabitants, about the time of Easter, when they were celebrating the solemnities of Serapis, tumultuously entered the church, forced St. Mark, then performing divine service, from thence; and binding his feet with cords, dragged him through the streets, and over the most craggy places, to the Bucelus, a precipice near the sea, leaving him there in a lonesome prison, for that night; but his great and beloved Master appeared to him in a vision, comforting and encouraging his soul, under the ruins of his shattered body. The next morning early the tragedy began afresh, for they dragged him about in the same cruel and barbarous manner, till he expired. But their malice did not end with his death; they burnt his mangled body after they had so inhumanly deprived it of life: but the Christians, after the horrid tragedy was over, gathered up his bones and ashes, and decently interred them near the place where he used to preach. His remains were afterward, with great pomp, removed from Alexandria tc Venice, where they were religiously honored, and he was adopted the tutelar saint and patron of that state.

He suffered martyrdom on the 25th of April, but the year is not absolutely known: the most probable opinion, however, is, that it happened about the end of Nero's reign.

His gospel, the only writing he left behind him, was written at the entreaty and earnest desire of the converts at Rome, who, not content with having heard St. Peter preach, pressed St. Mark, his fellow disciple, to commit to writing an historical account of what he had delivered to them, which he performed with equal faithfulness and brevity, and being perused and approved of by St. Peter, it was commanded to be publicly read in their assemblies.

St. LUKE.

This disciple of the blessed Jesus was born at Antioch, the metropolis of Syria, a city celebrated for its schools of learning, which produced the most renowned masters in the arts and sciences. So that, being born, as it were, in the lap of the muses, he could not well fail of acquiring an ingenious and liberal education. But he was not contented with the learning of his own country; he traveled for improvement into several parts of Greece and Egypt, and became particularly skilled in physic, which he made his profession.

St. Luke was a Jewish proselyte; but at what time he became a Christian is uncertain. It is the opinion of some, from the introduction to his gospel, that he had the facts from the reports of others, who were eyewitnesses, and suppose him to have been converted by St. Paul.

But, however this be, St. Luke became the inseparable companion of St. Paul, in all his travels, and his constant fellow-laborer in the work of the ministry. This endeared him to that apostle, who seems delighted with owning him for his fellow-laborer, and in calling him "the beloved physician," and the "brother whose praise is in the gospel."

St. Luke wrote two books for the use of the church, his gospel and the Acts of the Apostles.

His gospel contains the principle transactions of our Lord's life; and the particulars omitted by him are in general of less importance than those of the other evangelists.

With regard to the Acts of the Apostles, written by St. Luke, the work was, no doubt, performed at Rome, about the time of St. Paul's imprisonment there, with which he concludes his history.

In short, as an historian, he was faithful in his relations, and elegant in his writings; as a minister, careful and diligent for the good of souls; as a Christian, devout and pious; and, to crown all the rest, laid down his life in testimony of the truth of the gospel he had both preached and published to the world.

St. BARNABAS.

St. Barnabas was a descendant of the tribe of Levi, of a family removed out of Judea, and settled in the Isle of Cyprus, where they had purchased an estate, as the Levites might do out of their own country. His parents finding him of a promising genius and disposition, placed him in one of the schools of Jerusalem, under the tuition of Gamaliel, St. Paul's master; an incident which, in all probability, laid the foundation for that intimacy which afterward subsisted between these two eminent servants of the blessed Jesus.

The first mention we find of St. Barnabas in the Holy Scriptures, is the record of that great and worthy service he did the church of Christ, by succoring it with the sale of his patrimony in Cyprus, the whole price of which he laid at the apostles' feet, to be put into the common stock, and disposed of as they should think fit among the indigent followers of the holy Jesus.

And now St. Barnabas became considerable in the ministry and government of the church; for we find that St. Paul, coming to Jerusalem three years after his conversion, and not readily procuring admittance into the church, because he had been so grievous a persecutor of it, and might still be suspected of a design to betray it, addressed himself to Barnabas, a leading man among the Christians, and one that had personal knowledge of him. He accordingly introduced him to Peter and James, and satisfied them of the sincerity of his conversion, and in what a miraculous manner it was brought about. This recommendation carried so much weight with it, that Paul was not only received into the communion of the apostles, but taken into Peter's house, "and abode with him fifteen days." Gal. i: 18.

About four or five years after this, the agreeable news was brought to Jerusalem, that several of their body who had been driven out of Judea by the persecutions raised about St. Stephen, had preached at Antioch with such success, that a great number, both of Jews and proselytes, embraced Christianity; and were desirous that some of the superior order would come down and confirm them. This request was immediately granted, and Barnabas was deputed to settle this new plantation. But there being too large a field for one laborer, he went to fetch Saul from Tarsus, who came back with him to Antioch, and assisted him a whole year in establishing that church.

When the apostles had fulfilled their charitable embassy, and stayed some time at Jerusalem to see the good effects of it, they returned again to Antioch, bringing with them John, whose surname was Mark, the son of Mary, sister to Barnabas, and at whose house the disciples found both security for their persons, and conveniency for the solemnity of their worship. But soon after the apostles returned to Antioch, an express relation was made to the church by the mouth of one of the prophets who ministered there, that Barnabas and Saul should be set apart for an extraordinary work, unto which the Holy Ghost had appointed them. Upon this declaration, the church set apart a day for a solemn mission; after devout prayer and fasting, they laid their hands upon them, and ordained them to their office; which was to travel over certain countries, and preach the gospel to the Gentiles.

Paul and Barnabas being thus consecrated "the apostles of the Gentiles," entered upon their province, taking with them John Mark, for their minister or deacon, who assisted them in many ecclesiastical offices, particularly in taking care of the poor.

The first city they visited after their departure from Antioch, was Seleucia, a city of Syria, adjoining to the sea; from whence they sailed to the island of Cyprus, the native place of St. Barnabas, and arrived at Salamis, a port formerly remarkable for its trade. Here they boldly preached the doctrines of the gospel in the synagogues of the Jews; and from thence traveled to Paphos, the capital of the island, and famous for a temple dedicated to Venus, the tutelar goddess of Cyprus. Here their preaching was attended with remarkable success; Servius Paulus, the proconsul, being, among others, converted to the Christian faith.

Leaving Cyprus, they crossed the sea to preach in Pamphilia, where their deacon, John, to the great grief of his uncle Barnabas, left them and returned to Jerusalem: either tired with continual travels, or discouraged at the unavoidable dangers and difficulties which experience had sufficiently informed him would constantly attend the preachers of the gospel from hardened Jews and idolatrous Gentiles.

Soon after their arrival at Lystra, Paul cured a man who had been lame from his mother's womb, which so astonished the inhabitants, that they believed them to be gods, who had visited the world in the forms of men. Barnabas they treated as Jupiter, their sovereign deity, either because of his age, or the gravity and comeliness of his person; for all the writers of antiquity represent him as a person of venerable aspect, and a majestic presence. But the apostles, with the greatest humility, declared themselves to be but mortals: and the inconsistent populace soon satisfied themselves of the truth of what they had asserted; for at the persuasion of their indefatigable persecutors, who followed them thither also, they made an assault upon them, and stoned Paul, till they left him for dead. But, supported by an invisible power from on high, he soon recovered his spirits and strength, and the apostles immediately departed for Derbe. Soon after their arrival, they again applied themselves to the work of the ministry, and converted many to the religion of the blessed Jesus.

From Derbe they returned back to Lystra, Iconium, and Antioch in Pisidia, "confirming the souls of the disciples, and exhorting them to continue in the faith; and that we must, through much tribulation, enter into the kingdom of God." Acts xiv: 22. After a shor stay they again visited the churches of Pamphilia Perga, and Attala, where they took ship, and sailed to Antioch, in Syria, the place from whence they first set out. Soon after their arrival they called the church of this city together, and gave them an account of their travels, and the great success with which their preach ing in the Gentile world had been attended.

After some time Paul made a proposal to Barnabas, that they should repeat their late travels among the Gentiles and see how the churches they had planted increased in their numbers, and improved in the doctrines they had taught them. Barnabas very readily complied with the motion; but desired they might take with them his reconciled nephew, John Mark. This Paul absolutely refused, because, in their former voyage, Mark had not shown the constancy of a faithful minister of Christ, but consulted his own ease at a dangerous juncture; departed from them without leave at Pamphilia, and returned to Jerusalem. Barnabas still insisted on taking him; and the other continuing as resolutely opposed to it, a short debate arose, which terminated in a separation, whereby these two holy men, who had for several years been companions in the ministry, and with united endeavors propagated the gospel of the Son of God, now took different provinces. Barnabas, with his kinsman, sailed to his own country, Cyprus; and Paul, accompanied by Silas, traveled to the churches of Syria and Cilicia.

After this separation from St. Paul, the sacred writings give us no account of St. Barnabas; nor are the ecclesiastical writers agreed among themselves with regard to the actions of this apostle after his sailing for Cyprus. This, however, seems to be certain, that he did not spend the whole remainder of his life in that island, but visited different parts of the world, preaching the glad tidings of the gospel, healing the sick, and working other miracles among the Gentiles. After long and painful travels, attended with different degrees of success, in different places, he returned to Cyprus, his native country, where he suffered martyrdom, in the following manner: certain Jews coming to Syria and Salamis, where Barnabas was then preaching the gospel, being highly exasperated at his extraordinary success, fell upon him as he was disputing in the synagogue, dragged him out, and, after the most inhuman tortures, stoned him to death. His kinsman, John Mark, who was a spectator of this barbarous action, privately interred his body in a cave, where it remained till the time of the Emperor Zeno, in the year of Christ 485, when it was discovered, with St. Matthew's gospel in Hebrew, written with his own hand, lying on his breast.

St. STEPHEN.

Both the Scriptures and the ancient writers are silent with regard to the birth, country, and parents of St. Stephen. Epiphanius is of opinion that he was one of the seventy disciples: but this is very uncertain. Our blessed Saviour appointed his seventy disciples to teach the doctrines and preach the glad tidings of the gospel; but it does not appear that St. Stephen and the six other first deacons had any particular designation before they were chosen for the service of the tables; and therefore St. Stephen could not have been one of our Lord's disciples, though he might have often followed him, and listened to his discourses.

He was remarkably zealous for the cause of religion, and full of the Holy Ghost: working many wonderful miracles before the people, and pressing them, with the greatest earnestness, to embrace the doctrine of the gospel.

This highly provoked the Jews; and some of the synagogues of the freed-men of Cyrenia, Alexandria, and other places, entered into dispute with him; but being unable to resist the wisdom and spirit by which he spake, they suborned false witnesses against him, to testify that they had heard him blaspheme against Moses and against God. Nor did they stop here; they stirred up the people by their calumnies: so that they dragged him before the council of the nation, or great sanhedrim, where they produced false witnesses against him, who deposed that they heard him speak against the temple, and against the law, and affirm that Jesus of Nazareth would destroy the holy place, and abolish the law of Moses. Stephen, supported by his own innocence, and an invisible power from on high, appeared undaunted in the midst of this assembly, and his countenance shone like that of an angel; when the high priest asking him what he had to offer against the accusations laid to his charge, he answered in a plain and faithful address to the Jews, which he closed in the following manner:

"Ye stiff-necked, ye uncircumcised in heart and ears, ye will forever resist the Holy Ghost. Ye tread in the paths of your fathers; as they did, so do you still continue to do. Did not your fathers persecute every one of the prophets? Did not they slay them who showed the coming of the Holy One, whom ye yourselves have betrayed and murdered? Ye have received the law by the deposition of angels, but never kept it."

At these words they were so highly enraged, that they all gnashed their teeth against him. But Stephen, lifting up his eyes to heaven, saw the glory of God, and Jesus standing at the right hand of Omnipotence. Upon which he said to the council, "I see the heavens open and the Son of Man standing at the right hand of God." This so greatly provoked the Jews, that they cried out with one voice, and stopped their ears, as if they had heard some dreadful blasphemy; and falling upon him, they dragged him out of the city, and stoned him to death.

Stephen, while they were mangling his body with stones, was praying to Omnipotence for their pardon. "Lord," said he, "lay not this sin to their charge.' And then calling on his dear Redeemer to receive his spirit, he yielded up his soul.

TIMOTHY.

Timothy was a convert and disciple of St. Paul. He was born, according to some, at Lystra; or, according to others, at Derbe. His father was a Gentile, but his mother a Jewess, whose name was Eunice, and that of his grandmother, Lois.

These particulars are taken notice of, because St. Paul commends their piety and the good education which they had given Timothy. When St. Paul came to Derbe and Lystra, about the year of Christ 51 or 52, the brethren gave a very advantageous testimony of the merit and good disposition of Timothy: and the apostle would have him along with him, but he initiated him at Lystra, before he received him into his company. Timothy applied himself to labor with St. Paul in the business of the gospel; and did him many important services, through the whole course of his preaching.

This holy disciple accompanied St. Paul to Macedonia, to Philippi, Thessalonica, to Berea; and when the apostle went from Berea, he left Timothy and Silas there to confirm the converts. When he came to Athens, he sent for Timothy to come thither to him: and when he was come, and had given him an account of the churches of Macedonia, St. Paul sent him back to Thessalonica, from whence he afterward returned with Silas, and came to St. Paul at Corinth.

Some years after this, St. Paul sent Timothy and Erastus into Macedonia; and gave Timothy orders to call at Corinth, to refresh the minds of the Corinthians, with regard to the truths he had inculcated in them. Some time after, writing to the same Corinthians, he recommends them to take care of Timothy, and send him back in peace; after which, Timothy returned to St. Paul in Asia, who there staid for him. They went together into Macedonia; and the apostle put Timothy's name with his own, before the second epistle to the Corinthians, which he wrote to them from Macedonia, about the middle of the year of Christ 57. And he sends his recommendations to the Romans in the letter which he wrote to them from Corinth the same year.

When St. Paul returned from Rome, in 64, he left Timothy at Ephesus to take care of that church, of which he was the first bishop, as he is recognized by the council of Chalcedon. St. Paul wrote to him from Macedonia, the first of the two letters which are addressed to him. He recommends him to be more moderate in his austerities, and to drink a little wine because of the weakness of his stomach, and his frequent infirmities. After the apostle came to Rome, in the year 65, being now very near his death, he wrote to him his second letter, which was full of the marks of kindness and tenderness for this, his dear disciple; and which is justly looked upon as the last will of St. Paul. He desires him to come to Rome to him before winter, and bring with him several things which St. Paul had left at Troas. If Timothy went to Rome, as it is probable he did, he must have been a witness of the martyrdom of this apostle, in the year of Christ 66.

If he did not die before the year 97, we can hardly doubt but that he must be the angel of the church of Ephesus, to whom St John writes in his Revelations: though the reproaches which the Holy Ghost makes to him, &c., of having left his first love, do not seem to apply to so holy a man as Timothy was.

TITUS.

Titus was a Gentile by religion and birth, but converted by St. Paul, who calls him his son. St. Jerome, says, that he was St. Paul's interpreter, and that, probably, because he might write what St. Paul dictated, or explained in Latin what this apostle said in Greek, or rendered into Greek, what St. Paul said in Hebrew or Syriac. St. Paul took him with him to

Jerusalem, when he went thither in the year 51 of the vulgar era, about deciding the question which was then started, whether the converted Gentiles ought to be made subject to the ceremonies of the law? Some would then have obliged him to circumcise Titus; but neither he nor Titus would consent to it. Titus was sent by the same apostle to Corinth, upon occasion of some disputes which then divided the church. He was well received by the Corinthians, and very much satisfied with their ready compliance: but would receive nothing from them, imitating thereby the disinterestedness of his master.

From hence he went to St. Paul in Macedonia, and gave him an account of the state of the church at Corinth. A little while after, the apostle desired him to return again to Corinth, to set things in order against his coming. Titus readily undertook this journey, and started immediately, carrying with him St. Paul's second letter to the Corinthians.

Titus was made bishop of the Isle of Crete, about the 63d year of Christ, when St. Paul was obliged to quit that island, in order to take care of the other churches. The following year he wrote to him, to desire that as soon as he should have sent Tychicus of Artemus to him for supplying his place in Crete, Titus would come to him to Nicopolis in Macedonia, or to Nicopolis in Epirus, upon the gulf of Ambracia, where the apostle intended to pass his winter.

Titus was deputed to preach the gospel in Dalmatia; and he was still there in the year 65, when the apostle wrote his second epistle to Timothy. He afterward went into Crete; from which it is said he propagated the gospel into the neighboring islands. He died at the age of 94, and was buried in Crete. We are assured that the cathedral of the city of Candia is dedicated to his name; and that his head is preserved there entire. The Greeks keep his festival on the 25th of August, and the Latins on the 4th of January.

www.ingramcontent.com/pod-product-compliance
Lightning Source LLC
LaVergne TN
LVHW020928110826
845150LV00004B/801

* 9 7 8 1 4 2 5 5 5 3 9 0 6 *